Stephen A. Douglas and the Dilemmas of Democratic Equality

American Profiles
Norman K. Risjord, Series Editor

Thomas Jefferson
By Norman K. Risjord

Mary Boykin Chesnut: A Confederate Woman's Life
By Mary A. DeCredico

John Quincy Adams
By Lynn Hudson Parsons

He Shall Go Out Free: The Lives of Denmark Vesey
By Douglas R. Egerton

Samuel Adams: America's Revolutionary Politician
By John K. Alexander

Jefferson's America, 1760–1815: Second Edition
By Norman K. Risjord

Martin Van Buren and the Emergence of American Popular Politics
By Joel H. Silbey

He Shall Go Out Free: The Lives of Denmark Vesey,
Revised and Updated Edition
By Douglas R. Egerton

Stephen A. Douglas and the Dilemmas of Democratic Equality
By James L. Huston

Stephen A. Douglas and the Dilemmas of Democratic Equality

James L. Huston

ROWMAN & LITTLEFIELD PUBLISHERS, INC.
Lanham • Boulder • New York • Toronto • Plymouth, UK

The author acknowledges kind permission of Oxford University for permission to use the extended quotes in Robert W. Johannsen, ed., *The Lincoln-Douglas Debates of 1858* (New York: Oxford University Press, 1965).

ROWMAN & LITTLEFIELD PUBLISHERS, INC.

Published in the United States of America
by Rowman & Littlefield Publishers, Inc.
A wholly owned subsidiary of The Rowman & Littlefield Publishing Group, Inc.
4501 Forbes Boulevard, Suite 200, Lanham, Maryland 20706
www.rowmanlittlefield.com

Estover Road
Plymouth PL6 7PY
United Kingdom

British Library Cataloguing in Publication Information Available

Library of Congress Cataloging-in-Publication Data

Huston, James L., 1947–
    Stephen A. Douglas and the dilemmas of democratic equality / James L. Huston.
        p. cm. – (American profiles)
    Includes bibliographical references and index.
    ISBN-13: 978-0-7425-3456-8 (cloth : alk. paper)
    ISBN-10: 0-7425-3456-1 (cloth : alk. paper)
    1. Douglas, Stephen Arnold, 1813–1861. 2. Douglas, Stephen Arnold, 1813–1861–
Political and social views. 3. Legislators–United States–Biography. 4. United States.
Congress. Senate–Biography. 5. United States–Politics and government–1815–1861.
6. Democracy–United States–History–19th century. 7. Democratic Party (U.S.)–History–
19th century. I. Title. II. Series: American profiles (Lanham, Md.)
    E415.9.D73H87 2006
    973.6'8092–dc22
    [B]   2006012899

Printed in the United States of America

♾™The paper used in this publication meets the minimum requirements of American
National Standard for Information Sciences–Permanence of Paper for Printed Library Materials, ANSI/NISO Z39.48-1992.

Contents

~

Preface

For centuries, European politics had rested on the foundation that only the "best" should rule, and that the grouping of people into the few who issued commands and the many who obeyed them was a natural division of society, sanctified by theology and philosophy as well as common experience. Those who constituted the apex of the social order not only possessed wealth and political preferment, but they also had legal privileges that the rest of the citizenry did not. Inequality was enshrined in law and custom.

The American Revolution shattered the old European tradition of hereditary preferment and inequality. Destroying the legal basis of favoritism was, however, easier to do than defining what was to take its place. Most of the revolutionary generation was cautious about the amount of change they wanted to introduce, but they could not contain the Revolution's momentum: the forces it unleashed tore away at legal preferments and elevated the principle of equality. In the Declaration of Independence, Thomas Jefferson eloquently phrased the hope his generation had for an egalitarian future: "We hold these truths to be self-evident: That all men are created equal; that they are endowed by their Creator with certain unalienable rights; that among these are life, liberty, and the pursuit of happiness." What was missing was a definition of equality and a prescription for what policies would produce and sustain that condition.

After the War of 1812, the ideals of democracy and equality fully blossomed in the United States. In its wake came modern democratic politics, a rhetoric based on equality of citizens and a widespread assault on all forms of legal favoritism—the time older historians characterized as the "Age of Jacksonian Democracy" and the "Rise of the Common Man." Stephen Arnold Douglas (1813–1861) was a politician who came of age during the democratization of American politics, the time when egalitarianism became a national creed. This book seeks to examine the unfolding of the principles of democracy and equality in the United States through the life of one who was at the center of the storm.

The antebellum senator from Illinois is well known, for between 1846 and 1861 he played a pivotal role in the political controversy over slavery's expansion into the territories. For numerous biographers and historians, Douglas occupied the middle ground in the controversy as one who rejected the extremists of both the North and the South. Thus one obtains some of the more memorable titles about him: George Fort Milton's *The Eve of Conflict: Stephen A. Douglas and the Needless War* and Gerald M. Capers's *Stephen A. Douglas: Defender of the Union*. True as these characterizations are, Douglas's life reveals more about the political life of the country than just the forces tearing the nation apart. I have instead sought to place him in the perspective of American dilemmas over the meaning of democratic equality. Douglas once exclaimed, "I am a radical & progressive democrat"; the phrase deserves scrutiny because imbedded within it are troubling ambiguities.[1]

This book is organized around several themes involving Douglas, democracy, and equality. The first is how the Illinois Democratic Party was created and Douglas's role in it, and what in the 1830s was the content of equality and how the Democrats intended to acquire it. The second is how equality functioned in the 1840s Democratic program of Manifest Destiny. Next, this book will examine the confrontation between the North and the South over slavery and its expansion. This topic naturally breaks down into several constituent elements: Douglas and his vision of race relations in the United States; his promotion of the solution of popular sovereignty; his growing disenchantment with southern demands over the protection of slave property; and finally the meaning of majority rule, secession, and states' rights.

Stephen A. Douglas was not an overly complex figure. He never pretended to be a philosopher and, more than his fellow politicians, was given to action and practicality. For many researchers, his story is fairly easily presented. Nonetheless, certain questions about his life beg more probing. His early years remain somewhat mysterious, especially concerning his religious instruction, his love for Andrew Jackson, his silent rebellion against the formalism of New England life, and his instant adoption of a southern yeoman culture. Why Douglas demanded eternal landed expansion is something of a puzzle, as was his hostility to African Americans—the source of his prejudice is nowhere chronicled. Another powerful enigma is why Douglas never heeded or really replied to the free labor arguments and Slave Power apprehensions of his

Republican opponents; why did these propositions not cause him any anxiety about the political, economic, and social future of the United States? Finally, one especial puzzle has long bothered me: why could Douglas not let the South secede? Upon what basis did he insist that secession was not permissible? On this point, Douglas's views are just as important as Abraham Lincoln's, though scholars have surprisingly ignored them. Weaving its way in and out of these questions is the ideal of democratic equality and the paradoxes it raised for the early republic. I commenced this project convinced of the simplicity of the subject; I ended with a perplexity not well resolved.

Anyone daring to write a biography of Douglas immediately confronts the magisterial work of my mentor, Robert W. Johannsen. Johannsen's biography, 874 pages of narrative and 91 pages of endnotes, remains the ultimate source for those seeking detailed information on Douglas's life. The sources Johannsen used were the guides to the ones consulted in writing this book, and my presentation of the facts of the Little Giant's life was made by dutifully checking Johannsen's narrative. Needless to say, this brief study, in comparison to Johannsen's, slights various areas of Douglas's life; it also presents different interpretations. Nonetheless, the passage of time has revealed to me what a marvelous work of writing and research Johannsen's biography is.

I have used the term "democratic equality" as a way of probing the numerous political issues that dominated Douglas's life. Throughout this book, I refer to the "Gordian knots of democratic equality," a term that requires explanation. When Alexander the Great was conquering the world, he entered the kingdom of Phrygia. The king of Phrygia was Gordius. Gordius had tied a complicated knot, and an oracle had proclaimed that whoever untied the knot would be the ruler of Asia. Alexander found the knot too tedious, drew his sword, and severed it. From this story comes a definition that describes a Gordian knot as a problem that requires drastic action. However, I have opted for a different understanding. I choose the phrase "the Gordian knots of democratic equality" because defining and achieving a society of equals, a democracy, led to immensely complicated problems—a set of knots—that required much careful thought to unravel. But when people avoided the task of careful scrutiny and thinking, they were likely to "cut through" the problem without understanding the consequences. This was the fate of antebellum America and its quest for democratic equality. They grabbed the phrase "democracy and equality" and plunged ahead; but because they had not grappled with the problem in all its complexity, their haste led them into blunders that not only undermined their best intentions but almost put them on the path of repudiating their values.

In the American Profiles series, the biographies are usually published without comprehensive citations. In this work, the normal scholarly apparatus detailing controversies are omitted, but it troubled me to author a book that uses extensive quoting without indicating the sources. Fortunately, the editors at Rowman & Littlefield have consented to allow citations of quotations to appear as chapter endnotes. For readers who are more zealous in their quest for sources, for the historiography, and for additional evidence from primary sources, they may contact me by mail or e-mail at Oklahoma State University and I will gladly respond to their inquiries.

Readers of my previous book, *Calculating the Value of the Union: Slavery, Property Rights, and the Economic Origins of the Civil War* (2003), will undoubtedly note that in this current work my interpretations of Douglas, popular sovereignty, and property rights have shifted somewhat. The primary reason for this alteration has been additional research, especially Douglas's 1860 campaign in the South. Behind this modification of my views resides little stories about misplaced notes, faulty assumptions, and incomplete research, but these tales can be withheld for another time.

I want to thank the series editor Norman Risjord for his editorial suggestions; Laura Gottlieb, editor at Rowman & Littlefield, for her support in bringing this effort to a conclusion; and the staff at Rowman & Littlefield, especially Sheila-Katherine Zweibel, Andrew Boney, and Matt Evans, for their improvements. Two anonymous reviewers provided excellent suggestions that have enhanced the quality of the work immensely; to them I extend my sincere gratitude. The librarians at the various repositories holding manuscripts were more than willing to assist me, and I especially want to acknowledge my debt to the Special Collections Division of the University of Chicago Library where the large collection of Douglas's papers resides for agreement.

Notes

1. SAD to Caleb Cushing, February 4, 1852, Douglas, *Letters*, 237.

~

Abbreviations

CG	*Congressional Globe*
Douglas, *Letters*	Stephen A. Douglas, *The Letters of Stephen A. Douglas*, ed. Robert W. Johannsen.
Douglas Papers, Uchi	Stephen A. Douglas Papers, University of Chicago
Douglas Papers, Ill	Stephen A. Douglas Papers, Illinois State Historical Library
IllStLib	Illinois State Historical Library
Ill St Reg	(Springfield) Illinois Daily State Register
Ill St Jou	(Springfield) Illinois Daily State Journal
IndStHS	Indiana State Historical Society, Indianapolis
IndStLib	Indiana State Library, Indianapolis
LC	Library of Congress, Manuscript Division, Washington, D.C.
NYT	*New York Times*
SHSWisc	State Historical Society of Wisconsin, Madison, Wisconsin
SAD	Stephen A. Douglas
Uchi	University of Chicago

CHAPTER ONE

~

Creating Democracy, 1813–1840

"I have become a *Western* man[,] have im[b]ibed Western feelings principles and interests."[1] So Stephen A. Douglas wrote to his brother-in-law,
Julius N. Granger of New York. Douglas had arrived in Illinois in November
1833 and had at most only been in the state forty-five days. It certainly was
an odd response for such a recent immigrant. Did the New England culture
in which Douglas had been reared for nearly seventeen of his twenty years
on this earth mean so little? And just what aspect of the West was Douglas
talking about? Just what of the West had he acquired? From his Vermont boyhood, he probably acquired a strong love of debate, political action, and local
government—aspects derived from the famed New England town meeting. It
would seem, however, that he took some negative feelings with him. Even the
part of Vermont from which he hailed had a formal structure to it from which
he either openly or silently rebelled, and much of his life to follow became a
defiance against formality in all social and political realms. He also disliked the
rules for advancement and the want of opportunity that constrained him. Stephen A. Douglas wanted opportunity, and he wanted it immediately. For him,
the West was the West because it lacked the formality and the protocols of the
East, and it offered grand opportunities for a young man. Douglas would then
build these principles into the Illinois Democratic Party.

He was born in Brandon, Vermont, on April 23, 1813, the son of Stephen
A. Douglass and his wife Sarah (Fisk) Douglass, the couple having been married two years earlier. Family members traced their ancestors back to the migration of the Scottish Douglasses to Massachusetts in 1640. Eventually a branch

1

of the family sought cheap land to the West, and one Benajah Douglass bought some acreage in Brandon and established his family there. One of Benajah's sons, Stephen, rejected the occupation of farming and instead pursued medicine. He married and produced two children, a girl, Sarah Arnold Douglass, and a boy, whom he named after himself and who became the future Illinois senator. The young boy never knew his father, as he died only two months after Douglas's birth.

The death of the father plunged the family into straightened circumstances. Although the Douglasses possessed property and the father had been a doctor, the family belonged to the class of small farmers. Young Douglas had, in short, no social advantages in his youth and more than likely faced some deprivations. Sarah (Sally) Douglass moved her children onto a small farm a few miles North of Brandon that was owned by her brother Edward Fisk. Fisk, a bachelor at the time, wanted a housekeeper and used the boy as a farm laborer.

(The Douglass family did indeed spell their surname with two *s*'s, and so did Stephen. Later, when he was elected to Congress, he continued to have his name spelled Stephen A. Douglass in the *Congressional Globe*, the journal recording the debates in Congress. If one takes the *Congressional Globe* as a marker of change, then he changed the spelling of his name when he took a seat in the U.S. Senate in 1847.)

Brandon's social environment encouraged a rebellious spirit against established norms. Eastern Vermont was largely populated by old New England Puritans, and the region was stodgy in its social, religious, and political life. Western Vermont, which contained Brandon, differed. Religion in Western Vermont included Methodism and the Society of Friends. Douglas's grandfather, Benajah, had been a leader in creating a Methodist meeting in Brandon. Moreover, Western Vermont had defied New England Federalism and had voted for Thomas Jefferson's Democratic-Republicans. Benajah Douglass was something of a local politician and helped school the youth in the ways of Jeffersonian democracy.

Economic life in Brandon had limits. Most families relied on farming or some craft closely related to agriculture. While that economic base sufficed to provide most with a competence, population growth was slowly eroding the overall well-being of the people and was sending youth westward in search of better opportunities. Young Douglas's ambitions were growing—an element of his character that would never change. During his years as a farm laborer for his uncle, he learned some woodworking skills, which he enjoyed, and attended common school about three months out of the year. He learned the basics, excelled in mathematics and Latin, and started to have visions about college and an occupation other than farming. In an autobiographical sketch, Douglas later grumbled about only obtaining boarding and clothes from his uncle rather than pay. He did not want to be a farmer; he wanted more of a future than Brandon could offer. It was time for a personal revolt.

Revolt meant leaving Brandon for an apprenticeship in nearby Middlebury with a furniture maker named Nahum Parker. This arrangement lasted only eight months, for revealing reasons. Douglas was headstrong and wanted to be independent; Parker wanted a traditional, obedient apprentice. And then there was politics. The presidential election of 1828 pitted General Andrew Jackson, the Hero of New Orleans and the darling of the "common man," against the puritanical New Englander John Quincy Adams. Nahum Parker was an Adams proponent; Douglas and his fellow "mechanics" supported Old Hickory. During the campaign, Douglas and his friends tore down the "coffin handbills" that Adams supporters had posted around Middlebury and Brandon—these were handbills attacking Jackson for his execution of five deserters during the War of 1812. In his autobiographical sketch, Douglas would later claim that this election led him to Jacksonian principles and "confirmed my early attachment to the cause of Democracy."[2]

Douglas left Parker and returned to Brandon, where he resumed a cabinet-making career in the shop of Deacon Caleb Knowlton, but soon many features of his world changed. His home life with his mother on the farm had become complicated because his uncle, Edward Fisk, had married, and his grandfather, Benajah, had died. In the winter of 1829–1830, Douglas fell so ill that he had to abandon carpentry. Knowlton released him from his apprenticeship, and Douglas enrolled in Brandon Academy, a school that prepared youth for teaching or for entry into college. He was active in the school and participated in the debating society, and he eagerly learned about changes in politics, especially the rise of the Democratic Party under Jackson, and about its foe, at first called the National Republicans and years later the Whig Party.

His life turned a corner in late 1830. A visitor from Canandaigua, New York, Julius Granger, had met his sister Sally and had married her. The Granger family evidently found the Douglass women attractive, because a few months later, Julius's father, Gehazi Granger, married Stephen's mother. Douglas followed his mother to upstate New York. For him, the move had a number of vital consequences. First, he came to reside in an area close to the Erie Canal, where he could visibly see the effects of transportation improvements on economic life. Second, Canandaigua had an academy where Douglas could further his education. At the academy, he excelled in debate and sharpened his oratorical skills, abilities that in Illinois would propel him to the heights of electoral politics. Likewise, his studies at the academy must have given him a broad factual base of the nation's history, its politics, and the ideals of the founders, for as a youth he would be uncommonly educated on the issues of the day and their historical backgrounds. Third, the Granger family into which his mother had married was politically powerful, and the Grangers provided him with connections to established people. Those connections were most evident in his ability to leave the academy to pursue a law career. In those days, one could obtain certification for practicing law by working in a law office and later passing an examination. On January 1, 1833, Douglas entered the firm of Walter and Levi Hubbell to study law.

While in New York, he must have also learned about the new methods of organizing politics. He was there during the presidential election of 1832, and he lived in a household where politics was thoroughly discussed and among youth for whom politics was the soul of life. Martin Van Buren, the "Little Magician," had created in the 1820s a modern political party in New York. Instead of letting politics be ruled by an elite composed of elected officials who selected future candidates, Van Buren had established a system of conventions—for counties, for congressional districts, and for the state as a whole—where people of the same political persuasion met and made the nominations themselves. These conventions also drafted resolutions to declare their party's positions. To maintain the organization, Van Buren had set up "committees of correspondence" in the counties to coordinate election activities and had obtained newspapers to champion the party's cause. These techniques were new and shocked those who believed that individuals should either follow their social superiors or that candidates should announce their own availability and let the public pass judgment. The Van Buren system wanted organization because its promoters believed that the great mass of voters was inarticulate, but the party would give these people a voice. It was also a good way to consolidate people of similar thinking behind one candidate and increase that person's chances of electoral victory. Douglas must have absorbed at least the rudiments of this system while studying in upstate New York, because he immediately sought to install it in Illinois.

Douglas probably could have prospered and done well in New York, but his impatience at formality and rules propelled him to places where he could unleash his ambition. The laws of New York declared that to obtain a license to practice law, one had to have four years of classical education and three years of legal study. The twenty-year-old Stephen A. Douglas could not restrain himself for seven years. After six months of study, he made the decision to go west, where presumably the rules governing entrance into the legal profession were not so onerous. He announced his decision to his despairing mother, obtained three hundred dollars to tide him over initially, and received letters of introduction from Francis Granger and Mark Sibley, letters that he could show to westerners as proof of his character and ability—a vital asset for one going to the West with no connections. On June 24, 1833, at the age of twenty, Douglas began his westward journey.

Finding the right location to launch a rise to the top of American society proved exhausting and difficult. For a while, Douglas stayed in Cleveland, landing a position in a law firm, but was then smitten with illness for weeks. In October, with his finances disappearing, he took passage to Cincinnati, then to Louisville, and then to St. Louis. He expected to start anew in St. Louis but was unable to find a position. So he searched once again, this time in Illinois. He traveled to Alton, and from there to the small but thriving town of Jacksonville, located in the west central portion of the state. He had only five dollars. But again he could not find a law position in the town, and, given some tips of where some employment might be found, he traveled again until he arrived at the Illinois village of Winchester. At Winchester, his money ran out, and to earn a living, he opened a school in December 1833.

Douglas resided in Winchester until March 1834, living in a small apartment behind a general store. During these months, Douglas revealed an attribute that would explain much of his meteoric rise in the political world: an intense work ethic. After teaching, Douglas read law books, consumed newspapers, talked politics, went to the courthouse, and conversed with everyone he could. He found the early pioneers of Illinois open and friendly, and the opportunities limitless. After a few months, he closed his school. He then took an examination to practice law and barely passed it; he was warned that he needed more study. Douglas left Winchester for Jacksonville, the county seat, ostensibly to practice law, but in reality to engage in politics.

In Illinois, Douglas found a culture that did not prize dress, manners, and family connections, at least not as much as was typical in the East. He entered a society in which deference was fading, deference being a social custom in which members of the middle and lower classes bowed to the decisions and the alleged superiority of the upper class. Douglas eagerly embraced the informality of the West and the erosion of deferential behavior. According to one account, when Douglas arrived in Illinois, he "assumed a suit of Kentucky jeans and an arm-in-arm intimacy, in street and saloon, with men of the uniform and of the Jackson stripe."[3] Later, when he became one of the Illinois Supreme Court judges in 1841, an observer remarked that Douglas "is the most democratic judge I ever knew. He leaves the bench and goes among the people, and among the members of the bar, takes a cigar and has a social smoke with them, or often [sits] in their laps."[4] Douglas was known as a not especially punctilious dresser; at times he verged on the slovenly.

It is no wonder that Douglas raved about the opportunities of the West. Here no one stood astride the path of his ambitions, here were no rules and regulations formulated by alleged social superiors, here were no awkward apprentice systems demanding a servile demeanor, and here were no demands on personal behavior such as those insisted upon by the descendents of Puritans. Much of Douglas's life in Illinois was almost a conscious revolt against the formalism of New England, and he found in Illinois a release from all the confining behavioral standards of his home state. This attitude of revolt against upper-class standards of propriety also informed his political principles.

One feature of his New England culture, however, probably stayed with him: the need of family for discussing confidential and private matters. Douglas was an open and amicable youth and made friends easily. But he never developed close relationships with others. For those personal matters in his life, he wanted his family as confidants. So he wrote to them continuously, urging them to migrate from New York and join the "wealthy, intelligent, and enterprising citizens of almost every State in the Republic, or country, on the Globe."[5] Everyone in Illinois had the chance to be rich, and he told his brother-in-law that he would "be able to make a fortune in Lands without laboring any yourself."[6]

They never came, and Douglas was bereft of family life for nearly two decades. Later, when he campaigned for the presidency in 1860, he made small jokes about his westward move to a Massachusetts audience. In the East, he said, one of two sons went west and made a fortune and "a man of himself by his own energy. The other brother, perhaps being a little more obedient to parental authority, less energetic, less intellectual, and a little more lazy, prefers to stay at home, [than] to go forth to battle with the world." He summarized his comments by saying that the "energetic" went West, while the "timid" stayed home with the "old folks [laughter]."[7] Perhaps he was jesting, but perhaps as well there was a touch of sadness to his observation. As convivial and extroverted as the young Douglas was, he was also very much alone.

There was one other feature about western living he must have liked as well. Religion did not penetrate every aspect of life. The record on Douglas's religious practices is, to put it mildly, sparse. He may have attended some church services, and he may have gone during his early days in Illinois to a Baptist revival. Certainly he knew Reverend Peter Cartwright, a Methodist minister and Democratic politician, quite well. Yet, like his famous rival, Abraham Lincoln, he never became a member of a Christian denomination, and he seldom, it is surmised, attended services. Although Douglas would occasionally refer in his speeches to a deity, to the divine law, or to the precepts of Christianity, he did so in a generic way, indicating a sort of unreflecting acceptance of the cultural background of his society rather than any real active engagement in theology or church activity. In his autobiographical sketch, Douglas related that his mother was upset with his decision to go to Middlebury and required him to "avoid all immoral and vicious practices, attend church regularly, and obey the regulations of my employer."[8] The words "church" and "religion" are seldom found thereafter in his writings and activities. Douglas's religious experiences after his removal to Illinois were almost a nullity.

Illinois: Economy and Politics

The Illinois to which Douglas migrated was still a frontier state and was scarcely populated. In 1820, there were 55,211 American citizens in the state, and by 1830, only 157,445. Early migrants hailed from the South, and the lower half of the state was largely populated by persons from the border slave states of Kentucky, Virginia, Tennessee, and Maryland. In the center of the state, around Jacksonville, a mixture of northern and southern immigrants melded, with the upland southerners probably being most dominant. Douglas moved coincidentally with a mass of New Englanders, New Yorkers, and Pennsylvanians who had come to the state after 1830. This latter migration largely filled the northern portion of the state and thereby produced a cultural antagonism: northern Illinois was Puritan and Yankee, whereas southern Illinois drew upon the traditions, except for slavery, of the border South; central Illinois proved to be a mixture.

The state's economy began a transition in 1830 from self-sufficiency to commercial exchange. Southern migrants had generally been family-first farmers, meaning that they used farms to feed their families and to grow a few exchangeable crops to pay taxes and purchase necessities. They prized independence and kinfolk; they were not obsessed with making money through market transactions. New Englanders, New Yorkers, and Pennsylvanians had different economic orientations. They wanted to produce for a market, to invest earnings for future growth, and to accumulate wealth. Before long, the stereotypes of the Yankee swindler and the slow, slovenly southerner appeared, reflecting the different outlooks of the two groups and injecting a detectable hostility between residents of southern and northern Illinois. Nonetheless, after 1830, most of the state's inhabitants embraced economic development. They wanted more immigration in order to raise land prices, and they saw canals, roads, and railroads as the means to stimulate that immigration. At the time of Douglas's arrival, in short, Illinois was in the throes of commercial development.

Illinois politics mirrored this upland southerner/Yankee split. Early Illinois politics was rife with individual factionalism, much of it revolving around the person of Governor Ninian Edwards (governor 1826–1830). Parties did not really exist in 1834. Most individuals nominated themselves for state or congressional offices by announcing their candidacies in the newspapers or by spreading the word at the local courthouse. Thus, during elections, many candidates battled for victory, and the total vote was split among the many aspirants. This process suited the people of southern Illinois, for it belonged to their tradition of independence.

Northern Illinoisans felt differently. Many of them were familiar with the party machinery set up in New York by Martin Van Buren, which employed nominating conventions, party platforms, correspondence committees, and newspapers. The party then demanded from its members fidelity to candidates and party positions. In Illinois, a number of northern politicians moved to adopt the Van Buren system. Douglas joined this group.

Illinoisans had other political divisions. Most supported Andrew Jackson because they believed him to be a westerner who would support programs aiding their region. In the tumultuous battles during the Tennessean's eight years as president, however, Illinoisans showed various degrees of support for Old Hickory. The crucial battle was the war over the Second Bank of the United States. Jackson declared the bank to be a monopoly used by easterners to deprive farmers, mechanics, and laborers of their daily earnings, and the bank controlled the supply of credit to the nation and starved the West in order to fatten the East.[9] As Jackson fought with the Bank of the United States, trying to destroy it by withdrawing U. S. government deposits from its vaults, he split Illinois followers into "whole-hog" Jacksonians (those opposed to the Bank of the United States) and "milk-and-cider" Jacksonians (those who wanted to reform the Bank but not destroy it).[10] Illinois pro-Jackson forces met in December 1831 to advocate his position, while other Illinoisans opposed to Jackson gathered under the banner of Henry Clay. Neither developed into a political party in the state.

This was the politics of the state to which Douglas had migrated. Much of his New England culture he tossed aside, but he thoroughly embraced the eastern ideal of party organization. Indeed, he was to become one of the supreme party managers of his time. In his devotion to constructing party machinery, Douglas was a raging fire on the prairies; he was called a "steam engine in britches" for good reason, and his inexhaustible energy and devotion to politics helps explain the role of leaders in parties and why parties worked so well.[11]

The Road to Party Manager

Stephen A. Douglas encountered his first Gordian knot of democratic equality when he confronted the question of the mechanism that enabled people to exercise power over the government. How did the nation register the opinions of the masses, and how did those opinions then shape policy to augment the fundamental ideal of republican equality? Douglas took his answer from the New York experience, and he did so instinctively rather than philosophically. The masses needed to organize into parties; an electoral system without parties left people ignorant and dispersed. Parties united the masses and informed them of the best ideas and people so that their equality would be maintained. As well, the party became the best means to see to it that the inegalitarian instincts of would-be aristocrats were thwarted.

His rise to the summit of Illinois politics began in Jacksonville in 1834. Though Douglas came to the town to open shop as a lawyer, he was at best nonchalant about legal practice, and he soon recognized that the flood of lawyers in the state made it an unremunerative position. He had accumulated talents, however, from his education back in Brandon and Canandaigua: he had engaged in debates, had read widely, and had studied hard. He was only twenty years old in 1834, but he had already formed deep political convictions that prized openness, anointed Andrew Jackson a saint, revered the common man, and somewhat surprisingly rejected abolitionism. All that was needed was a forum to allow him to argue fiercely these convictions to an audience.

That forum came in the spring of 1834. Illinois experienced a sudden dwindling of credit that many believed was due to President Jackson's policy of removing federal deposits from the Bank of the United States. A town meeting was held on a Saturday at the Jacksonville Courthouse, and there the probank men, led by Josiah Lamborn, prepared resolutions castigating Jackson for his actions. At the meeting were also pro-Jackson men, such as S. S. Brooks and Murray McConnel, both of whom had befriended Douglas and had acted as his mentors. After Lamborn's speech, an offer of rebuttal was given, and instead of McConnel or Brooks taking center stage, the task was given to the recent Vermont immigrant. For an hour, Douglas roasted the probank faction and sent some of them steaming from the hall. As Douglas later said, "I was rather severe in my remarks upon the opposition."[12] The crowd responded to Douglas's performance with cheers and then adopted antibank resolutions. The twenty-one-year-old orator had just earned a local reputation, and it is reputed that at this meeting, the five-foot-four-inch-tall Douglas gained his nickname, "the Little Giant."[13]

In the division in the Jackson camp over the role of the United States Bank, Douglas was a wholehearted Jackson supporter who believed that any *true* Democrat followed the president in denouncing the institution, and those who did not had false hearts. He was virulent in his attacks, according to one reminiscer, a "bantam cock of the fight."[14] Douglas at this time also began identifying bank supporters with a word that evoked the specter of class-ridden Europe and the very substance of inequality: "aristocrats." For Douglas, the stakes were going to be the rights and privileges of the people versus the schemes of aggrandizement of the aristocracy.

A mere lad of twenty-one years of age, Douglas showed in Jacksonville most of the traits that would catapult him to the summit of Illinois politics. He had a passion for politics that overwhelmed all other considerations; he was thoroughly devoted to its pursuit, much more so than business, the legal profession, or, as it turns out, marriage. Aiding him on his quest for political advancement was his friendliness; he treated all people, rich and poor, equally and called them by their first names. Though his smallish size, short legs, and large head were potential political disabilities, he overcame them with his mastery of language, his ability to make his points understood, a wealth of information to draw upon, and at times vitriol to heap upon his adversaries—Douglas was never afraid to use sarcasm and scorn to embarrass an opponent. Above all, he threw passion into his speeches; people were drawn to him and his cause because of the intense earnestness with which he framed every sentence of every debate and speech. Humor was not the hallmark of his public performances; an unrelenting intensity was—he was a fighter. His pugnacity, earnestness, and intensity drew voters to him and made him, even from his youth, an important political leader.

Two objectives drew Douglas's exertions after that fight. One was to organize the Democratic Party and make it effective in uniting behind proper candidates, and the other was to advance himself personally. Douglas argued for a stronger Democratic Party organization in Morgan County (the county that contained Jacksonville), had the Jacksonville debate about the U.S. Bank published in newspapers throughout the state, and then campaigned for antibank candidates. Although lawyering in Jacksonville was supposedly his occupation, Douglas found the pursuit of his goals more agreeable at the state's capital in Vandalia. There he worked with a select group to piece together the Democratic Party.

Several Jacksonians saw the need for a convention system to unite people behind proper candidates. In St. Clair, Ottawa, and Cook counties, some conventions were held in 1834, but most were poorly attended. In Morgan County, S. S. Brooks and John Wyatt were advocates of the nomination system, and Douglas eagerly joined them in 1835. Shortly thereafter, a state convention of Democrats was held in Vandalia. The immaturity of Illinois's party system was exhibited by the appearance of representatives from only six of the state's sixty-two counties.

Douglas's prominence in political activity was acknowledged in another state convention held in December 1835. He was asked to author the party's declaration of principles and its resolutions. Here was a recognition of Douglas's literary talents and how valuable they were to the young Democratic Party. The platform had its interesting parts. Besides the passage of resolutions glorifying the presidency of Andrew Jackson and favoring the election of Van Buren, it also contained the stirring words that "all power of right, rests with the people, and emanates directly from them"; it proclaimed that conventions were a means to measure the wishes of the masses. As to specific issues, the Illinois Democratic Party—through the pen of Douglas—declared that Indian removal was "alike humane and wise," that the United States Bank was a "powerful instrument in the hands of an aristocracy," and that the spirit of the Democratic Party was "a resistance to monopolies."[15]

During the December meeting, many members expressed hostility to the convention system. In response, Ebenezer Peck, a delegate from Cook County, argued that conventions expressed the will of the people, while nomination by caucus—a meeting by party leaders for the purpose of nominating candidates—was elitist and undemocratic. Douglas also spoke to the assembled Democrats on this topic. He declared that conventions were the way to win elections; he and others had introduced the system in Morgan County the previous year and had been crowned with success. By contrast, caucuses divided and weakened the Democrats by fostering internal divisions. Douglas insisted that the enemy—the Whigs and their allies—were always plotting against the people, and only by the convention system could the people be protected from the nefarious designs of the aristocracy.

If the promoters of conventions argued that their system best echoed the "will of the people," others had their doubts. For the Whigs and not a few Jacksonian followers, the convention system was a means by which a few wire-pullers or, more candidly, some officeholders, manipulated the party to adopt their measures and their people. Instead of people running the conventions, the conventions, operated by a few officeholders, ran the people. There was some truth to this charge. The proponents of conventions wanted a more disciplined system to win elections, and they had already shown by 1835 that they were prepared to ostracize those who were unwilling to line up behind the right candidates.

While Douglas was helping to build the Illinois Democratic Party, he was coincidentally pursuing a career in government. At Vandalia, he immersed himself in party activity, writing anonymous editorials (sometimes getting into trouble over them) and making contacts with people who held his views. One such person was John Wyatt, a state legislator from Morgan County. Wyatt harbored a grudge against state's attorney John J. Hardin—also of Morgan County—because Hardin had not supported Wyatt for office and had effectively opposed the Jacksonian Democrats in the area. Wyatt recruited Douglas to exact some revenge. Wyatt soon had Douglas writing legislation for the state—once again, Douglas's education stood him in good stead—and together they fashioned a bill enabling the state legislature, instead of the governor, to appoint state's attorneys. Douglas and Wyatt were seeking to curtail the anti-Democratic faction in Morgan County, to allow their brand of Democrats to be appointed as state's attorneys instead of Whigs, and thereby to oust Hardin. The legislation was passed over the veto of the governor, thus enabling the legislators to select state's attorneys. At the same time, Douglas wrote other pieces of legislation establishing popular elections for certain county officers and revising the circuit court system of Illinois so that supreme court justices no longer bore these duties. All of this legislation had an explicit purpose: to remove judicial officers in Morgan County who opposed the Douglas brand of democracy.

Then, by a mere four votes, the legislature selected Stephen A. Douglas rather than John J. Hardin to be state's attorney for the first judicial district. At the time of his election, Douglas was only twenty-two years old, had barely passed his examination to practice law, and had no courtroom experience. The opposition, more openly calling themselves the Whigs, were outraged. They wanted a chance to embarrass Douglas and attempted to do so by pointing out some sloppiness in his writing of indictments. Douglas, however, met their criticism by denying any error on his part—and luckily was proven correct. His handling of the situation showed with crystal clarity his attitude toward elitism. When confronted by an established authority, Douglas fought back; he did not admit mistakes, he did not act contritely, and he did not defer to his social "betters." In many ways, his personality was like the Democratic Party—a revolt against deference and those who assumed social superiority.

Douglas did not acquire a reputation as an outstanding prosecutor, and in truth he was not enamored with practicing law. He obtained moderate success. Perhaps of more importance was his salary, $250 per year, which finally put him on a more solid financial footing, even though it was a meager amount. His appointment, however, aided him politically. Now he moved across the eight counties composing his district and met and talked politics with more people.

Perfecting the Party and Rising to National Prominence

Dissatisfied with his duties as a state's attorney, Douglas sought political advancement by running as one of several candidates for a seat in the Illinois House of Representatives. Using the convention system as his tool of organization, Douglas obtained solid backing from his district. His first election, though, was somewhat uninspired. Douglas favored having the state build canal and road improvements, but so did everyone else running for office in 1836. It was also a presidential election year, and while the nominee, Martin Van Buren, elicited little enthusiasm, the Democrats rolled to victory in Illinois and smashed the poorly organized opposition.

The Illinois legislative session of 1836–1837 proved to be a most memorable one. The legislators, a majority being Democrats, voted to move the capital from Vandalia to Springfield—which Douglas opposed because he wanted it placed in Jacksonville—and then expanded the state banking system by increasing the capitalization of the banks and the state's participation in it, and Douglas opposed this as well because it resembled too much the Second Bank of the United States. Douglas was responsible for making marital divorce in Illinois a judicial matter instead of one decided by the state legislature, and he also favored the secret ballot in elections. He supported resolutions brought in by a committee on the growing question of slavery and the abolitionist assault upon it; the resolutions declared that the national government had no role in the matter because it was entirely a state issue, and the rights of property in slaves had to be observed.

The major effort of the legislature was the passage of an internal improvements measure, subsequently labeled the "mammoth" bill. Douglas had his own ideas about how to proceed with funding internal improvements, and he wanted less grandiose plans. He lost. A spirit of grand adventure and, evidently, total financial lunacy seized the legislators. They passed a law allowing the state to obtain loans totaling $10,230,000, allocating from it some $500,000 for river improvements and spending the rest on eight railroads. The annual interest on the loans the state subscribed to was $800,000; the yearly revenue of the state was only $100,000. The legislators evidently believed the tide of immigration would be so overwhelming, the land sales so enormous, and economic development so instantaneous, that they could make ends meet. Douglas distrusted the financial arrangements of the bill, but so popular was the subject of internal improvements that he felt compelled to cast an "aye" vote on the legislation.

When the legislature closed its session in March 1837, Douglas made another climb into the hierarchy of the state party. He resigned his seat in the legislature in order to take the position of register of the Springfield Land Office, a federal appointment requiring the approval of President Van Buren. Douglas obtained this coveted post due to internal feuds in the Democratic Party, Douglas's advancement being championed by U.S. senator Richard M. Young. Young wanted to block the senatorial aspirations of rival William L. May, a congressman.

As the register of the Springfield Land Office, Douglas not only enjoyed a position of prestige but one that yielded a handsome income. His new employment carried a stipend of $3,000 a year, an amount much greater than Douglas had ever earned. This position also permitted him to engage in some land speculation. Being register of the Springfield Land Office as well allowed Douglas to converse continuously with Democratic leaders around the state. And Douglas was interested, because in 1838, congressional and gubernatorial elections would be held in Illinois, and Douglas had his eye on Congressman May's seat.

Douglas now resided in Springfield, and though always scheming about politics and building up the Democratic Party, he enjoyed an active social life. He was a bachelor and joined in the male activities of the day—some sports, much conversation at various public places, and considerable bouts of alcoholic consumption. Much of frontier life assumed the aspect of a fraternal order—women were scarce, and marriage was often delayed—and Douglas reveled in the male camaraderie. He had a natural inclination to participate in social gatherings; he was a hail-fellow-well-met personage, enjoying drink, coarse food, coarse language at times, and a hearty chew of tobacco. He was, however, an odd fit in this frontier society dominated by émigrés from Kentucky, Virginia, and Tennessee. They were often tall; Douglas was not. He stood only five feet four inches, possessing a large face, broad muscular shoulders, but short stubby legs. He had bold-blue gray eyes and long dark curling hair. His appearance might have been a detriment to his social and political status if it had not been for his amiable comportment, his strong convictions, and his forceful language. People were attracted—almost entranced—by his commanding personality.

A special characteristic of Douglas's impressed many people, a characteristic that had some bearing on his political beliefs. Many noted that as a bachelor Douglas was a slovenly dresser, often seen running around Springfield with documents, notes, and newspapers poking out of his pockets. Perhaps Douglas naturally gravitated toward a carelessness in dress, but as likely there was a political element to it. For Douglas, clothes did not make the man; that was a rule made by pompous easterners trying to find position not by merit but by wealth or family connection. Douglas lived a life where the inner qualities of humanity counted more than the outer garments of social sophistication—in fact, an Enlightenment point of view epitomized by Thomas Jefferson.

His sloppiness did not stop him from going to dances and parties. He attended these events and enjoyed himself immensely. He courted or flirted with a few of the single females of Springfield—the most famous being Mary Todd, the future wife of Lincoln—but without much success, and perhaps without much interest. His soul at the time was joined to the Democratic Party, and it would take several years before a woman could intrude on that bond. Douglas's excesses at parties and his enjoyment of alcohol became small legends in Illinois. Perhaps the most famous story—maybe true, maybe not—was his celebration with James Shields after Shields won election to the United States Senate from the Illinois legislature. It was said that at the victory party, Douglas and Shields leaped upon a table, danced together down the table's length, and scattered dishes and mugs as they went. True or not, the story certainly tells much about how a New Englander shed his cultural inhibitions.

The Vermont transplant quickly developed a rich appreciation for his adopted state, but he puzzled over the nickname of the people who lived there: the "suckers."[16] For reasons lost to the historical record, Illinois was called the "sucker" state. Douglas gave a humorous explanation of the origins of the label when he stumped Virginia in 1860. In his version, George Rogers Clark during the American Revolution marched to Illinois to combat the French at the town of Kaskaskia. It was a hot day, and the Frenchmen were "sitting quietly on a little verandah in front of their houses, sucking their juleps through a straw, and he rushed on them, crying 'surrender, you suckers, you!' [Great laughter.] The Frenchmen surrendered, and from that day to this, the Illinoisans have been known as 'suckers.' [Renewed laughter.]"[17]

Illinoisans looked optimistically to the future, trusting that government investments in canals and railroads would soon result in swarms of immigrants, upward leaps in land values, and a radiant prosperity that would touch every family. Such was not to be the state's destiny. In May 1837, a financial panic hit the nation and Illinois. The Panic of 1837 was a financial collapse originating in interest rate adjustments in London, which ended up sending many American banks into failure. As failures spread, depositors panicked and withdrew their funds. Weakened by having less money in their vaults, surviving banks curtailed loans dramatically, cutting off credit to businessmen and speculators. The contraction of loans brought business activity to a halt, resulted in workers being discharged, and thereby produced a general economic depression.

For Illinois, the Panic of 1837 was a disaster. The state had contracted a huge loan just months before the financial system collapsed, and now business came to a standstill. Illinois at one point had to forgo paying interest payments on its bonds, an action tantamount to declaring bankruptcy. An economic disaster of this magnitude would obviously have strong political repercussions, both at the state and federal levels, and at the heart of the debate would be questions about banking.

In preparation for the elections of 1838, the Democrats worked at perfecting their party's machinery. In July 1837, the Democrats held a state convention at Vandalia to set up the conventions at the county, district, congressional, and state levels. They determined that the nominating convention for governor and lieutenant governor would be on December 2 at Vandalia, and the delegates could be selected from each county as each county saw fit; the number of delegates permitted from each county would be equal to the number of representatives and senators each county elected to the state legislature. They also defined the basic committee structure of the Democratic Party. The delegates established a state central committee to direct efforts and to correspond with the county parties. The county parties were to set up similar committees to oversee their subdivisions (precincts), and these were often referred to as "vigilance" committees. The leaders wanted the state convention to publish an address to explain the principles of the Democrats and their position on the issues, and they urged all county parties to publish their resolutions and platforms in Democratic newspapers around the state. This organizational meeting also created corresponding committees for the congressional districts—three of them in 1837—so that congressional conventions could be held.

In the election of 1838, Illinois Democrats confronted internal fissures over the subject of banking. The Panic of 1837 had riveted attention on the role of banks in producing the financial collapse. One portion of the party followed President Van Buren, who argued that banking and government had to be "divorced." By letting bankers use government funds, bankers extended credit too freely—bankers did so by expanding the currency, then called banknotes—thereby enticing entrepreneurs into foolish business ventures. Eventually these speculative enterprises failed, and loans could not be repaid; bankers responded to nonperforming loans by contracting the supply of credit, and that in turn produced a financial panic and then an economic collapse. Van Buren believed a divorce of banking from government could be accomplished by an "independent treasury," a government office that merely collected debts and paid for services in gold and silver coin (called specie); it had no connection to private banking whatsoever. Van Buren believed the states should also divorce their government from banking as well.

These proposals of Van Buren's divided Democrats nationwide. Many Democrats thought that a prosperous economy without credit was impossible. Many wanted a national bank and some regulation of state banks. Others became true believers of the independent treasury and the hard money doctrine—gold and silver coins only. They demanded no monopolies in legislation, no special privileges to any group, and termination of government control of banking; in a broad sense, they were anticorporation and antibank. In the East, such individuals became known as Locofocos, the radicals of the Jacksonian Democratic party.

Stephen A. Douglas belonged to this portion of the Democratic Party. It was why he proclaimed in 1852, "I am a radical & progressive democrat."[18] All other Democrats needed to follow the party line, for Douglas was an extreme believer in party obedience. So in 1837 and 1838, Douglas, besides seeking his own advancement, wanted to purge the party of those Democrats who did not follow Van Buren. Among those who did not was Congressman May.

Douglas worked at establishing a Third District Congressional Convention to deny May renomination by the party and to obtain it for himself. He successfully did some wire-pulling and special pleading to round up support for the convention. In November, the Third District Democratic Convention was held in Peoria; only fourteen of the thirty-five counties in the district were represented, and only forty delegates showed up, most of them from Morgan and Sangamon Counties. They offered the Democratic congressional nomination to Douglas, not to May. And so Douglas, only twenty-four years old, became the party nominee for Congress.

He wrote one of the addresses for the Illinois Democratic Party in this election, and in it he defined the Democrats' position. He claimed that in Illinois two factions existed: "The one, the advocates of the rights of the People; the other, the advocates of the privileges of Property."[19] The Democrats descended from the party of Thomas Jefferson, while the Whigs were the rebirth of the party of Alexander Hamilton and John Adams, the Federalists. The Federalists, as Douglas loved to call the Whigs, believed government belonged only to the few, they conducted their meetings in secret caucuses instead of open conventions like the Democrats, and they sought to reward their favorites with monopolies, special privileges, and unfair advantages.

The egalitarian theme in Democratic pronouncements became stronger as the campaign progressed. After some difficulty in obtaining an appropriate gubernatorial candidate, the Democrats in convention declared that they were "the friends of order and justice, lovers of equal privileges, now, as always, contending for the rights of the many against the unjust aggressions of the few."[20] The Democrats' chief newspaper in Illinois, the Vandalia (and then Springfield) *Illinois State Register*, printed the resolutions and actions of the county conventions. Increasingly, such conventions declared that the Democrats were the party of the common folk, while the Whigs were the organization of the deceitful rich, always seeking further aggrandizement by political power and taking away the rights of the masses. The editor of the *Register* liked to quote Daniel Webster as proof of the Whig Party's favoritism to the wealthy: "*Let Congress take care of the RICH, and the rich will take care of the POOR.*"[21] The great leader of the Whigs, Henry Clay, was hostile to a "proprietary yeomanry," meaning that Clay did not favor small farmers owning their own land. The Whigs, stated the editor, based their party on the principle that "property makes the man!"[22] The egalitarian theme, deriving its strength from the banking issue, became the most prominent principle of the Democratic Party.

Douglas's congressional opponent was the Whig John T. Stuart, an imposing Kentuckian residing in Springfield, who was well known and liked. To win, Douglas had to conduct an arduous campaign, which lasted from March until August. Often Douglas and Stuart debated the issues in the small towns of central and northern Illinois. These jousts could last for hours. One of the more memorable moments of the debates came in Springfield, when Stuart, angry over some of Douglas's charges, clutched his arms around Douglas's head and marched him around; Douglas, in response, bit Stuart's thumb so fiercely that it left a scar for several years.

Banks occupied center stage in the battle between Douglas and Stuart. Newspapers in that day were not so interested in verbatim reports as much as informing the public on how well the paper's candidate did against the other candidate. Thus one person's speech was poor, boring, illogical, and uninspiring, while the candidate of the paper's choice revealed truth in a new way, kept the multitudes enraptured, and revealed such a keen intelligence that all were impressed. It would seem that Douglas pressed the party line every time he spoke: a specie currency was a good thing, national banks were engines of monopoly, the independent treasury was the only solution to the banking crisis, and Whigs were really Federalists who wanted to leech prosperity away from the people. The Whigs found Douglas a horrid example of demagoguery: full of "unequalled harrangues,"[23] his ideas on banks "are altogether without a parallel," and Douglas shockingly declared himself to have an *unconquerable hostility to all Banks.*"[24]

Whigs argued against the independent treasury by saying that it gave the president too much power and too much patronage, but the substantial difference was over a credit system. They did not see how a specie-based currency system could meet the needs of commerce. The Whig editor of the Jacksonville *Illinoisan* explained, "Experience has fully proven, that one dollar in specie in a vault is simply sufficient to meet three dollars in drafts in circulation"; he added, "We are in favor of the credit system, because it is friendly to the laborer and producer, and scatters its blessings upon the poor man as well as the rich."[25] Douglas's analysis of banking was standard Democratic fare and showed little subtlety. The Whigs did point out a shortcoming in Douglas, however. Douglas earnestly pleaded for the economic growth of the state, and the Whigs correctly pointed out that such growth was impossible without the use of credit.

His congressional race was extraordinarily close. At first, the Whigs expected an easy victory because of the reputation of Stuart and the youth of Douglas, but Douglas was a tireless campaigner whose commonplace arguments scored points with many Illinois residents. He had also taken time out to cultivate the votes of Irish laborers working on the canals. The balloting was so close that, though the vote was taken in early August, a victor was not declared until September: Stuart, 18,248; Douglas, 18,213. The Little Giant had missed election by only thirty-five votes.

Douglas had done much better than expected because he carried the canal counties laden with Irish working-class voters, counties in which he obtained 62 percent of the votes cast. The Whigs soon figured this out and began fuming about the influence of alien voters in state races. But Douglas could not bear the thought of having lost by such a small margin. He suggested a rematch with Stuart, but Stuart of course had no intention of running a second race.

The egalitarian quality of the Illinois Democratic Party did not diminish after 1838. On January 8, 1839, the Democrats hosted a celebration of their party in Springfield, and they exhibited the continuing growth of egalitarianism in the party. After many speeches, they gave toasts. Orlando B. Ficklin, a future congressman, tipped his glass to republican liberty based on "equal rights and sustained by the virtue and intelligence of the people," while another called metallic currency "every where the poor man's friend." Judge McRoberts declared that banks and chartered monopolies were the enemies of the people, for "they toil not, neither do they spin, yet Solomon in all his glory, was not arrayed like one of these," while John A. McClernand warned of the aristocracy of wealth and monopolists. Douglas was there as well, and he raised a toast to "democratic principles. Founded upon the inalienable rights of man—political equality, freedom of thought, of speech, and of conscience, appealing to the intelligence and virtue of the people, like the dews of heaven, shed their blessings upon all alike."[26]

Democrats held conventions in late 1839 in preparation for the election of 1840. The county conventions demonstrated how deeply the party system had rooted itself, in standardizing issues throughout the state and in spreading the committee system that was the heart of the party apparatus. The state convention met on December 9, 1839, and there Douglas, who was a delegate from Sangamon County, was a member of the committee that composed the address to the citizens of the state. The address insisted upon the rights of the common man and repeated the charges that Democrats had made about the Federalist ancestry of the Whigs and about the dangers of banks, corporations, and monopolies. It emphasized a strict interpretation of the Constitution so as to preserve states' rights, it demanded freedom of religion, and it called for an end to exclusive privileges. Within its rhetoric was a distinct class appeal: Whigs favored "the *rich* and the *well-born*" and ignored the "*mass of people*." Thus Whigs believed governmental power belonged to the talented wealthy instead of to the people. But Democrats believed in equal rights and in earning a position in society by one's talents and hard work. The state Democratic convention of 1839 probably represented the triumph of party principles in Illinois. Some 250 delegates gathered, and nearly every county of the state was represented.

The address laid out the issues for the campaign and then went on to stress party regularity and obedience. "Political infidelity, is an evil not to be overlooked," the broadcast read, "and one that we must treat of in plain English and in all frankness and sincerity." The party faithfully protected the rights of the masses; hence, any person abandoning the Democratic Party could be ostracized, for the party "can therefore outlive any individual who may abandon her cause."[27] These words of Stephen A. Douglas, written with such a zealous spirit, underscore the importance of party for him and his expectation that his fellows as well as himself would be faithful at all times to the organization. His emphasis on "party regularity"—that is, the duty of individuals to accept the positions of the party when the party spoke through the agency of conventions or meetings—should be kept in mind because even Douglas, one of the most insistent advocates of party regularity, would have to face the eventual collision of party demands and individual conscience.

Before the election of 1840 absorbed all his time, Douglas made some changes in his private life. He resigned his position as land register on March 2 and returned to practicing law to earn his living. He thus traveled on the judicial circuit, hunting up cases, at times meeting and discussing issues with Abraham Lincoln. By this means, he met and conversed with political leaders throughout his part of the state.

During the election campaign, Douglas was nothing less than a horrific tornado traversing the state, making over two hundred speeches and becoming the most prominent Democrat defending the Van Buren administration. Several times, Democrats and Whigs debated the issues, frequently bringing Douglas to joust with the eminent Springfield Whig Abraham Lincoln. A three-day debate occurred in November 1839, just before the state party conventions, and then the oratorical contests continued into the campaign of 1840. One of the meetings, held in Springfield, was instructive about the strenuous character of electioneering for both orators and audience. Douglas met former governor Joseph Duncan in debate; Duncan spoke for three hours, and Douglas took several hours to defend Van Buren. Later that night, John Ewing from Indiana spoke on behalf of the Whigs, and at the end he agreed to debate the issues the next day. Ewing then made a five-hour speech. Douglas rebutted him and "carried the war into Africa," using "bitter sarcasm and the most burning eloquence," speaking from dusk to 10 p.m., probably another three to five hours of speechmaking.[28] Politicians and audiences back then were certainly made of stern stuff!

Most candidates in the election of 1840 in Illinois campaigned on national issues because, in all honesty, they were largely in agreement on state issues. This election has been known ever since as the Log Cabin and Hard Cider campaign because the Whigs had decided to outdo the Democrats in wooing the common man; they were determined to compete for the franchises of common people and to avoid the descent into oblivion that had met the Federalist Party. Thus the Whig campaign was filled with mottos about the commonplace origins of the Whig presidential candidate, William H. Harrison: he had a difficult boyhood, he liked to drink "hard cider," and he had been reared in a "log cabin." On top of this appeal, Whigs staged torchlight parades, barbecues, and pageants. The Democrats were appalled at Whig electioneering tactics that avoided discussion of the issues. At a meeting of the central committee in Springfield in June, Douglas drafted an appeal to the Democrats of the state in which he deprecated the campaign of the Whigs and was mortified at the low level of political discourse: the Whigs were making a "moral degradation of the human character [and of] the intellect of man."[29]

An important theme in Douglas's speeches during this contest was his affirmation of the principle of democracy, of the right of the majority to rule. At a Sangamon County meeting in July, he gave a speech—unrecorded—and one of the resolutions of the meeting emphasized that the nation had to have rule by the consent of the governed, "that the will of the people, constitutionally expressed, is the supreme law of the land."[30] Here were clear foreshadowings of the doctrine of popular sovereignty that was to be the hallmark of his later years. Also rising to the fore was an issue not yet national in scope but one of troubling dimensions. Somehow abolitionism and the rights of African Americans were crowding into the set of economic issues that Whigs and Democrats usually debated. Douglas did not hesitate to label Whig presidential aspirant William H. Harrison an abolitionist, and the editor of the *Illinois State Register* freely used racist appeals to attract voters. Together the topics of majority rule and abolitionism would be the center of Douglas's political life in the 1850s.

Whigs won the presidency in 1840 but did not conquer Illinois. The exertions of the Illinois Democratic Party, with Douglas at its head, rebuffed the Whig charge. Douglas received much credit locally and nationally for the result. So it was that in 1840, Douglas was cresting to the top of Illinois state politics. He had been in the state a mere seven years; he had started out nearly penniless in his pursuit of fame and fortune; and by good luck, drive, and hard work he had entered the legal profession and become perhaps the prominent Democratic orator in Illinois, a founder of the Democratic Party, a holder of federal office (register of the Springfield Land Office), a state's attorney, a state legislator, a candidate for Congress, and one of the ruling members of the Democratic Central Committee. And in November of 1840, he was all of twenty-seven years of age!

Douglas, the Democratic Party, and the First Gordian Knot

Douglas's early fame rested on two pillars, his oratory and his activity in creating the Democratic Party in Illinois. Oratory was a staple of past politics, but party organization was a novelty, and even in the antebellum years, it was still in its infancy, and many parts were missing. Procedures for choosing precinct leaders do not seem to have existed, rules for convention delegates seem not to have been written, and duties for the central committee seem not to have been defined. The Illinois Democratic Party did not have a constitution elucidating its government and its selection of officers. Rather, the convention system that arose was almost a spontaneous act of interested partisans—in some cases, of interested officeholders. So far as is known, the party did not have a treasurer. At some point, the organization obtained more definition about its levels of governance and its officers at the county, district, and state levels, but that clarification evidently came after the Civil War. Organization had indeed happened in Illinois, but it was far from resembling the formal structures of twentieth-century political parties and had far more spontaneity to it than contemporary claims would lead one to believe.

A youthful Douglas came to dominate and lead this party within the space of perhaps a decade. How he managed to do so is a vital question, for the role of leadership has been underappreciated in historical writing for some years now. The basic difficulties confronting American parties have been ably laid out in the work of John H. Aldrich, *Why Parties?* (1995). Two problems dominated. First, there was the difficulty of "collective action." Such problems arise when all the members of a community would greatly benefit if all worked together cooperatively, but they do not do so because each member's self-interest leads him (or her) to leave the task to others. Many people hope to obtain the benefits of collective action without having to contribute any labor, and therefore nothing gets done and no one gets any benefit. In the case of parties in frontier Illinois, people of the same persuasion would have greatly benefited from having an organization that promoted individuals for office who held the same political perspectives and values, but most people were unwilling to take the time and effort to create such an organization.

A second problem concerning party formation involves information costs. Legislation can be tedious to read, and potential candidates may have backgrounds that most are unaware of. To gather information about the quality of legislation and how it affects people and to find out the qualifications of candidates is time consuming and costly. Most citizens have to spend their time earning their daily bread and feeding their families. They do not have the time to ferret out this information.

Citizens need agents to do this work for them. Those agents are political leaders. These leaders create stable organizations of like-minded people that voters of a certain persuasion can usually trust; they can interpret legislation to explain the tendencies of proposed enactments or to create laws that will be beneficial; and they can recruit candidates for the party by being in a position to know their backgrounds. Parties exist in large measure because they are shortcuts for getting information about the world and for organizing like-minded people to act together in the political realm. Thus leadership solves the twin problems of information costs and collective action.

Stephen A. Douglas is a classic example of how certain leadership traits in politics can vault a person to the forefront. Douglas was no grand specimen of finely chiseled manhood with abnormal abilities. As commentary after commentary revealed, he was short for the society he adopted, his head was somewhat oversized, and his legs were stubby. But he had personal qualities that more than made up for any deficiencies in stature. First, he was a genuinely friendly person who enjoyed conversation and conviviality. He mixed in with people and enjoyed their company. Second, he had skills that readily solved the problems of collective action. Douglas was excellent at writing and debating, results of his studies at Brandon and Canandaigua. At the core of politics is the skill of communication, and those who have advantages in this area can become leaders. Third, Douglas was a workaholic who enjoyed politics, speech making, and policy creation. He devoured newspapers, congressional debates, books, and pamphlets. Thus he became a solution to the problem of information costs: he kept up on developments and could inform others about them. This type of activity came naturally to him.

Certainly there were the usual other traits that counted in Douglas's rise to the top of the Democratic organization. He was smart, attentive, and lucky. Some opportunities fell into his lap, but he was quick-witted enough to seize them. And he did manipulate people and seemingly enjoyed the trickery that went along with politics. Yet Douglas earned his high position because he did the hard, laborious, unending work of politics that few others would. The simple truth is that citizens may harbor a general disposition toward officials or policies, but that disposition will remain invisible and unarticulated unless some person is willing to do the labor of bringing those people together and forging them into an entity to make their ideas known. Without leadership, the inarticulate remain inarticulate. And so the Democrats of Illinois turned to Douglas because he did the hard work of politics. Leadership was his reward.

Here arises the first Gordian knot of democratic equality: the relationship of the party to what it professedly stood for, the equality of citizens. Douglas's experience in fact points to two distinct questions about equality in the politics of frontier Illinois. One question involves party machinery and whether it did foster equality, and the other question pertains to the significance of casting aside deference in establishing egalitarianism. The first steps of Douglas and his society in pursuit of democratic equality had much to commend it.

The development of a party system to give people a greater voice in politics was probably a correct advance in political practice. Certainly parties could be abusive, and certainly party managers could foil as much as assist the "will of the people," but without such an organization, the people had almost no voice at all. Parties created communities of like-minded individuals and allowed them to vent their aspirations and their fears; without parties, people were too isolated to have much effect on policies in the statehouse or at the nation's capital.

And the rise of democratic sentiments in the United States in the 1830s produced the death of deference. The early story of Douglas's life is a perfect example of how citizens of the 1830s cast aside the deferential quality of early American life. This victory of the Jacksonians over the presumed superiority of an upper class, being a purely social rather than a legal victory, has perhaps been undervalued by scholars, but it has given the United States a unique culture. For a democratic nation to arise, the idea that the people were equal in some fundamental sense—religious, philosophical, or otherwise—had to be established. The Jacksonians substituted a benign faith in the essential equality of all human beings for the ancient ideal of naturally or divinely ordained superiors. Ending deference was a victory for democracy, for egalitarianism.

Democrats, however, did not define equality precisely, and they had difficulty forming policies that protected and amplified this equality. Equality before the law, before nature, and before nature's God were undoubtedly prerequisites for a democratic society. Tougher questions, however, were soon to follow, and the inability of the Democrats to define exactly what democratic equality meant made problems. These dilemmas showed themselves most emphatically in the realm of economic policy and in Manifest Destiny.

Notes

1. SAD to Julius Granger, December 15, 1833, Douglas, *Letters*, 3.
2. SAD, autobiographical sketch, in Douglas, *Letters*, 57, 58.

3. Daniel Roberts, "A Reminiscence of Stephen A. Douglas," *Harper's New Monthly Magazine* 87 (November 1893): 958.

4. Harvey E. Pratt, "Stephen A. Douglas, Lawyer, Legislator, Register, and Judge: 1833–1843," *Lincoln Herald* 52 (February 1950): 42.

5. SAD to Julius N. Granger, November 14, 1834, in Douglas, *Letters*, 10.

6. SAD to Granger, May 24, 1835, Douglas, *Letters*, 19.

7. Speech at Lexington, MA, in *New York Times*, July 21, 1860.

8. SAD, Autobiographical Sketch, in Douglas, *Letters*, 57.

9. Gerald Leonard, *The Invention of Party Politics: Federalism, Popular Sovereignty, and Constitutional Development in Illinois* (Chapel Hill, NC, 2002), 103–15.

10. Robert W. Johannsen, *Stephen A. Douglas* (New York, 1973), 25–26.

11. Allen Johnson, *Stephen A. Douglas: A Study in American Politics* (New York, 1908), 64.

12. Douglas, Autobiographical Sketch, in Douglas, *Letters*, 63.

13. James W. Sheahan, *The Life of Stephen A. Douglas* (New York, 1860), 20.

14. Roberts, "Reminiscence of Douglas," 958.

15. Douglas, *Letters*, 27–30.

16. SAD to Julius Granger, May 9, 24, 1835, in Douglas, *Letters*, 15, 1.

17. Staunton, VA, *Spectator*, September 4, 1860.

18. SAD to Caleb Cushing, February 4, 1852, Douglas, *Letters*, 237.

19. "To the Democratic Republicans of Illinois," Douglas, *Letters*, 42–49.

20. (Vandalia) *Ill St Reg*, November 4, 1837, June 8, 1838.

21. (Vandalia) *Ill St Reg*, June 22, 1838.

22. July 20, 1838.

23. *Jacksonville Illinoian*, February 3, 1838.

24. *Quincy Whig*, June 9, 30, 1838.

25. *Jacksonville Illinoian*, January 6, February 10, 1838.

26. (Vandalia) *Ill St Reg*, January 29, 1839.

27. *Ill St Reg*, December 14, 18, 1839.

28. *Ill St Reg*, October 2, 1840.

29. *Ill St Reg*, June 12, 1840.

30. July 10, 1840.

CHAPTER TWO

~

Democracy, Commerce, and Manifest Destiny

In the 1830s, Stephen A. Douglas felt the exhilaration of being at the forefront of tearing down class barriers, destroying deferential behavior, and glorifying the common man. He and his Democratic colleagues sang praises to equality and democracy while denouncing those who cautioned the people to respect property rights and order. He did not drop the banner of democratic equality as he entered into the 1840s but indeed hoisted it higher.

Democratic equality, however, was not a social condition acquired merely by exhortation. Democratic equality required a program, and therein lay several dilemmas. Douglas's economic policies were those of the Jacksonians—the policies of free trade and laissez-faire (the latter meaning that government should not intervene in the economy but leave it to the private actions of individuals). He had campaigned in favor of those policies during the 1830s and continued to do so after being elected to Congress in 1843. During his years in the House of Representatives, a new issue arose that involved the question of democracy—landed expansion. Shortly after his entrance into Congress, the nation acquired vast new territories in the West, and Douglas and his fellow Democrats lauded the acquisition as a means to preserve American equality. In this, he and the Democratic Party were deceived: laissez-faire economics and territorial expansion may have been many things, but they were not solutions to the Gordian knots of democratic equality.

Illinois Party Politics and the Ascent to Congress in 1843

Democrats had taken control of much of Illinois government by 1840 except for one crucial area: the judiciary. Ever since the days of Thomas Jefferson, those on the democratic side of politics distrusted the arbitrary power of judges, the lack of popular control over them, and the tendency of judges to favor vested rights and families of high standing. Democratic animosity toward the judiciary in Illinois erupted in 1839 because the Whig judges threatened the Democratic Party's electoral base.

Although the vote totals were quite close, Illinois was slowly turning into a Democratic state. In the presidential election of 1836, the Democrats obtained 54.7 percent of the vote, earned 50.8 percent in the gubernatorial race of 1838, and posted a victory in the presidential contest of 1840 with 51.0 percent of the popular vote. The closeness of the results meant that the Democrats had to hold on to all the groups that supported them, and one of the most important of these groups was the small community of Irish canal workers. Whig politicians sought to eliminate some Irish from voting on the basis that they were immigrants, not naturalized citizens. In a court case in Jo Daviess County, a judge decided in the Whigs' favor and declared that unnaturalized residents had no right to vote in Illinois state elections.

Douglas and other Democrats recognized the importance of the immigrant vote. They contested the ruling and took the case to the Illinois State Supreme Court, and there Douglas argued that unnaturalized residents deserved to vote because the state, not the federal government, set requirements for voting. The Constitution of Illinois only required that voters be male, white, and twenty-one years of age—the state Constitution did not require naturalization. Douglas won the case, however, not because of the merits of his argument, but because he discovered a clerical error made by the clerk of the circuit court. Democrats were nonetheless put on notice that the Whigs intended to deprive them of the immigrant vote.

Coincident with the alien voting case, there arose another controversy involving the Illinois State Supreme Court. The Democratic governor, Thomas Carlin, tried to remove a secretary of state, a Whig, who had been appointed nearly ten years earlier. The secretary of state refused to yield his position. The question of the right of a governor to appoint his own cabinet eventually landed in the state supreme court, with Douglas and other Democratic luminaries arguing for the governor's right of appointment. Only four judges composed the Illinois Supreme Court in 1839; two excused themselves from the case, and the remaining two were Whigs. The Whig justices then decided in favor of the sitting secretary of state and against the Democratic governor.

The Democrats responded by attacking the court in the election of 1840. They warned that the Whigs wanted judges to have life appointments and that the judges were thwarting the popular will. Indeed, Douglas's argument before the court was based on a strict reading of the state constitution, emphasizing its popular sovereignty essence: "All power is inherent in, and derivable from the people; that our government was instituted by them, for their mutual benefit and protection."[1]

After three attempts to remove the secretary of state, the governor finally won. Because of the Democratic triumph in the election of 1840, the Illinois Senate fell into Democratic hands. The governor then removed his Whig opponent and requested that the senate give the position to Stephen A. Douglas. On November 30, 1840, the senate confirmed Douglas's appointment, and he again became a public official. However, the position of secretary of state of Illinois had few duties and was perhaps more appropriate for a politician at the end of his career than at the beginning. Douglas probably did not look at it as other than a mere way station to something more prominent and important.

Illinois Democrats vented their anger at the state supreme court in December 1840 when they began altering the institution. First, they expanded the number of justices from four to nine. Second, the justices would act as circuit court judges as well as supreme court judges; the Democrats ended the practice of having judges distinctly for the circuit courts. A battle flared up between the Whigs and the Democrats over the proposed changes in the state supreme court, and the Democrats triumphed. The governor sent five names for the newly created justiceships to the state senate, and among these was Stephen A. Douglas. Douglas wanted the position and had worked strenuously behind the scenes to get the judiciary reform measure passed in the legislature. He then resigned his position as secretary of state on February 16, 1841—he barely served three months—and on March 1, 1841, he became a supreme court judge of Illinois. For his actions and his command of the party faithful, Douglas was called "Generalissimo" of the Democrats of Illinois, and from this time on, he was often referred to as "Judge Douglas."[2]

Although many had their doubts about the legal ability of the twenty-seven-year-old Douglas, he ran an efficient court that disposed of cases quickly, and Douglas's opinions on several important cases stood the test of time. Abolitionist William H. Herndon, no political friend of Douglas's, said that as a judge, Douglas was a "broad, fair, and liberal-minded man."[3] An eminent Whig lawyer, Justin Butterfield, offered "that little squatty Democrat" a begrudging compliment; Butterfield thought he could best Douglas in the courtroom, but Douglas "listens patiently, comprehends the law and grasps the facts by intuition; then decides calmly, clearly and quietly and then makes the lawyers sit down."[4]

During his tenure as a supreme court judge, Douglas presided over two prominent cases. The first involved fugitive slaves. New Englanders had commenced a broad immigration into Illinois and had brought with them some individuals who were avowed abolitionists. It was only a matter of time before someone acted on his or her beliefs and assisted slaves. One such person was Quincy physician Richard Eells, who was arrested for aiding a fugitive slave. Eells's lawyers contended that due to a U.S. Supreme Court decision (*Prigg v. Pennsylvania*), only federal authorities, not state authorities, could enforce the Fugitive Slave Act, and therefore Eells should be released. Judge Douglas decided against Eells because the State of Illinois had passed its own fugitive slave law, and, because each state had the right to maintain the peace, Eells could be arrested by Illinois officers. Douglas then handed down a monetary fine ($400) but did not impose a prison term; he felt that the fine served as a warning that more severe consequences might follow if Eells persisted in illegal behavior.

The second case involved the arrival of Mormons into Illinois. The Mormons originated in upstate New York in the 1820s and derived their theological views from the religious visions of Joseph Smith. From his visions, he published *The Book of Mormon* in 1830 and created the Church of Jesus Christ of Latter-Day Saints. He attracted followers, and they decided to set up their own community devoted to practicing their particular religious tenets. Hostility in New York led the Mormons to move to Ohio, and then again to Missouri. In Missouri, violence against the Mormons rose to such a pitch that in 1838 Governor Lilburn Boggs, a Democrat, issued an "extermination order"—that the Mormons had to be subordinated or driven out of the state. The Mormons thus resettled in Illinois in 1839 around Nauvoo, a place within Douglas's judicial circuit. The entrance of several thousand new persons into Illinois had distinct political repercussions: those several thousand new persons meant also several thousand new voters. Both Whigs and Democrats vied for the votes of the Mormons, but it turned out that the Democrats won the contest.

Douglas faced the Mormon issue in court because the Missourians had charged Joseph Smith and several of his followers with treason to the state of Missouri due to an election-day altercation in 1838. Smith had fled to Illinois, and the governor of Missouri tried to extradite him back to Missouri for trial. Smith was arrested in Nauvoo and held for trial in Quincy. There Douglas dismissed the case against Smith on procedural grounds, not on the merits of the case. Later, Smith again faced extradition because in 1842 someone attempted to assassinate ex-governor Boggs, and the Missourians held Smith accountable. On the advice of Illinois governor Ford, Douglas, and others, Smith in 1843 surrendered himself to the United States District Court in Springfield, was tried, and was then released, as there was no evidence to connect him with the assassination attempt.

The fortunes of the Mormons and the destiny of Stephen A. Douglas then parted company. Douglas soon resigned his judgeship to run for Congress in mid-1843, and thus he was removed from the dilemmas of the Mormons and their relations with others. The Mormons, though, continued to suffer persecution, this time in Illinois. In 1844, Smith ran for the presidency and was arrested for trying to commit treason to the state (the charge being that he was in a conspiracy with foreign nations). He was taken to Carthage, where an anti-Mormon mob stormed the jail and killed him. After that, the Mormons left Illinois in 1846 to head west, eventually settling in the present state of Utah.

The Mormon episode revealed several of Douglas's important characteristics. When the issue of religion flared up in Illinois in the 1840s, Douglas had no apparent connection to a church. Frontier Illinois voters evidently did not place much pressure on their politicians to have strong religious connections. And in this episode with the Mormons, Douglas clearly showed his hostility to government-imposed restrictions on freedom of conscience. As to religious doctrine, the policy of the Democrats was, in the words of the *Illinois State Register*, "to let them [Mormons] alone. . . . Every man has a right to worship God as he pleases."[5] Throughout his life, Douglas demonstrated an intense dislike of religious leaders imposing their views on public affairs.

Douglas resigned his judgeship on June 28, 1843, so that he could plunge back into the whirlpool of electoral politics, having been on the bench for only two years. However, those two years displayed a crucial aspect of Douglas's character: he had profound sympathy for and acted charitably toward the persecuted and socially ostracized. In the cases of both the Irish and the Mormons, he reacted against the prejudices of the arbiters of society and embraced the causes of those dismissed from the charmed circles of polite society. Here was his egalitarianism at work. Certainly some political calculation entered into his thinking—both the Irish and the Mormons were significant voting blocs in a competitive electoral district. But such overtures could also harm his fortunes as well; the unpopularity of the Irish and the Mormons could cost him votes. The fact is that Douglas almost always sided with the people of whom polite society disapproved.

His sympathies had one limitation. His outcasts were those of European descent, not of non-European descent. Douglas always raised the banner of liberation for the oppressed European; he had no feeling for non-Europeans, especially Native Americans and African Americans. How Douglas learned this antipathy for African Americans is unknown. Perhaps he had some incident with black people early in his life that has never been revealed, perhaps he learned his prejudices from the upland southerners he joined culturally in Illinois, or perhaps he simply absorbed the general cultural disposition of European Americans to disparage non-Europeans. Certainly Douglas never lived in communities that had an appreciable number of black people until he moved to Springfield—neither in Vermont nor in New York. The sources of Douglas's racism are destined to remain a mystery.

But in his concern for the lowly, Douglas mirrored perfectly the attitudes of Jacksonian Democrats. The people who professed allegiance to the Democratic Party tended to evince concern only for the European part of humankind; often they held an utter contempt for those not of European descent. The Democrats of antebellum America wanted an egalitarian community of Europeans only—equal rights, access to productive resources, and a society characterized by the middle. They did not want that equality extended to non-Europeans, and they did not want non-Europeans included in their community. Historians have generally called this situation an example of "herrenvolk democracy"—democracy only for the master race or dominant ethnic group, and subjugation for those different. Because most modern notions of democracy are *inclusive* (bringing all people within the political structure) instead of *exclusive* (providing democracy only for a few), modern students have trouble understanding the Democrats of antebellum America. It does look like a grand contradiction: Europeans wanted equal rights and opportunities for themselves but then would not extend equality to others. It may not be the easiest mental framework to understand, but it is the one that existed. And Stephen A. Douglas demonstrated it as well as anyone—both the good and the bad of the antebellum Democratic Party.

Congressional Politics

As was once remarked of Abraham Lincoln, so it could also be said of Stephen A. Douglas: his ambition was an engine that knew no rest. While being an Illinois Supreme Court judge had its advantages, Douglas preferred electoral politics. Part of the reason for his leaving the bench may have been that Illinois representation in Congress increased from three to seven members after the census of 1840. New opportunities thus unfolded for the politically ambitious. Douglas moved his residence out of the old Third Congressional District, where the Whigs held sway, and made Quincy his home in 1841. Quincy belonged to the new Fifth Congressional District, and the possibilities of a Democratic victory were good.

A return to electoral politics would also return Douglas to issues he was familiar with. Illinois was a growing state with distinct interests and needs. The state required a transportation system to move its agricultural products to markets. Rivers and the Great Lakes were a part of that transportation system—that is, once obstacles in the rivers had been removed, harbors had been built on the lakes, and canals had been constructed to tie all the water routes together.

Another transportation alternative was the railroad, whose potentialities were just being understood. Markets for Illinois agricultural products were the East Coast, parts of the South, and Europe. Because farmers near the Great Lakes exported a significant percentage of their crops overseas, they had an obvious interest in policies that stimulated foreign trade. Hence the economy of Illinois led its representatives to champion obvious federal policies: federal assistance for internal improvements and a low federal tariff that allowed farmers to sell their products to foreign markets.

Douglas's decision to run for Congress came at a moment when the Whigs suffered internal division. Although the Whigs had won nationally in the election of 1840, their presidential candidate, William Henry Harrison, died shortly after taking office, and the vice president, John Tyler of Virginia, succeeded him. Leading Whigs, especially Henry Clay of Kentucky, wanted to press the Whig program of high tariffs to stimulate manufacturing, distribution of surplus federal revenue to the states for funding internal improvements, creation of a new national bank, and slowing down American migration to the West by keeping land prices high. Tyler, however, was a states' rights Whig and did not want any of this program. An uproar swept over the Whigs, and they became a bitterly divided party. Conditions were thus ripe for a Democratic revival. The economic issues that had marked Jackson's presidency were now in full force in American politics—a national bank, western land prices, the tariff, and internal improvements.

On June 5, at the small town of Griggsville, some thirty-seven delegates met to select the Democratic congressional candidate for the new Fifth District. Former governor Thomas Carlin led in the early voting for the congressional nomination, but the delegates took a half-hour recess, returned, and promptly voted Douglas the candidate. Douglas, presiding as judge not far away, immediately accepted the nomination. Douglas was probably the strongest candidate the Democrats could have chosen, but it was also likely that Douglas worked his contacts to steer the nomination his way. In the platform, the Fifth District Democrats declared their allegiance to "eternal truth and justice—they acknowledge and sustain man's political and social equality—his right of self-government."[6] They then denounced the Whig tariff of 1842 and their attempts to resurrect a national bank.

Douglas's Whig opponent was Quincy lawyer Orville H. Browning, a Kentucky émigré with rather formal manners. He and Douglas agreed to debate in a number of towns throughout July. Protectionism and national banks were the focus of both men's arguments. Browning stood for a high tariff to create a home market to stimulate manufacturing, and a national bank to regulate the currency. Douglas declared himself for "glorious free trade," holding that "the tariff arrays the rich against the poor." As to banks, Douglas, according to one person, was opposed to banks of all kinds and believed in a "hard money system." These debates lasted for hours in each community, and by the August 7 voting date, both men were exhausted.

Even allowing for distortion, the Whig reaction to Douglas was interesting. The Whigs were taken aback by Douglas's style. Douglas talked probably twice as long as Browning. When it was his turn, he "threw out a keg of cider and a coon skin, rolled up his sleeves, and went to the attack." In his argument, the "young Sampson of the locofoco party" was full of errors and issued to the audience a "tirade of nonsense and falsehood." One Whig observer did Douglas some justice, however. "I admit what he said," wrote the Whig, "he said well, and with *much energy of manner*; but there was no argument, no reason, no patriotism; it was all bold and vague assertion, without proof, intended to work on the passions and prejudices of his party."[7]

This latter charge actually held some merit, for Douglas in his speeches often rolled out one fact after another without any central principle holding everything together. His speeches displayed an amazing command of factual information—not always scrupulously used, for in political contests, Douglas had no intention of being objective—and he usually gave his audiences a simple rendition of the controversy at hand. He stuck to the basic propositions of his party—equality before the law, no special treatments for anyone, no monopoly, no corporations, and opportunity for all. He rammed facts into these categories regardless of whether they made sense or not. And at all times, his earnestness suffused his words. He seldom made jokes, and his intensity was revealed in his emphatic physical movements during his presentation; he waved his arms, shook his fists, and pranced about the podium. It was hardly any wonder that Whigs, who prided themselves on self-control, found Douglas's speaking performances an unholy spectacle, the ravings of a demagogue.

Douglas won election to Congress on August 7 by a close margin, 8,641 votes to Browning's 8,180. Democrats in the state rejoiced, for they had nearly swept the congressional races, winning six of seven, losing only the district that housed the Whig stronghold of Sangamon County. Overall, the Democrats distanced themselves from the Whigs and started a political dominance in the state. Adding all the ballots cast in the congressional races of 1843, the Democrats earned 49,482 votes, 52.7 percent of the total, while the Whigs got only 42,288, or 45.1 percent; the remaining 1,947 votes were cast for the Liberty Party, an abolitionist organization (2.1 percent), and some scattered votes for others (116, or 0.1 percent).

The first session of the Twenty-eighth Congress commenced on December 4, 1843, and so Douglas as well as the rest of the Illinois delegation scurried to Washington, D.C. The capital city was nothing to brag about, and even Illinoisans—supposedly representing the frontier—found the place dirty, unkempt, half finished, and unhealthy. Douglas, after visiting his family on his way to the District of Columbia, found boarding and prepared to begin life as a national legislator, a role he occupied until his death.

Whigs and Democrats had the 1844 presidential election on their minds, however, and most of Douglas's first taste of congressional activity was jockeying for position on the issues and forming the alliances that would produce victory in November 1844. Douglas was a firm backer of Martin Van Buren, former president but loser of the election of 1840. Sharp divisions appeared within the Democratic Party that made Van Buren's nomination problematic. South Carolina's states' rights champion, Senator John C. Calhoun, distrusted Van Buren and worked against him. Within the South generally, a sentiment existed that Van Buren was not a strong candidate. Westerners also formed a distinct group within the party, and they smarted under the belief that the development of the western states had been sacrificed to the economic interests of the East.

Douglas may have been a freshman legislator, but he was not a bashful one. He earned a reputation for his first major speech in Congress by arguing for a bill that would refund Andrew Jackson the fine of $1,000 that a judge had sentenced him to pay in 1815 for imposing martial law in New Orleans. Douglas insisted that Jackson had suspended normal civil proceedings to enable the city to survive the British attack and that as soon as the emergency had passed he lifted the order. The Illinoisan identified strongly with Jackson, saying that a blot on Jackson's name was a blot on the history of the United States. The bill passed the House and the Senate by overwhelming majorities. Some months later, Douglas visited Jackson at his plantation in Nashville, and there Jackson thanked Douglas for his powerful speech.

In another incident, Douglas showed that he was willing to use his stump-speaking techniques in the halls of Congress to defend Democratic ideals. In this case, it was the right of states to elect congressmen either by creating separate congressional districts or by electing all of them at large (that is, the state's voters cast ballots for a list of candidates, and those who obtained the most became the state's congressmen). Douglas spoke for the committee on elections and insisted that the Constitution clearly divided the spheres of activity between the states and the federal government; the Constitution gave election procedures to the states, and therefore Congress should admit those who were chosen in the manner prescribed by a state, in this case, the at-large procedure. When attacked for his views, Douglas responded in Illinois fashion. Massachusetts congressman John Quincy Adams, former president and the epitome of

New England cultural reserve, was aghast: "In the midst of his roaring, to save himself from choking, he stripped off and cast away his cravat, unbuttoned his waistcoat, and had the air and aspect of a half-naked pugilist."[8] Douglas, however, won the day.

As was true throughout his life, Douglas never showed deference, and he never shied away from battle. Sharp-witted, sarcastic, and earnest, he commanded attention. Before long, he crossed swords with the South Carolinians, who took it upon themselves to preach to everyone else the meaning of the Constitution. The issue was river and harbor improvements. For Douglas and the Illinois delegation, river and harbor subsidies were of vital concern to their farmer constituents. Because the improvements were to be given to the Mississippi River system and the Great Lakes, Douglas believed they came under the interstate commerce clause of the Constitution and were legitimate appropriations for the national government. South Carolina's Robert Barnwell Rhett raised the red flag of danger: given Douglas's views, all rivers and harbors were interstate and international in character, expenditures would grow, the federal government would pay all existing state schemes, and soon the federal government would grow into a leviathan. Douglas justified his Democratic credentials by referring to the policies of Andrew Jackson, who had favored internal improvements if they had an interstate nature. The South Carolinians dismissed this reliance upon the deeds of Jackson, finding Jackson's opinions irrelevant. Representative Isaac Holmes did capture Douglas's unusual worship of Jackson, however, when he observed that Douglas based his advocacy not on principle but on the acts of one man: "Jackson said so; ergo it is so."[9] Here Douglas got his first taste of southern extremism.

Congressmen debated many other important matters, such as the tariff, national banks, and the gag rule (used to stop the presentation of antislavery petitions in the House of Representatives), but Douglas did not contribute to these discussions, partly due to health problems. One other subject did emerge that for him became supreme above all others: territorial expansion. Toward the end of the session, after the Democratic National Convention had chosen James K. Polk for the party's presidential nomination rather than Van Buren, the question of Texas annexation and the boundary of Oregon swept away other issues. In a speech praising the Democratic Party, Douglas put his stamp of approval on expansion. Oregon and Texas, he said, must be brought into the Union before England subverted American prospects, ruined the U.S. cotton trade, and eliminated western grains from the English market. While he had a commercial vision in his claims for Texas and Oregon (and Cuba), he also emphasized the expansion of American political practices, to extend "the principles of civil and religious liberty over a large portion of the continent."[10]

Douglas returned home to campaign for reelection to Congress in 1844, and afterward to work for Polk's election in November, but certain aspects of his political career in Congress were beginning to take shape. First, Douglas was given to arduous labor. His speeches did not come from mere sentiment. He did the hard work of finding information and then using the facts, whether accurately or not, to make a coherent argument. A Douglas speech in Congress was filled with historical knowledge; when he dealt with international affairs, he researched treaties and their backgrounds. Douglas did not go into debate unarmed, and he used his memory, quick wit, and sarcasm to effect when challenged.

He also attended to the Democratic Party machinery at all times, and did so by several means. The first was by staying in contact with newspaper editors, especially the Springfield *Illinois Daily State Register*. Generally, the relationship between Douglas and the paper, which was the voice of the Illinois Democratic Party in the antebellum years, was cordial, although at times the paper questioned Douglas's ability to bring home the river and harbor bacon the residents so badly craved. Charles Lanphier owned and edited the Springfield paper after 1846, and he and Douglas worked together quite well. Douglas promoted other newspaper editors and stayed in touch with a considerable number of them. Probably the most notable individual he promoted was James Sheahan, who in the 1850s became editor of the Chicago *Daily Times* and later wrote a biography about Douglas. As well, Douglas kept in contact with important individuals in the state legislature—he was very much interested in becoming a U.S. senator—and he sought to promote his friends to federal offices. In the nineteenth century, the procedure of getting political friends appointed to jobs in government was called patronage. Douglas's correspondence is filled with Illinoisans asking for favors, and Douglas sent scores of letters to presidents seeking places for his friends. Sometimes Douglas succeeded, and sometimes he failed and became vexed and angry; the process consumed much of his time and energy.

Jacksonian Economic Issues and Democratic Equality

When Douglas entered Congress, economic issues fueled the debate between the parties. That the economic agenda shaped partisan differences had been true since the election of Andrew Jackson in 1828, and that agenda consisted of the appropriate federal policies toward banks, internal improvements, the sale of western lands held by the federal government, and the tariff. These struggles to determine government involvement in the economy constitute one of the mother-lode areas of the Gordian knots of democratic equality. The problem, simply put, is how meaningful can political equality in a democracy be if the society is marked by extreme economic inequality? The extent of economic inequality may be shaped by legislation, and thus the matter of economic policy is crucial for a democratic polity.

Whigs generally argued for government intervention in the economy, whereby Congress spent money on internal improvements, kept the tariff high to force Americans to manufacture for themselves, restrained westward migration so as to produce more cities engaged in commerce and manufacturing, and regulated the amount of credit in the financial system by establishing a national bank. Whigs expected the United States to remain agricultural, but they wanted more development in commerce and industry. Moreover, Whigs accepted economic inequality in society, a society divided into income classes. For them, this was the obvious result of unequal talents, and any attempt to create a general economic equality could only be obtained by denying the talented the chance to exercise their abilities, and such denial cost society so much in forgone improvement that it was foolish to attempt; moreover, to deny a person the right to accumulate all that he or she wanted was a profound violation of an individual's natural rights.

Democrats usually exhibited unity on their economic platform, but they had some difficulty with the question of equality. Democrats opposed high tariff duties, favored low western land prices, generally believed that the state governments should handle internal improvements except for arteries that were truly interstate in nature, and distrusted banks and banknotes. Most Democrats believed that the nation should be a land of small farmers for as long as possible and should not use government to prod the population into manufacturing before its appropriate time. A widespread attitude among Democrats was that an active, powerful national government made policies that gave unnatural advantages to the wealthy and limited the opportunities of commoners; in short, an energetic government redistributed income from the poor to the wealthy. Upon this reasoning, Democrats claimed that they stood for equality while the Whig program gave the propertied elite more power and wealth.

Yet problems suffused the Democrats' stand. They did not deny that people had different talents that led to unequal outcomes; rather, they said that government should not magnify such outcomes by policies that favored the rich and wellborn. Democrats basically accepted the results of a natural inequality in society; they advocated a laissez-faire program. Many expected the United States to remain a small farmer society for generations, and such a society would be roughly egalitarian because farmers by their own exertions could only do so much to earn extra wealth. For some Democrats, equality meant exact equality before the law, and no special privileges to any group. Even still, the party's leaders, and not a few of its idealists, offered no program for reaching and maintaining economic equality in American society. Their solution was a laissez-faire solution, and ultimately—as they well knew—laissez-faire would fail to sustain equality. Over time, the United States would fall into a crass inequality such as existed in Europe when excess population could not become farmers by removing to unoccupied land.

The question of equality divided the Democrats into several groups. One extreme faction was the "agrarian" wing of the party. Composed mainly of easterners, some southerners, and a few working-class leaders, they argued for a nation composed of farmers who only partly raised crops for a market. They distrusted commerce, banking, and economic development in general. Another faction, one almost directly opposite of the agrarians, was the commercial Democrats, who believed that equality could be maintained through the process of market expansion and economic growth. They did not fear commerce or industry so long as both evolved naturally and were not forced upon society by foolish federal policies. These Democrats favored what today would be called economic development. The difficulty with their position, however, was that it naturally produced inequality. And of course there were those Democrats who opted for some combination of the agrarian and economic development visions.

Stephen A. Douglas was a commercial Democrat, not an agrarian Democrat. He wanted economic development, and his years in the House of Representatives and the Senate of the United States were devoted to obtaining policies that allowed the western states to mature economically. After 1846, the bulk of his political skill was devoted to questions arising from Manifest Destiny and slavery's future, but he always gave some time to arguing for policies to enhance western development. By looking at his record on the tariff, banks, internal improvements, and western lands, Douglas's views on political economy can be found, as well as his quizzical stand on equality.

Douglas's tariff stance mirrored perfectly the sentiments of the Old Northwest, the states surrounding the Great Lakes. When the tariff issue waxed hot in the 1830s and 1840s, he used standard arguments. In the election of 1844, he addressed partisans in St. Louis and denounced the Whig tariff of 1842 as an act of oppression to "plunder [the] American laborer for the benefit of a few large capitalists." Although the tariff of 1846 drastically reduced tariff duties and seemed destined to become a hot political issue, a soaring prosperity after 1848 lulled the tariff issue to sleep until 1858. Thus, for most of his years in Washington, Douglas did not confront a citizenry engaged in questions of foreign trade. Probably the most telling remark he made about the tariff came in 1855 when he declared, "I am a free trade man to the fullest extent that we can carry it."[11] He later explained his policy stances to his father-in-law in 1859. The issue of protection had ended; it "has ceased to be a political issue," and the country had settled for the Democratic position of a tariff sufficient to generate enough revenue for the legitimate needs of the federal government, but duties so arranged as to give some protection to American manufacturers.[12]

Douglas made too few remarks about the tariff to probe to any depth his sympathies on the subject, but he seems to have represented faithfully the general Democratic position. During a debate over a donation of public land to Iowa, however, his understanding of economic operations was clarified and placed distinctly within the free trade camp. In his remarks, he interjected, "Gentlemen do not seem to be able to comprehend how it is that two parties can make a contract by which both parties will be benefitted. Why, sir, it is only upon that principle that the world is benefitted by the exchange of different productions. The whole system of exchange and of commerce is predicated upon the principle that exchange is beneficial to both parties."[13] And here is in truth the heart of free-market economics: contracts made between individuals, so long as they are not coerced, benefit both parties. Exchange of goods is not a matter of a winner and a loser, but of both participants achieving gains. This declaration puts Douglas solidly in the camp of free-market economics, in domestic and foreign trade, and marks him as favorably disposed to increased commercial activity.

Enhanced commercial activity could not occur without transportation links to important markets, and Douglas thus became a leading spokesman for land grants to railroads and funding for harbor and river improvements. Indeed, the need for federal aid for transportation facilities for the West was the backbone of westerners' complaints that their section was ignored while Congress pampered the South and East by lavishing money on them. By the mid-1840s, a rivers and harbors movement had emerged to put pressure on Congress for appropriations, a movement that some southerners saw as a means to effect a coalition between the South and the West.

In giving land to railroads, Douglas displayed some ingenuity and interesting thinking. He did not disparage state-owned enterprises, and when he had been a state legislator, he had argued in favor of public enterprise; evidently his model was the Erie Canal, owned and operated by the state of New York. In the case of private companies, he wanted the legislation to have appropriate state oversight of the corporation's behavior. By the mid-1840s, talk of a transcontinental railroad had begun, stimulated by a proposal of Asa Whitney of Illinois. Douglas did not like the proposal, because Whitney wanted to become the president of a company that would obtain 144,000 square miles from the government, thereby earning an obscene profit. Douglas clearly thought in terms of states' rights: he pondered about whether to donate land to states and then let them build the railroads or to assign the task to a private company rather than having the federal government do the work.

In a pioneering measure, Congress in 1850 gave away about one and a half million acres of public land to Illinois to build a railroad (the Illinois Central), and Douglas was questioned about the constitutionality of such a measure as well as its practicality. Then a senator in 1850, Douglas explained that the land given was in a checkerboard pattern, with one square being given to the company and an adjacent square to be sold at public auction. The reason the scheme would work was that internal improvements created migration to these lands because now farmers had the ability to ship crops to markets. That condition also made the land more valuable, so its market value rose. Douglas calculated that without the railroad, the price of the land at sale was $1.25 per acre, but no one bought the land because of its isolation from markets. By granting some land to make transportation available, the land attracted immigrants, and the value rose to at least $2.50 per acre. Hence the government actually gained, because the land, formerly unsellable, was now sold at an enhanced price, and the revenue that was gained more than offset the value of the lands given away.

Most of Douglas's energies on economic policy centered on getting federal aid for river and harbor improvements and canal construction. He was probably not a free agent on the subject because his constituents demanded not only his exertions but results. At the same time, he confronted southerners—especially Cotton State southerners—who questioned his Democratic credentials and his allegiance to states' rights principles. During the vital session of 1846, Congress passed a rivers and harbors bill that Douglas had labored to secure, only to witness President Polk veto it because of states' rights principles and the limited powers of the national government. In a subdued response to Polk's message, Douglas emphasized how he agreed with the limited powers of the central government but that he still believed that if Jackson had approved internal improvements, then the constitutionality of the proceedings should not be questioned. He continued to be miffed at the scruples of extreme states' rights southerners on the subject.

Although funding for river and harbor improvements passed Congress during the administrations of Zachary Taylor and Millard Fillmore (1849–1853), Douglas came to doubt the wisdom of the approach that he and his colleagues were taking. By 1852, Douglas announced that Congress's method of fostering harbor construction for the Great Lakes was incorrect. The funding was too small, and too many projects were included. To get proper funding, he proposed giving the states the ability to pass tonnage taxes on commerce, as had been done in colonial days, to permit permanent structures to be made. That certainly changed the nature of the debate. Instantly his Democratic colleagues asked where he found the constitutional power of the states to levy tonnage taxes, and soon the Senate was in an uproar.

Experience had proved to Douglas that the problem was that insufficient funding given to harbor improvements led to the building of weak structures; storms then blew away whatever had been built. He found the origins of the problem in the motives of legislators: they all wanted a piece of the funding so that they could tout their records to their constituents. But that process divided the pool of funds so much that no single location received enough money to make permanent structures. Douglas came to the conclusion that distant government was not well suited to handle local problems, a position that matched his insistence on local popular sovereignty.[14] There was an economic equivalent, however, to his political formulation. He laid down as a distinct rule that when possible, Congress should allow economic activity to be undertaken by businessmen rather than by government. The reason was that "business men, experienced men, whose fortunes and hearts are enlisted in the work," will increase the likelihood of success.[15] Distant politicians did not have the concentration necessary to see great works through to completion. And this attitude squared well with the laissez-faire orientation of the party, the belief that business life should usually be left to businessmen with little interference from government.

The disposition of public land posed a small dilemma for Douglas, especially as he was in Congress when the agitation for a homestead bill rose in popularity. The homestead ideal was to offer to actual settlers on the public domain (the land owned in the West by the federal government) a farm of 160 acres without charging a price: free land for actual settlers. Douglas's use of land actually depended on charging a price. In the debates in Congress in 1854 over the homestead, Douglas said little and voted for the measure. Publicly he sided with the settler and against charging high land prices. One surmises that Douglas's sympathies for the small farmer outweighed his desire to establish transportation routes.

Douglas's stand on the disposition of public lands took clear form in the proposal of Dorothea Dix to use proceeds from the sale of land to fund asylums for the insane. He did not like the proposal primarily because it detracted from development of the West. Soon all sorts of uses of the western land for charitable purposes would be concocted, and then how could the West develop? Douglas only approved land giveaways under the condition that they serve transportation needs and raise the price of the land yet unsold.

Douglas actually participated little in economic debates after 1846, and in one area the lack of information is especially irksome—finance. Illinois had a wretched experience with banking in the 1830s and early 1840s, leaving many Whigs and Democrats hostile to financial institutions. Hostility to banking, however, clashed with the desire for economic growth. Illinoisans were farmers, artisans, and merchants: they produced goods for a market. This naturally led to the need for a medium of exchange. By the 1840s, due to the Panic of 1837, many Americans, and certainly a majority of Illinoisans, viewed paper money with deep suspicion. They wanted the medium of exchange to maintain its value—that is, its purchasing power. In the mid-nineteenth century, most Americans agreed that the articles that most kept their purchasing power were gold and silver coins, and so they demanded that any paper money be redeemable in the appropriate amount of gold and silver coin. Thus many came to believe that the only trustworthy medium of exchange was gold and silver coin—the position of the Illinois Democratic Party. Therein lay the problem: a commercial economy requires some method of paper transactions instead of reliance solely upon gold and silver coins. Illinois had in the 1840s a commercial economy; it needed a commercial financial system.

Illinois Democrats believed in hard money and wanted to avoid legalizing banks. Whigs, being more commercially minded, wanted the state to approve the New York free banking system, which permitted any group to form a bank after filing an application with the state authorities and agreeing to make reports on their financial transactions. The free banking system had the virtue of removing governmental favoritism from banking by avoiding the granting of monopoly privileges to anyone and by disallowing the government from engaging in banking itself; the free banking system thus had an egalitarian appearance. Between 1847 and 1852, the question of hard money or a free banking system dominated Illinois politics. An attempt to extend the state bank failed in 1848, and in 1849 a constitutional convention tackled the financial question. Democrats tried to get a prohibition against banking altogether but failed. Northern Illinoisans were unhappy with the financial situation and wanted a free banking system in Illinois. In 1851, the Illinois legislature, after a two-year battle, passed a free banking system for the state, and then the popular governor, Governor Augustus French, vetoed it. The legislature overrode the veto, and then in a special election, voters approved the free banking system with a majority of 54 percent of the votes cast.

Douglas was an antibank Democrat, but the record of his reasoning about banks is virtually nonexistent. On another subject, Douglas once lashed out at "miserable corporations, which hung, like an incubus, upon the energies of the state, [and who] cling to their corporate privileges."[16] This statement was made about a transportation corporation, but it could have easily been extended to banks and the privileges they received from government authorities. In a debate over a Polk administration measure to divorce the federal government from banking altogether and place government monies in a special repository, Douglas blurted out, "[I am] in favor of a metallic currency."[17] Douglas worked to defeat the general banking system in the 1851 referendum and lost. He accepted defeat because "we as good democrats are forced to submit to the will of the people when expressed according to the forms of the constitution."[18] Douglas's opinion on banks represents the one area in which his commercial orientation was paradoxical, for commerce without banking is an impossibility.

Running throughout the debate over economic policy between the 1830s and 1850s was the subtheme of democratic equality. Democrats assumed, as did many others, that for a democracy to exist, the general condition of the people had to be one of economic equality. Under that circumstance, there was no large poverty class to disturb politics about the existing distribution of wealth. A highly inegalitarian society—the few rich and the multitudinous poor—did represent a danger under democratic government, because the poor, being a majority, could vote and seize power, could take away the wealth of the elite, and could thereby cause a civil war. Most political philosophers agreed that if a society exhibited a widespread condition of poverty, then such a society required a political system run by a small group who used the power of the state to restrain the masses; such a system of restraint was aristocracy.

Douglas had an egalitarian streak, but his desire for commercial development did not easily coexist with it. He talked about equality, but the policies he favored brought about inequality. He rejected the prospect of keeping the United States an agrarian nation. While discussing a route for a railroad to the Pacific, Douglas said that territories developed to maturity by a process of growth: railroads, or transportation facilities in general, attracted farmers and then teamsters; a dense population arose; and after the farmers came laborers. Douglas found this economic evolution natural and beneficial, but it was not a scenario portending egalitarian development. In the mid-nineteenth century, the phrase "dense population" and "urban laborers," or wage earners, meant the existence of widespread poverty. For that generation, poverty indicated those who owned no property and were doomed to live on starvation wages. Douglas was virtually admitting that economic development resulted in the emergence of a large poverty class. Thus his vision of development was fundamentally inegalitarian.

Here was one of the most powerful of all the Gordian knots of democratic equality: what economic policies best nurtured and maintained a democratic polity? Douglas's solution to this Gordian knot was commercial expansion. Growth of means of transportation, growth in building up capital stock, and growth in enterprise by expanding the market system were fundamental to his idea of equality. Douglas and his contemporaries could not bear to think of putting limitations on individual behavior and acquisitiveness—a potential alternative policy to that of growth. For Douglas, therefore, a perpetual expansion of the economy was needed to provide new generations the opportunity to succeed at becoming property holders. Democratic equality was not to be won by legislation that limited behavior, but by perpetual economic growth.

Market economics do not by themselves bring equality—far from it. Market economics reward people differentially, giving greater rewards to some than to others. To counteract this difficulty, Douglas tied his vision of commercial expansion to another vision: geographical expansion. By adding more territory to the nation, Douglas realized that the surplus population of the East (the "dense population") could always be moved west, thereby preventing the growth of an unpropertied pauper class, the bane of democracy. And so Douglas prepared again to cut a Gordian knot of democratic equality, but this time the cutting was not metaphorical but descriptive: democratic equality was to be achieved by the sword.

Manifest Destiny

Americans had a monstrous appetite for land, and expansion had been the order of the Euro-Americans since the founding of Jamestown in 1607. At the start of the Republic under the Constitution in 1789, the country totaled 888,685 square miles. By the Louisiana Purchase (1803), it doubled to 1,715,877 square miles, and a treaty with Spain in 1819 (Florida and elsewhere) added another 72,003 square miles. While Douglas was a representative in Congress, the nation absorbed another 1,204,740 square miles (Texas, Oregon Territory, New Mexico Territory, and California). Most of the accessions of land were greeted with glee among the citizenry, save a few dour Federalists, but the last acquisition was accompanied by bitter political contest, for the nation acquired much of that land by war.

Desire for land sprang from several sources. Probably the basic cause for the westward movement of Americans was the agrarian nature of their society. Sons of farmers wanted to become farmers. Lack of available farmland in the surrounding vicinity led these young people to push westward in search of acreage they could claim for themselves. This was the process pushing migrants out of the northern states. In the South, the same process was in operation with ever greater force because the crops of cotton and tobacco diminished the fertility of the soil, making a search for new land in the West even more imperative.

A belief in the importance of land to gain social status also contributed to the Americans' urge to acquire new territory. From the British and European heritage came the conviction that to be somebody in society, one had to own land; to be landless was to be a nobody, an outcast. In the United States, these ideas were recast as the cult of the yeoman farmer, the view propounded by Jefferson that farmers who owned their own soil were the backbone of republics; they were independent souls who did not rely on others for their livelihood. Americans, for economic and social reasons, ceaselessly sought to acquire new lands; their pursuit of new land was so relentless that it could be termed an unconquerable lust.

One last condition governed American attitudes toward the West. No power resided there. Eastern Canada had population and was protected by Great Britain. Indian tribes populated the Louisiana Territory and the lands next to the Pacific Ocean, but they numbered probably only one hundred thousand on the Great Plains and were politically divided and geographically dispersed. Mexico supposedly governed Texas, California, and New Mexico after winning independence in 1821, but its government was really centered around Mexico City and the area beneath the Rio Grande River. Mexico sent few forces into its northern possessions and governed them in name only. Meanwhile, the United States grew in population and wealth. The United States became powerful in the 1840s, but the West was a land without the presence of a power; it was in truth a power vacuum. For that reason alone, regardless of any other, the United States would have moved in to fill the vacuum.

The incident that touched off America's conquest of the rest of the continent was Texas's independence. Americans had settled in Texas after 1821 under various conditions set by the Mexican government. By 1836, relations between the Texans and the Mexican authorities had worsened so much that the Texans declared independence and won separation from Mexico. However, Texas and Mexico disagreed over the southern boundary of Texas, the Mexicans claiming the Nueces River as the boundary, while the Texans insisted that the boundary was the more southern river, the Rio Grande.

The United States looked covetously upon Texas, but domestic considerations stopped presidents Jackson and Van Buren from advocating that land's absorption into the Union. President John Tyler, however, was, unlike most other Whigs, an expansionist, and he sought the annexation of Texas. Complicating his efforts was the slavery issue, with northerners fearing that the addition of Texas to the country would augment the power of slaveholders in the national government. Making the slavery issue more contentious was the presence of Calhoun as secretary of state, because Calhoun argued for annexation precisely on the basis that it was necessary for the health of the peculiar institution.

As the politicians debated about the wisdom of expanding the nation's borders, a wave of excitement surged among elements of the population, especially among writers for the Democratic Party. Increasingly shrill cries for the absorption of all western lands into the United States commanded public forums, for to idealists expansion meant the expansion of American democracy, American opportunity, and American equality. Often the source for these ideas was the magazine *The United States and Democratic Review*, edited by John L. O'Sullivan. Such journalists wrote that it was now the mission of the United States to expand the reach of liberty and democratic government to all nations, and one way to accomplish this divinely sanctioned goal was to incorporate new lands into its jurisdiction. By 1844, Massachusetts representative Robert Winthrop had given, somewhat derisively, a name to this sense of mission: Manifest Destiny.

At the same time that the Texas situation was erupting politically, Illinoisans were seized by the travel accounts of the green and fertile valleys of Oregon. Starting about 1839, reports of the glories of Oregon's climate, resources, and soils flowed into the state and stimulated a migration to that distant territory. By 1843, Illinois politicians insisted on the need of the United States to acquire Oregon Territory—all of it, up to the 54th parallel and beyond (which is close to the present boundary of southern Alaska).

Expansion became a vital issue in the election of 1844. Van Buren lost renomination as the Democratic candidate because he counseled caution about Texas annexation, a position that disturbed southerners. Democrats turned to Polk as their standard-bearer, a move that angered Van Buren and his followers. The Whigs nominated the strongest figure in their party, Henry Clay, but Clay disliked reckless expansionism. Polk and the Democrats embraced Texas annexation and the acquisition of all of Oregon.

Douglas had been a Van Buren supporter, but he had little trouble switching his loyalty to Polk. He then began a long career espousing the glories of American expansion. On June 3, 1844, toward the end of the congressional session, Douglas delivered a long speech glorifying the nomination of Polk by the Democratic Party. After dismissing the Whig economic program and praising Polk's fidelity to Democratic ideals, he launched into the issue of expansion, claiming that both Oregon and Texas needed to be absorbed into the United States. Chief among his many justifications for acquiring more territory was a desire to spread democratic ideals over the hemisphere.

After the session ended, Douglas scurried home to campaign for reelection to Congress and then assist the Democrats in the presidential campaign. He faced only ineffectual opposition in the Fifth Congressional District of Illinois and won by a vote of 9,799 to 8,043 (53.9 percent). In the Illinois congressional elections, the Whigs suffered a catastrophe, receiving only 38.7 percent of the votes cast; the Liberty Party (an abolitionist organization) obtained 1.9 percent, while the Democrats earned a whopping 59.4 percent.

Immediately after his reelection, Douglas turned to the presidential contest. His reputation was growing beyond Illinois, for he was invited to a gigantic rally (estimated by an optimistic Tennessee reporter at 50,000) in Nashville in August. There assembled an amazing array of Democratic Party luminaries—Levi Woodbury, Lewis Cass, and Robert J. Walker, among others. Douglas spoke for two hours at the courthouse on annexation and the "evils" of a protective tariff. A Nashville reporter simply noted, "As a popular debater, Judge Douglas is equalled by few men."[19] In Illinois, the Democrats again romped over the Whigs: Polk earned 57,920 votes (54.1 percent), Clay 45,528 votes (42.5 percent), and Liberty Party candidate James G. Birney 3,570 votes (3.3 percent). Illinois was becoming a thoroughly Democratic state.

Letting pass an opportunity to be chosen as senator from Illinois—deciding instead to wait until 1846—Douglas returned to Washington, D.C., in December 1844 for the short session of Congress and emerged as a leading northern spokesman for Manifest Destiny. His views about territorial expansion started solidifying, and he developed ideas to counter the Whig antiexpansionist position. His arguments contained flaws and unusual interpretations of past documents, but then he was defending a political cause, not seeking to prove a mathematical theorem. The Senate refused to ratify a treaty annexing Texas. Douglas sought to bring Texas into the Union by passage of a joint resolution calling for the "reannexation of Texas" in accord with the Louisiana Treaty of 1803. When given the chance to expound upon his opinions, Douglas insisted that the United States had the right to annex because of a commitment in the Louisiana Purchase Treaty of 1803 to accede to the wishes of Texans for admission when they requested it. The Adams-Onis Treaty of 1819 changed American claims to Texas territory, but, Douglas insisted, it did not change the commitment to annex when Texans so requested. One of the key points of his presentation was that his source for the concept of reacquiring Texas came from none other than President John Quincy Adams, who had sought when president to obtain Texas in 1825 and again in 1827. Adams was sitting in the House when Douglas made his assertions and was caught totally off guard; he offered only a feeble response. Later, a set of resolutions offered by Milton Brown of Tennessee replaced those of Douglas, and the Brown resolutions became the ones jointly passed by the House and Senate.

Douglas also let it be known that Oregon was to be absorbed into the United States with the northern border of 54°40'. In a lengthy speech on January 31, 1845, Douglas explained why expansion was good for the United States, how it improved the lot of mankind, and how it averted the dangers of aristocratic England. The federal nature of the republic allocated most power over domestic affairs to the states, thus permitting greater deviations among the states than had been true in past empires. Moreover, distance no longer presented the problems it had in older times, for the telegraph and the railroad had overcome the temptations of distant portions of an empire to ally themselves with foreign nations to secure protection and trade. Because of the alliance of transportation and communication technology with the federal nature of the Constitution, "we might extend our republic safely to the extreme parts of the continent, and even further if necessary." Moreover, Douglas saw the American West as the prize in a competition between the political systems of the United States and Great Britain. These political systems stood for different ideals. The American system meant self-government and freedom; the British Empire meant aristocracy and class oppression. "Even a blind man could see," said Douglas, that Great Britain feared the liberating example of the United States upon Europe, and it was the policy of the British Empire "to check the growth of republican institutions on this continent, and the rapidity with which we have progressed."[20]

Annexation of Texas proved to be the bottle that held the genie of discord. By the end of the session, Congress passed joint resolutions annexing Texas, rather than a treaty, which the Senate steadfastly refused to ratify, and so Texas was later enabled to enter the Union. As had been predicted by Van Buren and many Whigs, the Mexican government refused to recognize the annexation and instead hoped to bring that land back under their suzerainty.

Into this volatile situation came the new president, James K. Polk. Polk was a tight-lipped, righteous Presbyterian who viewed suspiciously the desires of others and especially those seeking government favors. He wanted a frugal government; he believed in low tariffs, abstention from federal funding on internal improvements, a divorce of government from banking, and a limited federal government that gave most authority to the states. He also favored an aggressive foreign policy to achieve continental expansion. Much of this program was indeed acceptable to the majority of northern Democrats, but it did exude a distinctive southern flavor. Northern Democrats began to find the flavor increasingly distasteful as Polk's patronage decisions tended to favor southerners and as the cabinet appointments decidedly snubbed important northern leaders. The most important of those northern leaders was Van Buren.

Polk wanted to settle the Texas boundary, obtain California from Mexico, and establish the Oregon boundary with England. In Polk's efforts to settle the Oregon questions, Britain at first refused his overtures, but when it looked as if the two nations might come to blows, the British government renewed talks. The Oregon dispute ended in 1846 when both nations accepted the 49th latitude as the border between the United States and Canada, a border that many Americans thought fair but one far beneath Douglas's and the Great Lakes

Democrats' hopes for 54°40'. Mexican relations proved to be the real shocker. Mexico severed relations with the United States upon the annexation of Texas, but Polk nonetheless pressed Mexico to sell her North American possessions and to agree to the Texans' claim that their border was the Rio Grande River rather than the Nueces. Polk sent U.S. forces into Texas as a show of strength, but it was read by the Mexican authorities as a hostile act. Then Polk sent Louisiana senator John Slidell to negotiate, but the Mexican foreign secretary refused to deal with him. On top of this, the United States had monetary claims, worth about $3.5 million, against Mexico for loss of property of American nationals. To push the Mexican government, Polk ordered troops into the territory disputed by Mexico and Texas. The inevitable happened, and on April 25, Mexican forces fired on American soldiers, killing and wounding sixteen. Even before this incident, Polk had drafted a declaration of war. Learning of the battle, he asked Congress on May 11 to declare that war "exists by the act of Mexico herself." This Congress did, and the Mexican War began. American forces proved victorious over a weak Mexican government, and a treaty of peace, the Treaty of Guadalupe Hidalgo, was negotiated on February 2, 1848, was accepted by the United States Senate on March 10, and was ratified by the Mexican government in May. By this treaty, the United States obtained the territories of California and New Mexico, as well as recognition of its annexation of Texas with a border at the Rio Grande.

Expansion and relations with Mexico dominated Douglas's congressional efforts between December 1845 and the first months of 1848. He locked horns with states' rights southerners again over internal improvements, one of whom called Douglas and the Illinoisans "pretended Democrats." Stephen threw the insult back at the states' righters by saying that some other Democrats did not believe in 54°40', and thereby were violating the pledges of the 1844 Democratic Convention. Soon, however, Douglas and the northwest Democratic Party had to retreat because Polk produced a treaty settling the Oregon dispute at the 49th latitude.

When the nation was at war with Mexico, Douglas was one of the administration's most ardent supporters. He claimed that Mexico had started "a war of aggression" and that the boundary was indeed at the Rio Grande River. Moreover, Mexico had to accept whatever actions Texas took as an independent nation, because the Texans had earned their sovereignty: "[The Texans] held it by virtue of [their] Declaration of Independence, setting forth the inalienable rights of man, by men who had hearts to feel and minds to comprehend the blessings of freedom." Those who argued against the Mexican War were almost traitors; they had called it "an unholy, unrighteous, and damnable cause. . . . Is there not treason in the heart that can feel such sentiments?" In a fit of spread-eagle nationalism, and in language not conducive to rational considerations of public policy, Douglas trumpeted the emotion of nation love: "Patriotism emanates from the heart, fills the soul, infuses itself into the whole man, and speaks and acts the same language."[21]

In a later Congress, Douglas justified taking one-half of Mexico (that is, California and New Mexico) as payment due to the United States for Mexico's having initiated the war. He said the Polk administration did not commence the war to steal land from Mexico; the war was Mexico's doing, and now an indemnity must be paid: "Conquest was not the motive for the prosecution of the war; satisfaction, indemnity, security, was the motive—conquest and territory the means."[22] Douglas's eagerness for more land led him later to advocate the absorption of *all* of Mexico by the United States, and he came to be one of the most aggressive expansionist politicians in the nation, arguing that eventually the country would incorporate all of Canada, Central America, and even beyond. No limits would Douglas recognize in his willingness to expand the American form of government over the globe, for the cause of the United States was the cause of freedom, democracy, and local self-government.

Manifest Destiny was the commanding issue of the day, but it did not consume all of Douglas's time in Congress. He became the House chair of the Committee on Territories in December 1845, and then when elected to the Senate was awarded that body's chairmanship of the equivalent committee. In these appointments, the Democratic leaders acknowledged the abilities of the Illinoisan: a strong command of factual information, a fierce partisanship, and a willingness to fight for Democratic positions. As chair, he drafted bills to organize the territories of Nebraska and Oregon, he sponsored a homestead act, and he worked to get the states of Iowa and Wisconsin admitted to the Union. Territories often asked for land grants for various purposes, and Douglas communicated these requests to his peers. He of course pursued internal improvement projects, and he engaged in various and sundry debates, such as one over naturalization laws. At one point, he became angry at the reporting of debates by the *Washington Union* and wanted its reporters dismissed from the halls of Congress, a little tempest that had sectional overtones to it. He congratulated the people of France for having revolted against its monarchy in favor of republicanism—and then added a bit of nationalist bravado: "All republicans throughout the world have their eyes fixed upon us. Here is their model. Our success is the foundation of all their hopes."[23]

Nor did Manifest Destiny concerns deter him from building his personal following in Illinois. In the summer and fall of 1846, he not only campaigned for reelection to Congress (winning 57 percent of the vote), but he also earned a seat in the United States Senate. James Semple determined not to remain in office, so his seat became open. To get it, Douglas had to undermine some opponents by patronage appointments and to confront one of the favorite Democratic sons of southern Illinois, John A. McClernand. His efforts worked, and in December 1846, the Democratic caucus nominated him. He won election in the state legislature by a vote of 100 to 45 (he determined not to take his seat in the Senate until December 1847, remaining in the House of Representatives for the second session of the Twenty-ninth Congress). He then moved to spread his influence, making sure that a friend of his, William A. Richardson, became the new congressman from the Fifth Congressional District of Illinois; approving the appointment of Charles Lanphier to the editorship of the Springfield *Illinois State Register*; and later healing any wounds with McClernand.

Douglas earned a national reputation from his activity in Congress between 1844 and 1848. He was one of the foremost exponents of landed expansion and one of the most strident glorifiers of the American experiment in federalism and self-government; he boldly justified the Mexican War and demanded territory as the price Mexico had to pay for its impertinence in foreign affairs. His rise in the national Democratic Party matched his fame. He was given chairmanship of the Committee on Territories in both the House and the Senate, and his pugnacious speeches were admired by his Democratic coworkers.

During his rise to national prominence, Douglas's private life changed little. Like most congressmen, he boarded at one of Washington's many hotels. His habits did not change especially. In Washington, Douglas was known for his western ways: chewing tobacco, enjoying alcohol with the men, and dressing in a less-than-punctilious fashion. He did enjoy the social life in the capital, as the president and various other officials held balls, levees, and parties. Perhaps indicative of a change in temperament—a tiring of the bachelor's life—Douglas began courting women with more earnestness than he had in the past. His attention to the young belle Phoebe Gardner started Washington tongues gossiping, and later he seemed interested in the charms of a Mary Corse.

His private life took a decided turn, however, with the entrance of Martha Martin. While a first-year congressman, Douglas established a friendship with David S. Reid, a representative from North Carolina, whose uncle, Robert Martin, was a large plantation owner. When Robert Martin visited Washington, he brought along his two daughters, one of whom was eighteen-year-old Martha. Douglas and the young woman struck up a friendship that turned into a courtship lasting three years. In April 1847, they were married. Douglas planned to establish his new family in the booming Illinois city of Chicago and accordingly established a residence there, but his wife spent most of her time in North Carolina or Washington. She bore him three children: Robert

Martin Douglas in January 1849, Stephen Arnold Douglas Jr. in November 1850, and a daughter who died soon after her birth in 1853. Douglas finally reestablished a family environment, a condition that had been absent from his life since 1833.

Marriage helped to curb some of Douglas's bachelor habits. His dress and deportment improved. One presumes his tobacco chewing was confined to certain quarters. And Martha also remedied some of Douglas's overindulgence in alcoholic beverages, although the Douglas household would never be known for practicing temperance.

A specter did haunt the Douglas household, however, and it was one that was a constant and unwelcome visitor to many mid-nineteenth-century domiciles: ill health. Warning signs were beginning to appear in Douglas's life that he needed to take more care of his physical condition. In his first term as a congressman, illness incapacitated him for nearly two months. His 1844 speaking engagement in Nashville was cut short due to sickness. Martha was never especially robust, and her health stopped her from the move to Chicago. During the presidential campaign of 1848, they were both struck down with sickness, so much so that Douglas even failed to engage in campaigning. Martha was permanently weakened after her second childbirth and had only a few years left to live.

Douglas's marriage into a prominent North Carolina family had a number of repercussions beyond his family life. Unlike many northern politicians, Douglas now had constant interchange with southerners on a social basis and understood them and their tendencies far better than other northerners. Thus Douglas had personal experience to back up his claims that white northerners and white southerners had much in common and should remain united under the Constitution, allowing some deviations to occur through the mechanism of states' rights. And because of his constant trips to North Carolina, Douglas saw slavery in a way that other northerners could not: as a daily experience over long stretches of time. The written record is actually rather silent on this point, for Douglas did not discuss it in his letters, speeches, or reported conversations, but his observations of the peculiar institution must have softened his culturally inherited disposition against it. He did not find slaves physically abused, and he probably believed that most slave masters conducted themselves with a fair measure of humanity, compassion, and paternalism.

Because of his marriage, slavery intruded in a powerful way into his financial life. Originally, Robert Martin was going to bestow upon the newlyweds a Mississippi plantation, but Douglas, fearful of the northern political repercussions of such a gift, dissuaded him from doing so and instead suggested that Martin might make a provision about slave property for Martha in his will.

Robert Martin died shortly thereafter (June 1848), and in his will he gave Martha 2,500 acres of Mississippi land and over one hundred slaves. Stephen A. Douglas was named in the will as a manager of the plantation and to receive one-fifth of its profits.

Although technically Martha owned the plantation and the slaves (under some additional requests by Martha's father that the slaves be freed, if they desired, upon Martha's death and transported to Liberia, or given to the Douglas children), Stephen A. Douglas just became one of the nation's wealthy elite. The worth of the slaves, at an average of $500 per slave, was no less than $50,000, and the value of the land probably equaled that of the slaves. Very few Americans in 1850 had a net worth of $100,000.

Although Douglas often said that he wished to divest himself of his southern property and move everything he owned to Chicago, he never did so. Rather, he actively participated in overseeing the management of the plantation, and later in the 1850s, he undertook some unusual legal maneuvers so that he could join a partnership with a different planter. In any case, his share of the profits may have been considerable and may have enabled him to speculate in Chicago lands. During the 1850s, Douglas purchased several thousand acres of land in western Chicago and made considerable sums from their resale. However, Douglas never had an easy time financially; his campaigns were expensive, as were his domestic habits, and he carried a considerable load of debt. In fact, besides his salary from being a senator, the proceeds from Martha's Mississippi plantation were almost the only steady source of income he possessed. And in its own way, the story of Stephen A. Douglas and his relations with the inherited Mississippi plantation yields a deep understanding of why slavery endured and so easily conquered idealism. Douglas said he wanted to end his association with slavery and move all his possessions to Chicago; he never did. How difficult it was for him—and, one can imagine, for thousands of other slaveholders—to end a relationship that produced so much personal profit.

The Gordian Knot and Manifest Destiny

Many contemporaries, and especially Stephen A. Douglas, did not see the outward movement of American borders as merely a response to the absence of rivals; rather, they saw it as the march of democracy and the spread of American ideas about self-government and equality. Manifest Destiny and westward expansion had a distinct and important relationship to the Gordian knot of democratic equality: acquisition of new land was a solution to the problem of how to create and sustain equality in a democracy. But the solution of Manifest Destiny was in truth a twisted answer that beclouded the problem instead of solving it.

Douglas had a number of reasons for celebrating Manifest Destiny and for connecting it to American democratic practices. By removing to the West himself, Douglas had left the clogged eastern arteries of commerce, industry, and agriculture and had fallen into a land of open possibility—open because no one else was there to claim it. As he once said, "I came out here when I was a boy and found my mind liberalized and my opinions enlarged when I got on these broad prairies with only the Heavens to bound my vision."[24] An Ohio representative put the feeling into more exact words: the West was a "theater for enterprise and industry," and people wanted "a West for their sons and daughters where they would be free from family influences, from associated wealth and from those thousand things which in the old settled country have the tendency of keeping down the efforts and enterprises of young people."[25]

Douglas also made allusion to a prominent doctrine in nineteenth-century political economy: the role of population increase. "This is a young, vigorous, and growing nation, must obey the law of increase, must multiply, and as fast as we multiply we must expand."[26] Moreover, "Increase is the law of our existence and of our safety. Just as fast as our population increases our territory must expand. You cannot arrest this law."[27] In the economic thinking of the time, human population grew rapidly and overwhelmed the ability of a fixed amount of land to provide sufficient foodstuffs to ensure a high standard of living. People used this theory whenever they talked about the "density of population," and they believed that as population increased, a surplus population was created that could not acquire farms but could only seek out a bleak existence in cities. There the surplus population became a source of cheap labor for manufacturing and other nonagricultural pursuits. Most important was the type of society that formed because of a high population density. It was highly inegalitarian, with a few industrialists, merchants, and landlords at the top, and a mass of miserable, unpropertied urban workers at the bottom. Given its grotesque inequality, such a society could not sustain a democratic form of government because the poor people would unite politically to get the possessions of the wealthy, thereby igniting class war.

Among the proponents of Manifest Destiny was the belief that the democratic nature of the United States, and its yeoman farmer base, could only be sustained through landed expansion, by which the surplus population could be drained away from the congested eastern states. Westward expansion was thus held out as a solution to the Gordian knot of democratic equality. But it was not a solution at all; at its best it was only an evasion. Americans, like Douglas, expected that the lands acquired would undergo normal economic evolution and pass from an agrarian stage to a commercial one. Few prophesied that the West would forever remain a land of small farmers. Once one conceded that commercial activity would take root, then one admitted that western lands in the not-too-distant future would generate a surplus population; thus would arise again the problem of inequality in a democracy.

Land acquisition schemes embedded in the dreams of Manifest Destiny always ran into one embarrassing obstacle: the lands dreamt about belonged to someone else. Mexico owned California and New Mexico, while the Indian tribes in the West either held title outright or by ancestral possession. To obtain this land, the people living there had to be conquered—and all in the name of democratic equality. The advocates of Manifest Destiny did not disguise this fact: their democracy belonged to Europeans only, and among some, only to Anglo-Saxons. The Indians and Mexicans were either barbaric or backward people who failed to develop the commercial potentials of the land they held—and by this logic, they had no right of possession; they had no property rights that Americans were bound to respect. The talk of inferior races and the superiority of the Anglo-Saxon race was thick in the 1840s. Daniel Voorhees of Indiana, a congressional representative at the time of the Civil War, demonstrated the congruence between antebellum Democrats and racism. In an 1860 oration entitled "The American Citizen," he said that the history of mankind was the story of two forces battling each other, democracy and aristocracy. He praised self-government, dreaded centralization, and extolled states' rights—but only for Anglo-Saxons. He totally rejected the "theory of absolute human equality." As far as the Indians were concerned, the Anglo-Saxons had the "direct sanction of God, to exclude and exterminate, and to reduce to subserviency" those people. At the end of his address, he then declared the need to absorb all of Mexico, Cuba, and Central America.[28]

Douglas was more guarded in his comments than were many of his Manifest Destiny peers, but nonetheless he uttered the same sentiments about displacing non-Europeans to get their lands. He did not want to give Indians any permanent rights to land because that then precluded use by American citizens, who were the representatives of the "onward march of civilization." He disliked the talk of Indian rights that might keep a portion of the continent "a howling wilderness . . . roamed over by hostile savages."[29] If Douglas shied away from language as thoroughly racist as Voorhees, his policy nonetheless came close to producing the same result.[30]

Manifest Destiny was in truth the outgrowth of the Democratic Party's failure to resolve the democratic yearnings of the nation's citizens with an economic framework that gave citizens a sense of proprietorship. Instead of unraveling the Gordian knot of democratic equality by solving the problem, that is, by advocating measures that limited the size of farms, the size of families, or the ingress of immigrants, or by offering some other political legislation that limited acquisitiveness of individuals and provided some means of property acquisition for all, the Americans—and the Democrats in particular—refused to place any restriction on individual acquisition whatsoever. Because of their failure to deal with the problems of population growth and of ensuring the possibility of independent employment for all the nation's citizens, the Democrats (and the Whigs as well) created the circumstances that led hundreds of thousands to seek property ownership by plundering others.

And so, once again, the Gordian knot of democratic equality was not unraveled. Instead, the problem was cut by the sword of Manifest Destiny. And from that cutting of the cord was to come even more awful results.

Notes

1. Johannsen, *Douglas*, 86.
2. Johannsen *Douglas*, 97.
3. Pratt, "Stephen A. Douglas, Lawyer, Legislator, Register and Judge: 1833–1843," pt. 2, *Lincoln Herald*, 52 (November, 1950), 42.
4. Gerald M. Capers, *Stephen A. Douglas: Defender of the Union* (Boston, 1959), 17.
5. Johannsen, *Douglas*, 109.
6. *Ill St Reg*, June 16, 1843.
7. *Quincy Whig*, July 5, 12, 17, 1843.
8. John Quincy Adams, *Memoirs of John Quincy Adams*, ed. Charles Francis Adams (Philadelphia, 1874–1877), 11:510–11.
9. Holmes quote, CG, 28-1, 528–30.
10. CG, 28-1, 602.
11. *Ill St Reg*, October 4, 1844; CG, 33-2, 1060.
12. J. Madison Cutts, *A Brief Treatise upon Constitutional and Party Questions, . . . as I Received It Orally from the Late Senator Stephen A. Douglas, of Illinois* (New York, 1860), 160.
13. CG, 32-1, 351.
14. SAD to Joel Matteson, January 2, 1854, in Sheahan, *Life of Douglas*, 361–62.
15. CG, 34-1, 1831–32.
16. *Ill St Reg*, October 18, 1849.
17. CG, 29-1, 574.
18. SAD to Lanphier, December 30, 1851, in Douglas, *Letters*, 235.
19. *Nashville Union*, September 2, 1844.
20. CG, 28-2, 225, 226.
21. CG, 29-1, 497–99, 815, 816.
22. CG, 30-1, appendix, 222.
23. CG, 30-1, 569.
24. Johannsen, "Douglas and American Mission," in *Frontier Challenge: Responses to the Trans-Mississippi West*, ed. John G. Clark (Lawrence, KS, 1971), 112.

25. Allen Johnson, *Douglas*, 88.

26. Albert K. Weinberg, *Manifest Destiny: A Study of Nationalist Expansionism in American History*, (Baltimore, MD, 1935), 205.

27. Johannsen, "Douglas and American Mission," 121.

28. Daniel W. Voorhees, *Speeches of Daniel W. Voorhees of Indiana*, comp. Charles S. Voorhees (Cincinnati, 1875), 40, 42–57.

29. Johannsen, "Douglas and American Mission," 130–31.

30. H. M. Flint, *Life of Douglas, to Which Are Added His Speeches and Reports* (Philadelphia, 1865), 38.

CHAPTER THREE

~

The Compromise of 1850

The years between 1846 and 1850 were for Stephen A. Douglas both a climax and a prelude. Manifest Destiny grabbed hold of the politics of the country and by 1848 had created the transatlantic republic. Yet in those four years also commenced the battle for the Union that consumed the remainder of Douglas's life. Out of the territorial expansion question rose the issue of slavery's role in the newly acquired territories, with the South ultimately demanding that the peculiar institution be allowed into the territories, and the antislavery North insisting that it be prohibited. For Douglas, the sectional antagonism endangered his sense of both the mission of the United States and the special role of the Democratic Party. He grappled for a solution to the sectional hostility that arose from the slavery expansion issue, and he found it in the doctrine of popular sovereignty. However, hidden in the doctrine of popular sovereignty were two more Gordian knots, and they were the problems of initial definitions and moral principles in a democratic polity.

The Wilmot Proviso Controversy

Questions about slavery soon found their way into debates over the acquisition of Texas and then the Mexican War. Whig Julius Rockwell of Massachusetts objected that perpetuating slavery by expanding its boundaries had now become the central purpose of the federal government. Rockwell said that the policy of slavery expansion was wrong because slavery was an "incubus" that ruined a land because labor was not paid a fair reward. More forceful was Ohio's Joshua Giddings, who warned of the rising strength of the "Slave Power," and reminded northerners that at present the South had the "balance of power, and subjected the free labor of the North . . . to the tender mercies of a slave-holding oligarchy."[1]

Congress had experienced sectional animosities before, but they reached new heights in August 1846 due to the action of Pennsylvania congressman David Wilmot. To a bill giving the president money to negotiate an end to the Mexican War, he offered an amendment, forever after called the Wilmot Proviso, prohibiting slavery in any land acquired from Mexico. In the House of Representatives, the amendment passed by a vote of 80 yeas to 64 nays, with all but 3 negative votes coming from the slave states. On a motion to table the bill (to remove it from consideration for the session), the vote was 78 yeas to 94 nays; and finally, the bill passed by a vote of 85 yeas to 80 nays. Almost all votes on the Wilmot Proviso produced a sectional split, with northerners voting for the measure and southerners against it. All three times, Stephen A. Douglas voted with southerners. Somehow Douglas instinctively knew that this measure was dangerous to the Union and to his party. The bill, however, failed to win the approval of the Senate, and so it did not become law.

Congress met for its second session of the Twenty-ninth Congress in December 1846, and soon thereafter the Wilmot Proviso became the center of controversy. In the debates over the fate of the territories, the northern and southern positions became clear. For southerners, their property rights were being questioned on an institution that represented just under 20 percent of all the nation's wealth. Once the federal government started denying the validity of property rights in slaves in the territories, the federal authorities might do the same in other areas of federal jurisdiction. Moreover, southerners wanted their honor to be unblemished; they refused to be singled out and treated differently from other members of the Union; this was the essence of their demand for "equality within the Union." Led by John C. Calhoun, southerners insisted that they had a right to migrate to the territories with their slave property, and that neither the federal government nor a territorial government could outlaw slavery.

Northerners countered by saying that slavery produced an anemic economic system that provided only profits for a few slaveholders while plunging the rest of society into poverty. They insisted that northern labor—they called it "free labor"—could not reside next to slave labor and thrive; only one labor system could inhabit the territories, for free labor and slave labor were natural enemies. The reason for the enmity between them was that slave labor was impoverished labor, while free labor, when given appropriate rewards, was productive and beneficial to all.

Northerners also constantly voiced a fear about additional slave states and the extra slave state representation in the federal government that would result from slavery's expansion. The additional numbers in Congress would give more strength to the "Slave Power," a power that northerners defined as the slave owners who, through their congressmen, looked after the economic interests of slavery at the federal level, insuring that only legislation favorable to slavery became law. Among some northerners, the Slave Power was a synonym for an aristocracy, one bent on destroying civil liberties, establishing slavery in the northern states, and turning white free laborers into slaves.

Some northerners opposed slavery because they thought the institution immoral. Northern moralists argued—usually with vehemence—that slavery was a violation of God's law because slavery reduced a person to the status of an animal and denied the New Testament's command to obey the golden rule. Abolitionists, persons agitating for the immediate end of slavery, propagated these views and flooded the nation with pamphlets and speeches against slavery; they espoused most clearly the moral attack on slavery. They and a few prominent religious leaders drew furious rebukes from the South. Southerners found plenty of biblical citations justifying the practice of slavery. Most of this particular debate over the morality of slavery was outside the halls of Congress, but on occasion it intruded into debate, and southerners heatedly rejected the characterization of slavery as an immoral practice. Most northerners, however, were not abolitionists and talked more about their trepidations toward the Slave Power and their concern for the future of free labor.

What stunned contemporaries, however, was the breakdown of party allegiance in Congress. Representatives voted along sectional lines on the Wilmot Proviso, not along party lines. Most fascinating to observers and participants was the spectacle of the northern Democrats leading the charge against slavery's expansion. David Wilmot was a devoted Jacksonian Democrat, as were many of the prominent speakers for the proviso in the House. Southern leaders saw the sectional split and wrung their hands over its political portents—a North united politically against slavery.

Northern Democrats had various motivations for bucking party loyalty and seeking an end to the expansion of slavery. The heart of the revolt was in New York, and the Democrats there, called Barnburners (who in order to rid the barn of rats would go to such extremes as burning the barn down), held grudges against the South and the Polk administration. New York Democrats had wanted Martin Van Buren to be the party's nominee in 1844, but southerners had refused to accept him and had steered the convention to Polk. When Polk became president, he damaged his standing with New Yorkers by his patronage policies. Other northern Democrats were upset with the almost single-minded devotion of the Polk administration in pursuing southern economic goals: the tariff of 1846 angered Pennsylvanians, while Polk's veto of river and harbor appropriations annoyed the Democrats of the Great Lakes. Beyond the specific complaints of Barnburners and others, however, was a fairly widespread conviction that slavery was a relic of barbarism that ill fitted the democracy of the United States. Moreover, many northern Democrats fell prey to the idea of the Slave Power, and they saw in the actions of Polk an almost conspiratorial drive to use the federal government to bolster the economic strength of slavery.

In the crossfire of verbal sectional barbs in Congress stood Illinois's Stephen A. Douglas. Even before the Wilmot Proviso was presented, Douglas registered his dissent over the introduction of slavery into every issue that came before Congress. On a deficiency bill in the spring of 1846, he defended the Polk administration's war against Mexico and dismissed all the rhetoric about conspiracies to extend slavery as being the work of either demagogues or cunning politicians. Such exclamations did not aid the slave, he said, but only increased the animosities between northerners and southerners: "He had no favor [to bestow] to the fanatics upon either extreme."[2] Later, he quipped that he had no desire to take up "abstract questions having no bearing upon our legislation."[3] During a debate in 1849, he showed his disgust at the antislavery agitation and the emotional outbursts it was producing in Congress, saying, "I wish to banish this whole agitation from these halls."[4]

Douglas constantly butted heads with southerners over questions relating to slavery, and one of the more memorable occasions came during his first year as a United States senator. The Senate was discussing a set of resolutions offered by antislavery Democrat John P. Hale of New Hampshire to protect property in Washington, D.C. A number of inflammatory speeches came from Calhoun and Jefferson Davis of Mississippi about the security of their property and the insecurity of the Union if their slave property was not protected. Douglas interjected that these types of speeches only manufactured abolitionists in the North. The iron-jawed Calhoun looked at Douglas and declared, "We are only defending ourselves." And Douglas shot right back at the senatorial titan, "No, they are not defending themselves." They spoke with heat, he continued, and threw out threats, thereby creating tens of thousands of antislavery votes. The other Mississippi senator, Henry S. Foote, countered Douglas's assertions; "But if the Senator from Illinois thinks that a middle course in regard to this question [on slavery] is best calculated to serve his purposes, he is mistaken." Douglas then came as close to revealing his attitude toward slavery as he ever did: "[The North cannot say that slavery is] a positive good—a positive blessing. . . . We have moulded our institutions in the North as we have thought proper; and now we say to you of the South, if slavery be a blessing, it is your blessing; if it be a curse, it is your curse; enjoy it—on you rest all the responsibility!"[5]

Douglas was probably confused over the appropriate way to handle the question of slavery in the territories, but he could not fail to notice how the subject was destroying the northern wing of the Democratic Party. In 1847 and 1848, northern Democrats gave consistent testimony to their dislike of slavery for moral, economic, and social reasons. In the Great Lakes states, the refrain of revulsion against slavery came from the region's Democratic editors: "We are no advocates of slavery," affirmed a Detroit editor as he quoted a Boston paper,[6] while the *Cleveland Plain Dealer* contained an editorial entitled "The Wilmot Proviso—Stand By It."[7] Even Charles Lanphier, Douglas's friend and owner of the *Illinois State Register*, wrote that it was generally agreed "in the South as well as the North that it [slavery] is a physical evil, an incubus upon the prosperity of every state where it exists."[8]

Northern Democrats responded in various ways to the challenge of slavery's possible expansion into the territories. A large group, led by the Barnburners, wanted the Wilmot Proviso. This group constituted the majority of northern Democrats going into late 1847. Among many northern Democrats was a further belief—probably the one most prominent among them—that slavery could not go into the territories because local laws prohibited it. The western territories had been acquired from Mexico, and Mexican law had prohibited slavery since 1824. Thus the land in the West was already free, and Congress had no power to introduce slavery into land already free. In the midst of this northern Democratic commentary were forthright expressions about the superiority of free labor and the dark designs of the Slave Power.

Fissures in the Democratic Party frightened Douglas, but in 1847 and early 1848 a practical solution to the problem of slavery's potential expansion eluded him. He probably believed that slavery would not go west. Moreover, he undoubtedly felt, like the rest of his party, that slavery had already been barred because municipal law in California and New Mexico, at the time of acquisition, had prohibited slavery. He told the Senate in January 1849 that New York Democrats were "against the extension of slavery over a country now free. I know of no man who advocates the extension of slavery over a country now free. If there is such a man on this floor, I am not aware of the fact."[9] The Wilmot Proviso, Douglas explained, was an unnecessary affront to southerners, and northern Democrats adopted it at the price of shivering the party into sectional fragments.

Douglas's initial solution was to extend the Missouri Compromise line of 36°30'. In 1820-1821, Congress had run into the problem of slavery's extension into the Louisiana Territory. Congress's solution then was to draw a line across the Louisiana Territory, at 36°30', and declare slavery prohibited above the line, permissible below it. The compromise seemed to satisfy northerners and southerners for twenty-six years, and Douglas saw no reason why the line could not be extended to the eastern border of California. When Wilmot first proposed his proviso on August 8, Representative William Wick of Indiana tried to amend it by eliminating the prohibition and substituting the Missouri Compromise line. It was defeated. Douglas liked the idea, though, and pushed it several times in 1847 and 1848.

As of 1848, Douglas did not believe the Missouri Compromise line violated the Constitution. Some southerners did, but on the whole, southerners favored the extension of the line to the Pacific (thus creating two Californias). James Buchanan of Pennsylvania blessed the compromise line, and numerous authors of letters written to Douglas's Illinois colleague, Sidney Breese, also thought the line the best measure to break the impasse between North and South.

But the Missouri Compromise line was not to be the solution to the dilemma of slavery's expansion into the territories. Northerners, along with some southerners, consistently voted it down. Much of the push to establish the line as the basis for a new compromise came in efforts to permit Oregon to become a territory. Various representatives and senators tried to inject into the territorial legislation a provision establishing the 36°30' line as a boundary for the existence of slavery. Armistead Burt of South Carolina led this drive in the House in January 1847, and his amendments were voted down—Douglas always voting yes. When Douglas moved to the Senate, he tried repeatedly to place the 36°30' line in the Oregon territorial legislation, but to no avail. One attempt to establish the 36°30' line in the Senate was rejected by a vote of 2 yeas to 52 nays, with only Douglas and Indiana's Jesse D. Bright voting for it. In another case, the Senate managed to pass such a measure, only to have the House of Representatives eliminate it. For Douglas, the fate of the Missouri Compromise line during the debates over the establishment of Oregon Territory was absolutely crucial. He read out of this experience that the old compromises over slavery were now dead, and new ones needed to be manufactured.

Lewis Cass then built the armor with which Douglas would gird himself for the rest of his life—the doctrine of popular sovereignty. Cass was a prominent Democratic senator from Michigan and an eager aspirant for the Democratic presidential nomination in 1848. He had at first supported the Wilmot Proviso, but he quickly backed down when he saw the furious southern opposition to it. Cass finally wrote a long letter to A. O. P. Nicholson of Tennessee to explain his position on the Wilmot Proviso and slavery's possible expansion, and in it Cass seized upon the doctrine of popular sovereignty, a doctrine that had been earlier aired by several Democratic politicians. The key part of the letter included this passage: "[The intervention of Congress in the territories] should be limited to the creation of proper governments for new countries, acquired or settled, and to the necessary provision for their eventual admission into the Union; leaving, in the meantime, to the people inhabiting them, to regulate their internal concerns in their own way[;] they are just as capable of doing so, as the people of the states."[10]

In Cass's letter, two principles stood out. First, Congress should not intervene in domestic affairs of settlers in the territories; this was the principle of nonintervention. For Cass, nonintervention was a constitutional truth; for others, like Douglas, it was a compromise on how to handle the question of slavery in the territories without generating vicious debates in Washington. Second, Cass put the decision of slavery squarely on the settlers—it was theirs to determine. Letting settlers take care of these matters seemed the best way of solving the dilemma. What Cass did not fully explore, but which the Democratic Party and Douglas soon picked up, was calling this method of dealing with the territories a democratic solution. Let the people involved determine the fate of slavery by a vote; this was the principle handed down by the revolutionary forebears—rule by the people, popular sovereignty.

The idea of popular sovereignty was in the air. Others besides Cass were broaching the idea, if not giving it a precise name, and Douglas had evoked the principle on several occasions. As the chairman of the Committee on Territories in both the Senate and the House, Douglas continually marveled over the diversity of the constitutions that territories created when asking for admittance into the Union. One of the more pregnant discussions in the House of Representatives occurred over the admission of Florida and Iowa. Freeman Morse of Maine objected to Florida's constitutional provisions that forever denied emancipation by the general assembly and prohibited free blacks from coming into the state. Douglas admitted that he had troubles with both constitutions and that some elements in the Florida constitution were "positively obnoxious." But, he added, if Congress started placing restrictions on some constitutions, the number of restrictions would only increase. The United States had a "variety of climate, soil, productions, pursuits, and customs." Each area had to legislate for itself, and therefore differences between them would arise. States would naturally vary in their legal frameworks. The only rule that Congress could possibly follow was that the governments created by state constitutions were "republican" in form. Therefore, Congress should accept the decisions of local assemblies about the types of constitutions that suited their needs best.[11]

Douglas's role in the birth of the doctrine of popular sovereignty was minor, but he soon marched under its banner, figured out its power, and then became its leader. Popular sovereignty became the theme of much of the rest of Douglas's life. While time has eroded the luster and polish of the ideal of popular sovereignty, the strength of the democratic sentiment lying in the doctrine must be recognized. Democracy in the United States was a new thing, the equality preached by politicians was a new thing, and in Europe the future of democracy as a system of governance was in doubt. In the 1840s, the word "democracy" had magic to it because it indicated an act of faith in the goodness of the common man and a prayer that self-government by the masses was possible. But what was missing was a definition: in popular sovereignty, who were the populace—who were the people?

The Election of 1848

Cass created the doctrine of popular sovereignty not only to help a divided country find a peaceful settlement over the slavery expansion question, but also because he had strong presidential aspirations, and 1848 was a presidential election year. Popular sovereignty was a way that he could woo southern Democrats to his standard. Cass had challengers, of course: Levi Woodbury of New Hampshire was popular among many Jacksonians, and James Buchanan of Pennsylvania also coveted the office of the chief magistrate.

New York politics imperiled Democratic Party unity. Barnburners desired to have the party subdue southern dominance and give northern Democrats more influence in policy formulation and patronage decisions. Others followed the Polk administration. This situation led New York Democrats to produce two slates of delegates for the national convention: one composed of administration supporters who rejected the Wilmot Proviso, and the other peopled by Barnburners who insisted on the Wilmot Proviso. At the Democratic National Convention in Baltimore in May 1848, the credentials committee concocted a formula that allowed representation for both slates of delegates in the convention, but that was not acceptable to the Barnburners. They bolted the convention. Then, through a series of meetings in New York, they created the Free Soil Party, a coalition of antislavery Democrats, "Conscience" (antislavery) Whigs, and some political abolitionists. They nominated none other than Martin Van Buren for the president and Charles Francis Adams, a Conscience Whig from Massachusetts, for vice president. This new party drew its strength from Democrats in New York, some antislavery regions throughout New England, and New England enclaves in Michigan, Ohio, Indiana, Wisconsin, and Illinois.

Douglas had a low opinion of the Barnburners and was upset at their betrayal of party unity. For Douglas, fidelity to political party was a quality that made a politician virtuous and true; the Barnburners had deserted the party and had hence become traitors. He ascribed some of the motives for the Barnburner revolt to personal dislike of Lewis Cass. Douglas fretted about the impact of the Wilmot Proviso Democrats in the northern part of Illinois—the region where they were strongest—but it turned out that there was little to fear. The Free Soil movement in Illinois fizzled badly.

The Democrats nominated Lewis Cass for the presidency on a platform that called for congressional nonintervention in the territories and intimated that the slavery question should be decided by popular sovereignty. The Whigs countered with the nomination of Zachary Taylor, a Mexican War hero and a Louisiana slaveholder; the Whigs failed to produce a platform at their convention, hoping that the lure of a victorious war general would be enough to give them victory. Before long, it became clear that the Free Soil Party had limited appeal and that the real contest was between Taylor and Cass. This election witnessed the oddity of distinctly different sectional appeals in different parts of the nation. In the South, Whigs touted Taylor's southern ancestry, arguing that he would certainly be a foe of slavery's restriction, and they charged Lewis Cass with Wilmot Provisoism. But northern Whigs claimed that Taylor was a friend of restricting slavery's expansion, while Cass was in favor of it. Democrats likewise had different appeals depending on their section: southern Democrats said Cass was of course proslavery, while northern Democrats said that Cass was against slavery's expansion.

Douglas's activity in the 1848 election turned out to be circumscribed. His father-in-law died, and Douglas journeyed to North Carolina in midsummer to take care of details. The trip gave him a chance to speak to southern audiences, which he did with relish. At New Orleans, he gave a speech based on economic issues and asked his audience, "Are you in favor of a national bank—of a high tariff—of distribution of the proceeds of the sales of public lands—of the bankrupt law?" He in short relied on standard Jacksonian issues to bring people to the Democratic Party. He justified the Mexican War and found fault with the Whigs and their nominee, but he extolled the virtues of the Democratic Party and Lewis Cass. As to the Wilmot Proviso, he pledged never to support it, and if he were required by the Illinois legislature to vote for it, "I will not hesitate to resign my post and retire to a private state." He had nothing to say about the merits or demerits of slavery, as each state had to decide the question for itself, and both Illinois and Louisiana had made their respective decisions. As for slavery's expansion, he offered a vague notion of popular sovereignty—let the people concerned vote on the institution—but he insisted that intervention by the federal government would be a "usurpation."[12] Douglas gave a variant of the speech in Montgomery, Alabama, and was preparing to assault the Whigs in Illinois at the end of the congressional session in August. However, illness intervened. When Douglas returned to his wife's residence in North Carolina, he came down with a fever and had to sit out the remainder of the election.

Illinois Democrats did far better in the elections of 1848 than did the national party. Once again, Democrats won six of Illinois's seven congressional seats. Out of 102,823 votes cast, congressional Democrats obtained 62.6 percent, the Whigs a meager 34.3 percent, and the Free Soilers only 3.1 percent. In the presidential election, the Democrats proved their electoral power by giving Cass 56,300 votes, while Taylor received 53,047, and Van Buren got 15,774. Some observers might have fretted that a portent of the future could be gleaned by adding the Free Soil vote to the Whig vote, making the Democrats actually a minority party in the state. But in 1848, no one knew where that Free Soil vote would eventually go. What counted was that Illinois radiated a Democratic glow. In other states, however, the presidential race did not end with Democratic victory; Zachary Taylor was elected president with 163 electoral votes to Lewis Cass's 127.

Congressional Stalemate, 1848–1849

In the short session of Congress between December 1848 and March 1849, Douglas tried to obtain a bill establishing territorial government in California. In this he would be frustrated, but his efforts showed a vital aspect of Douglas's democratic faith. Douglas did not believe in a freewheeling democracy without rules, without structure. Before the people voted on subjects, constitutions needed to be written and procedures established. Thus he argued that California needed government: "I trust, sir, that Colt's pistols will not continue to be the common law of that land." On another occasion, he again pleaded for Congress to implement territorial government for California, "for our brethren are being murdered, and, that, too, for want of law. The inhabitants of California are given up to every sort of crime and outrage, in consequence of the neglect of our duty"; shortly thereafter he warned that congressional inaction was letting California fall into "the horrors of an anarchy."[13] He exaggerated the situation, as California had unusually law-abiding residents, but his remarks were in line with his basic thinking. Democracy was not a system in which anything was allowed, but a system confined by a fundamental agreement—a constitution—that listed minority rights and the procedures that the majority had to follow. He firmly believed in the law and in the rules that governed conduct; his was not the democracy of momentary passion and emotion.

Douglas and his followers tried ingenious ways to get California admitted. He offered a bill that treated all the territory acquired from Mexico as belonging to one state, he allowed this entity to bypass the territorial stage, and he permitted it to write a state constitution immediately. His attempt elicited little support. He later tried to get California into the Union alone and granted

Texas the possibility of absorbing all the Mexican cession beneath 36°30'; again it failed. So Douglas tried a third time, allowing California to enter as a free state and part of California to be merged with New Mexico and given the opportunity to become a slave state, and it failed. In another effort, Wisconsin Senator Isaac P. Walker offered an amendment to an appropriation bill that would automatically extend the Constitution and the laws of the United States over all the West and would permit the president to establish governments of a transitory nature, but there was no success here either. The session ended with no provision for territorial government in California and New Mexico.

Southerners looked on Douglas's efforts at conciliation with disgust, for they wanted access to the territories as a matter of right and as proof that northerners would not block future acquisitions of potential slave territory. Calhoun was leading southern radicals on the question of southern rights in the territories, and he was especially opposed to permitting California to enter the Union as a free state. His distrust of the federal government was so deep because the power of the federal government could not be wielded solely by southerners, by slaveholders, and northerners were not to be trusted on questions relating to slavery because they had no interest in its maintenance and prosperity. To stop northern aggression on slavery, Calhoun wanted the number of slave states and free states to be equal. Then the power of the sections was equal in the Senate, and the South, if its states acted in unison, could veto any federal legislation that threatened to damage slavery. Admitting California as a free state would probably permanently upset that balance in the North's favor, and Calhoun adamantly opposed this. His position on the equilibrium of the sections had grown to the point that he had developed a theory about it called "the concurrent majority."

Calhoun's abstractions did not entrance his fellow southern legislators. They rather increasingly turned to the doctrines of property rights in slaves to justify their positions on slavery's possible expansion into western territories. The laws that enabled slavery to yield profits to the slave owner were the laws that defined slaves as property like cattle or domestic animals. Southerners believed that as northerners had the right to take their forms of property into the territories, so they had a right to do likewise—and for southerners, slaves were property.

Douglas occupied a strange place in these sectional debates. During a discussion over a petition for the colonization of "Colored Persons," John P. Hale rose to counter suggestions that northerners were guilty of sectional aggression. Rather than being assertive, Hale said, the North had "been so pusillanimous, so cowardly, so craven, and so submissive on the subject" that southerners always won the legislation they wanted; the Slave Power ran the United States, and northerners always caved in to slaveholder demands. Douglas quickly obtained the floor and rebuked Hale for saying northerners had been craven and cowardly: "Northern men have always maintained their rights." But he then launched into a discussion of leaving slavery exclusively to the states and letting settlers in the territories decide for themselves questions about the peculiar institution. Only the willingness to compromise and the exclusion of "the agitation from these halls" were important to Douglas.[14]

What was missing in Douglas's response was any consideration of the basic Provisoist complaints: the power of slaveholders, the property rights argument of the South, and the dangers to free labor from a competition with slave labor. When Douglas argued about slavery, sectionalism, and expansion, he very seldom—and in some instances, never—brought these matters up. Rather, he directed his arguments away from the core of antislavery hostility toward slavery as an institution, and he went instead to matters involving the possibilities of slavery's expansion, the need for intelligent compromise, the necessity of abandoning vituperative language, and, eventually, the folly of treating slavery as a moral issue instead of as a practical political problem. He either refused to understand the fears of antislavery spokesmen, found them groundless, or dreaded to answer them directly because he worried that public debate on them might lead the public to the wrong conclusions. His attitude toward the free labor ideal and the existence of the Slave Power is elusive because he simply did not directly engage these topics.

Southern Anxieties

The questions about slavery's expansion refused to die. Between March and December 1849, the issue grew to threatening proportions, and the threat was to the continuation of the Union. In 1848, Californians found gold in their state; that mineral produced a gold rush that within one year gave California enough population to justify writing a constitution and seeking admittance into the Union. So California started to loom large in everyone's calculations.

The new Whig president, Zachary Taylor, though a Louisiana slaveholder, had free soil notions about the West. He did not believe that slavery could exist there, and he tried a strategy of ending the crisis by bypassing Congress. He sent emissaries to both California and New Mexico to stimulate the people there to write state constitutions knowing that they would prohibit slavery. Taylor would then recognize California and New Mexico as states before Congress met in session, and when Congress did convene, they would have to accept the new states as deeds that could not be undone. California did formulate a state constitution, but the plan unraveled because some of the details involving Utah failed to materialize.

Southerners now became even more distraught. Calhoun had tried to rally southern congressmen and senators to a defense of the South and its share of the western territories by issuing a manifesto promising the birth of a purely southern political party. He had been only partly successful, as most of his colleagues did not sign his "Address of the Southern Congressmen in Washington." But most did not expect Zachary Taylor to show free soil tendencies. This absolutely panicked southern Whigs because they could not expect to exist as a party in the South with a leader who agreed with the antislavery rabble in the North. California's possible formulation of a free state constitution, and the threat of the South becoming a minority in the Senate and thus in the entire federal government, fanned flames of desperation. At a Mississippi gathering of Southern Rights advocates, the proposal was made that a convention should be held in Nashville to map out nonnegotiable southern demands concerning slavery and the Union.

As the first session of the Thirty-first Congress approached, Douglas and the northern Democratic Party squarely confronted the slavery extension issue and the possibility of southern secession. One individual wrote to Democratic senator William Allen of Ohio, "What shall the Western Democracy do? If forced to vote on the question of Slavery in California they must vote for freedom. [We] cannot compromise."[15] For Douglas, the problem came in two forms. First, the Illinois legislature, though strongly Democratic, was filled with individuals sympathetic to free soil principles, especially the members from the northern counties. Some state leaders, moreover, were upset with Douglas's failure to support the Wilmot Proviso. So the free soil sympathizers managed to have the state legislature pass a resolution instructing the state's elected federal officials to obtain congressional laws that ensured "that there shall be neither slavery, nor involuntary servitude" in the western territories.[16] Many expected Douglas to resign his seat, and, given the fact that he had said he would when in New Orleans only a year earlier, Douglas was on the horns of a dilemma.

Douglas did not resign, of course. He dutifully reported the Illinois resolutions to the Senate with little commentary. As for the content of the resolutions, Douglas explained that the mechanism for obtaining free territories was vague; the resolutions did not call for Illinois federal officials to vote for the Wilmot Proviso, only that slavery not be allowed in the new territories. How that might be arranged was left open to interpretation. Therefore, Douglas could claim that as long as these territories came into the Union as states without slavery, he had obeyed the essence of the Illinois legislature.

To shore up his political support in Illinois, however, Douglas returned to the state and in October 1849 gave a long address on political subjects at the Representatives Hall in Springfield. It was a typical Douglas oration lasting several hours. He described his actions on all relevant issues and finally turned to the Wilmot Proviso and explained the history of the slavery agitation in Congress, an agitation he wholly deprecated. Praising the Missouri Compromise, he then stated that it had failed to serve as a compromise for the newly acquired territories, noting that the Missouri Compromise "had become canonized in the hearts of the American people, as a sacred thing, which no ruthless hand would ever be reckless enough to disturb," an observation he failed to remember when he framed the Kansas-Nebraska Act five years later.

He argued that the Wilmot Proviso was unnecessary because the western territories were bound to become free states for three reasons. First, climate dictated that slavery could never be profitable in the West, so slaveholders would not migrate there. Second, "by the universal acknowledgement of all intelligent men, the whole country was then free—free by law, free in fact," because Mexican law prevailed. Third, the people who would migrate to the West were going to be northerners, and they would not vote to establish slavery. The Wilmot Proviso was thereby a "mischievous and a wicked measure." He told Illinoisans forthrightly that he desired the territories to become free states and that the real effect of the Wilmot Proviso was to superheat southern fears about the security of the peculiar institution to the point that they contemplated secession—all for no good reason, because the territories were going to be free regardless of the Wilmot Proviso.[17] And missing from his speech was any acknowledgment of the basic complaints of antislavery advocates: the might of the Slave Power, the potential of slave labor–free labor competition, and the consequences of the property rights doctrine lodged in the southern demands for territorial recognition of slavery.

Problems stemming from the Wilmot Proviso affected Douglas in other ways. The Illinois legislature had botched the selection of a United States senator, the legislators desiring someone who supported the Wilmot Proviso. Casting aside the sitting senator, Sidney Breese, the legislature chose James Shields, a Mexican War veteran and Irish immigrant who seemingly had spoken in favor of slavery's restriction. But the United States Senate refused to seat Shields because he did not meet the naturalization and age qualifications stipulated by the Constitution, and the Senate told Illinois to make another selection. Governor French might have appointed a different person to fill the vacancy—this is what Douglas wanted—but instead he threw the problem back on the legislature. There ensued a three-way race for the senatorship; Shields eventually won again, and by this time he had reached the appropriate age, so the Senate accepted him. In the effort to get the Senate's approval of Shields, Douglas had to make sure that Shields was on the correct side of the slavery question. Shields assured Douglas that his position was the same as the one given by Douglas in his Springfield speech.

Though the slavery expansion issue dominated much of Douglas's political life, it did not consume everything. He had just moved to Chicago, was involved in some land speculation, and was building a house. His wife, Martha, living in North Carolina, bore him a son in January 1849. Somewhat ominously, Martha remained in a weak condition after childbirth, although she joined Douglas in Washington, D.C., during the 1849–1850 session of Congress. The child remained in North Carolina under the care of Martha's family.

In legislative affairs, Douglas had other matters to attend to besides the slavery expansion question. It was this Congress that passed the Illinois Central Railroad Act granting public land in alternate sections to the state to finance the railroad's construction. And though Douglas never quite admitted it, the Whig administration of Zachary Taylor (and then Millard Fillmore) was far more disposed to finance river and harbor proposals than was the Democratic regime of Polk. Throughout the ordeal of the entry of California into the Union and related matters, Douglas carefully nurtured existing territories, like Minnesota, and brought their needs to the attention of Congress. He also continued to sponsor a homestead measure and Pacific Railroad legislation.

Yet these other topics paled before the immensity of the issues surrounding slavery's expansion into the territories. Talk of secession filled the air. Southerners simply were not going to let the North have possession of the new territories from which would arise new free states that would overwhelm the number of slave states; that condition would give the North the preponderance of votes in the federal government and the ability to pass any law that section favored. Southern radicals operated under the belief that if they lost the battle for the territories, slavery itself would perish. And southerners simply had too much wealth in slaves and too much emotion invested in the existing racial social order to permit any tampering with their slave system.

Upset, angry, and adamant, many southerners were in no mood for pleasantries with northerners. The Democrats of the Northwest found the behavior of southern radicals unbearable. Illinois congressman Thomas Harris wrote to Lanphier that the "southern fanatics [practice] an unyielding proscription of northern men. No northern man can ever be endured by them, unless he goes as far as they in abusing the whole North." And the goal of southern radicals? "These Calhoun men are aiming to create a sectional division—& to effect disunion."[18] Northern Whigs felt the same pressure. Another Illinois congressman, William H. Bissell, wrote, "The Southerners are insolent, overbearing & bullying beyond all endurance."[19]

The issue of slavery's expansion into the territories had shivered the Democratic Party into fragments. In the South, several camps existed: the Calhounite radicals, the border state moderates who accepted a loose definition of popular sovereignty, and some border and Deep South Democrats who found popular sovereignty acceptable so long as the decision on slavery was delayed until the moment when a territory wrote a state constitution. However, many southerners indicated that they preferred the imposition of the Missouri Compromise line of 36°30'. Among northern Democrats was the Wilmot Provisoist faction, who desired an absolute prohibition against slavery's possible expansion, while others stood under the banner of popular sovereignty. And some Democrats just did not care, because they thought slavery would never migrate to the West, and they believed that the institution posed no danger to the North. More generally, the essential problem was that, in one way or another, northern Democrats knew they could not survive politically if they allowed slavery to expand, while southern Democrats wanted explicit language indicating that slavery could expand and would not be singled out as a different form of property.

Douglas slowly moved toward popular sovereignty as the solution to the nation's ills about slavery. During the first session of the Thirty-first Congress, he expanded upon most of the ideas he had outlined in his 1849 speech at Springfield. California's actions probably acted as the greatest influence on his decision: the state had voted to become a free state and to prohibit slavery. "I predicted that the people would decide against slavery if left to settle the question for themselves," he wrote to Lanphier. Free Soilers were wrong: a congressional prohibition against slavery was not needed to keep the institution from spreading. "The result has shown that we were right & they wrong."[20] Popular sovereignty thus guaranteed that the West would become a batch of free states because most settlers would come from free states and would vote for freedom; thus northerners—Douglas's constituency—obtained their goals. At the same time, the doctrine of popular sovereignty did not insult the South and seemingly gave an equal chance for the peculiar institution to spread. But because of climate and the overwhelming number of northern migrants, the equal chance was entirely an illusion. Douglas still had to overcome some other opinions and deal with some other arguments, but the direction of his thinking was generally set.

Making the Compromise of 1850

To help steer the nation out of crisis, Henry Clay came out of retirement and was elected to the Senate by the legislature of Kentucky. Clay had earned the nickname "the Great Compromiser" because he had guided the nation past two other sectional collisions and had manufactured two memorable compromises, the Missouri Compromise of 1820-1821 and the Tariff Compromise of 1833. Failure to win the presidency in 1844 had sent him sulking back to Lexington to live out his days as a retired legislator. Seeing the dilemma in his country over the admission of California and the fate of the territories, however, reactivated his political fervor, and he returned to the Senate to save his country, so he hoped, one more time.

When early efforts to admit California to the Union failed, Clay presented to the Senate a set of resolutions that he believed represented a fair compromise between both sections on all existing controversies over slavery. His resolutions called for the admittance of California to the Union as a free state, the organization of the territories of Utah and New Mexico from the rest of the Mexican cession without reference one way or another to slavery, the establishment of appropriate boundaries for Texas and New Mexico, the absorption of Texas's debt by the federal government, a new fugitive slave law, the abolition of the slave trade in Washington, D.C., a declaration that the abolition of slavery in the District was inexpedient, and an affirmation that Congress could not regulate the domestic slave trade. Meanwhile, Douglas was busy in his Committee on Territories writing bills for the admission of California and for territorial governments for New Mexico and Utah (or Deseret, as the Mormons called it.) In his bills, Douglas called for the implementation of popular sovereignty in the territories by leaving all questions about domestic regulations to the settlers themselves. Douglas's proposals were before the Senate by late March, but they were then circumvented by the furor surrounding Clay's proposals.

Henry S. Foote had been pressing for weeks for the Senate to establish a select committee to take the Clay resolutions and transform them into bills that the Senate could consider. On April 18, 1850, in an atmosphere nearly producing physical violence, the Senate approved Foote's select committee, with Henry Clay as chairman. Douglas declined to serve. The select committee then produced the bills to compose a new sectional compromise. There were three. The first, known as the Omnibus, answered the territorial questions by bringing together the admission of California, territorial governments for Utah and New Mexico, and the boundary of Texas and New Mexico. The Committee of Thirteen had taken Douglas's work practically line for line, except for Douglas's declaration of popular sovereignty, putting in its place a statement prohibiting territorial legislatures from passing laws on slavery. The second bill was the fugitive slave law, and the third the termination of the slave trade in Washington, D.C. Although Douglas behaved as an unswerving supporter of the Omnibus, he had little hope of its passage. He frequently said that the best chance of winning approval for these measures was to place each territorial subject in a separate bill.

The debates over Clay's resolutions and then the Omnibus were something to behold. At the start of the session, Douglas adhered closely to the views he had enunciated at Springfield just a few months earlier. Senator John P. Hale sparked numerous debates by introducing petitions from some of his constituents asking for disunion or for a prohibition of slavery's introduction into the territories. Douglas did not like the petitions and wanted them tabled; and as for the one about the territories, he said the territories were already free due to prior Mexican law. This statement drew an immediate rebuke from Jefferson Davis of Mississippi, destined to be Douglas's most belligerent foe in the session. Douglas reiterated his belief that the Mexican prohibition made the Wilmot Proviso a useless but insulting redundancy. He then added that the Wilmot Proviso violated "the great fundamental principle of self-government." In the territories, neither the South nor the North had rights; "why, Sir, the principle of self government is, that each community shall settle this question for itself." He responded then to another southern complaint that northerners were assaulting the South; Douglas said that the charge was not true, but that the "impression has unfortunately gone abroad that southern men ask men from the North to come to their aid and help them to extend slavery into Territories now free."[21] Davis then replied, as he would endlessly throughout 1850, that southerners had an absolute right to go into all territories of the Union because Congress had no power to discriminate against the rights of property that southerners had in slaves.

Douglas continued to rely upon multiple solutions to the territorial dilemma. He could support the 36°30' line, but he knew now that such a line could not command a majority in both houses of Congress. He used the Mexican law argument about the territories, but southerners never accepted it. He had mentioned earlier letting climate determine the question of slavery's expansion and would say so again. Popular sovereignty had not yet become for Douglas the sole healing salve for the nation's sectional wounds. At least on one score, however, he felt there had been progress. Given the explosive nature of southerners and their open talk of disunion, northern Democrats began to retreat from the Wilmot Proviso.

The great debates over Clay's resolutions had come in March, before the select committee had been formed. Calhoun, near death and having his speech read by James M. Mason of Virginia, bemoaned the fate of the minority slave states as they faced the triumphant northern majority. On March 7, Massachusetts senator Daniel Webster shocked the antislavery activists of his region by accepting the Clay resolutions and calling them an adequate compromise between the sections. In his analysis of the issue of slavery in the territories, he decided that the question was bogus because climate prohibited slavery's establishment. Four days later, New York's William H. Seward derided Webster's capitulation and warned that conscience was beyond the control of mere mortal law: there was governing the slavery question "a higher law than the Constitution." Southerners immediately seized onto the phrase "higher law" and inferred that northern antislavery agitation now refused to be bounded by governmental statute—a disaster for slaveholders should the attitude become pervasive.

Douglas had his turn as well. On March 13 and 14, he delivered a lengthy address on the issues confronting the sections. His approach was to analyze the territorial issue by dressing down the extremists, both North and South. For northern firebrands, he used Webster's speech as a starting point. Generally, Douglas found the speech admirable and its tone of reconciliation exactly the medicine needed to cure sectional fevers. Webster, however, had gone out of his way to attack northern Democrats for acquiring Texas and starting the Mexican War, the incidents that had led to the explosive issue of slavery's expansion. Douglas insisted that the Democrats had acted out of the highest patriotism. He declared that the future of the nation lay in the Mississippi Valley, where true patriotism would rule, a land that knew "no ultraisms, no strifes, no crusades against the North or the South." He then demonstrated that Texas and California, if left to their own devices, would have strengthened the free states if abolitionists had not interfered. The Wilmot Proviso was pure evil: "the most insidious, dangerous, and fatal form, to the acquisition of any territory whatever." He based his vision of the future of the territories on the likelihood that free settler migration and climate would result in free states. The rest of the territories, he predicted, would follow the example of California in choosing freedom over slavery.

What was interesting was that this was one of the few times in his life that he dealt directly with the charge that the Democrats had acted to enhance the "slave interest." For four years, northern Whigs and Barnburners had screamed warnings about the growing power and unrepublican intentions of the "Slave Power," and nary a word—from either southerner or northerner—was uttered to refute the charge. Douglas limited his discussion of the "slave interest" exclusively to the acquisition of territories and new slave states. He avoided the questions that antislavery leaders raised about the nature of the interest, the domineering qualities of slaveholding representatives, how much control of the government slavery actually exercised, and whether the continued presence of slavery did indeed erode republican institutions and individual liberty. Douglas brushed these concerns aside and would do so for the rest of his life. He frequently operated in this manner in debate: he limited the general propositions of others to a selected few areas and then talked those areas to death. This is why after a Douglas speech, logical as they usually were, one had the sense of a question not answered.

He then turned to southerners and made South Carolinians squirm angrily in their seats. As to the Calhoun school that shouted southern rights and northern aggressions, Douglas disagreed "in *toto*." Sections had no place in the Constitution, for that document recognized no geographical divisions. In a fit of nationalism, he declared that the territories belonged to one people, one nation. Congress did have the power to regulate those territories: "It is no violation of southern rights to prohibit slavery, nor of northern rights to leave the people to decide the question for themselves." He then gave a historical presentation to show that congressional prohibition of slavery in the territories had been useless; territorial settlers had always decided the question of slavery based on their own experiences and the climate of the region. Douglas's example was his own state of Illinois, where settlers had defied the Northwest Ordinance of 1787 and had tried to establish slavery. But, Douglas said, slavery was terminated in Illinois not because of congressional statutes but because slavery had been unprofitable due to climate and soil conditions. Congressional laws that operated against a local majority's opinion, he summarized, were "dead letter[s] upon the statute book." Douglas made his plea for popular sovereignty, "that great Democratic principle, that it is wiser and better to leave each community to determine and regulate its own local and domestic affairs in its own way." Here in the open was Douglas's marriage with popular sovereignty.[22]

At one point, Douglas got to the heart of the southern argument. Addressing their conviction that their property rights were being violated, Douglas claimed that property rights in slaves had no meaning in the territories. Northerners agreed to do justice to southerners when states defined Africans as property, as the Constitution required, but the territories were a different circumstance altogether. Local communities simply had to construct their own laws about property. He then referred to the multiplicity of laws concerning property in other states: those regarding banks and liquor were two of his examples. These were local laws about property, and no state had the right to impose these local laws on a territory. The same reasoning held for slavery. The property rights argument of southerners was empty.

Douglas later amplified his position on property rights in slaves. Because Jefferson Davis pressed the subject of property rights in slaves mercilessly during the session, Douglas clarified his explanation. He disliked the radical southern claim that rights in Africans had to be specifically exempted from territorial legislation. Why was only this form of property so listed, he asked? It amounted to special recognition of one form of property to the detriment of others—northerners asked for no special laws concerning their property. While Douglas believed Congress did have the power to exclude slavery from the territories, he was more willing to leave that power to actual settlers. Nevertheless, Douglas indicated that all property had to have local sanction in order for that property to exist.

Douglas then went forward to scold northerners for thinking that somehow the territories might be snatched away from freedom and put into the maw of slavery. To the undoubted consternation of the southerners in the audience, he proclaimed, "The course of freedom has steadily and firmly advanced, while slavery has receded in the same ratio." He predicted that seventeen new states would emerge from the territories, and they would all be free. Moreover, the country had no territory at the time that was suitable for slave labor—it was at its natural limits. On March 14, Douglas then reiterated his belief in the governance of Mexican law on the issue of slavery, and again he stressed the role of climate—"climate regulates these matters." He finished by lauding Henry Clay and moderation: "The people of the whole country, North and South, are beginning to see that there is nothing in this controversy which seriously affects the interests, invades the rights, or impugns the honor of any section or State of the Confederacy."[23]

Douglas's analysis of the southern position, while meeting the property rights argument frontally, still missed a vital aspect of southern desperation, especially in the Cotton South. Exactly what were southern fears composed of? Why would slavery restriction hurt them? How powerful was the economic interest of slavery? Douglas may have known some of the answers. He was far more familiar with slaveholding than most northerners, and he had intimate connections with the large planters of North Carolina because of his wife and his friendship with former North Carolina representative David Reid. Yet Douglas did not speak about the depths of southern apprehension. It is as though he believed the entire controversy had no grounding in real political stakes or economic interests.

Douglas's position on slavery itself was hazy because he avoided discussion of the topic purposefully. Nonetheless, it seems clear from his statements in Congress that he disliked slavery, that he did not want it to spread—especially to the existing western territories—and that he probably believed it hindered economic development. Under the circumstances of climate, race, and certain exotic staples like cotton, slavery might be made profitable, but the system did not embody progress in the way that Douglas envisioned—a way that was epitomized by the technological wonders of his time, the railroad and telegraph, which conquered time and space and fit into his idea of endless American expansion. At least for the United States and its territories as they existed in 1850, Douglas saw slavery confined to a particular area of the nation and doomed to be a shrinking component of national life.

Whether he foresaw the eventual demise of African slavery in the United States is more conjectural. Given some of his statements, one could surmise that he predicted the future triumph of freedom throughout the country. But other statements of his testified to slavery's longevity. He accepted the existence of slavery so long as climate and race resulted in profitable production. Later in the decade, he admitted that if the country acquired new lands that could sustain slavery—such as in the Caribbean and Central America—then slavery would be established there. The logic of his reasoning on slavery did not lead to its eventual collapse, yet his ebullience about American institutions did.

He made his claims about the shrinking power of slavery and his predictions for the triumph of northern freedoms before southerners assembled in the Senate of the United States. Why he expected them to take his comments with good grace is strange. Normally, one would predict that individuals being told of their being shorn of power, and possibly of profitability, would react excitedly and pugnaciously. Instead, Douglas seemed to believe that southern slaveholders would sit idly by and allow themselves to be relegated to obscurity, and do it with good humor.

He, in short, did not weigh the slavery issue in terms of political power, economic interests, or social necessities. Instead, he felt that passion and emotion ran amok on the slavery issue, the passion of the slaveholders to rule without interference, and the emotion of abolitionists who refused to obey civility and statute law. Douglas's word for the unrestrained passions of abolitionists and fire-eaters (extreme states' rights advocates) was "fanaticism." Douglas had mentioned several times before that the struggle over slavery in the territories derived from "fanatics upon either extreme."[24] In the world that Douglas inhabited, the form of fanaticism he most often encountered was the religious zealotry of the abolitionists and their determination to make every issue a moral issue—an issue involving the commandments of God. Douglas insisted that slavery was a political problem, not a religious one; he felt that agitators, by making slavery an issue involving biblical strictures, only inflamed passions to the point that compromise was impossible. Hence Douglas warred on the emotionalism connected with the slavery issue. But he never quite grappled with the possibility that much of the fears of both northerners and southerners concerning slavery's fate came from the way the slave system spun off economic, political, and social effects. It was not simply mindless emotion that governed people's actions and words, but well-considered fears about what slavery meant for the American future.

The Senate debated the compromise measures between April and July. Hostile forces sought to add amendments suitable to their particular desires, while the compromisers tried to preserve the integrity of Clay's original purpose. Operating against the compromisers was the hostility of the Taylor administration and the threat of a veto. However, Taylor died on July 9, and Millard Fillmore became president; and Fillmore let it be known that he favored sectional reconciliation along the lines suggested by Clay. The Senate considered the Omnibus for final passage on July 31, when suddenly all the work of the compromisers fell apart. Radicals North and South voted together on a series of amendments that removed all the sections involving territorial government, California, and boundary disputes. Nothing of substance was left in the bill; it had effectively been defeated. Southern fire-eaters and northern antislavery orators rejoiced and raised their arms in triumph as the compromisers slumped down in their seats in abject defeat. Henry Clay left the Senate in disgust.

The task of picking up the pieces of the shattered compromise fell to Douglas, and he rose to the occasion. He never had much faith in the Omnibus approach, and now he was given the chance to pass the component parts of the compromise separately. Although no record exists of his calculations, he must have figured that he could obtain a winning coalition on each measure because of the way senators and representatives would shift between opposition and support. For example, the southern fire-eaters would support a fugitive slave law, but northern Wilmot Provisoists would not; likewise, the Provisoists would support the abolition of the fugitive slave trade in the District of Columbia, but southern fire-eaters would not. Only when all the measures were combined together did the fire-eaters and Provisoists act together. The key would be to have one stable group that supported all the compromise measures throughout: that group was a small number of northern conservative Whigs, some border state representatives, and most distinctly the popular sovereignty wing of the Democratic Party. Douglas worked with the speaker of the House of Representatives, Howell Cobb, and with the president, who promised to use his influence to secure passage of the bills. Douglas made no speeches about the issues in the last few months of the session but rather managed the pressure applied to wavering lawmakers.

With the compromise broken into separate pieces of legislation, the Senate acted quickly and passed them on to the House. In a mere two weeks, the territorial bills received the Senate's approval, a testament to the political acumen and arduous labor of Douglas in marshalling the winning forces on the floor of the Senate. Even his adversary, Jefferson Davis, admitted Douglas's achievement: "If any man has a right to be proud of the success of these measures, it is the Senator from Illinois."[25] Douglas missed the vote on the fugitive slave bill, as he was in New York City negotiating a financial problem, but he left no doubt that he approved of it. In early September, the prohibition of the District of Columbia's slave trade also received approval. By September 7, the four territorial bills of the compromise had passed the House, and it would only be a few more days until the House agreed to the final measures on fugitive slaves and the slave trade in the District. Collectively these measures became known as the Compromise of 1850, and the nation leaped over the great hurdle of disunion and achieved a sort of sectional harmony. The forces of sectionalism had been vanquished and the Union preserved. In this outcome, Stephen A. Douglas played a decisive role. His fame was now national.

Just at the moment when he should have been allowed to celebrate, however, he faced another challenge. This one came from outraged citizens in Chicago upset over the provisions of the Fugitive Slave Act. This part of the Compromise of 1850 allowed southerners to capture runaway slaves more easily by enabling federal marshals forcibly to enlist northerners to form posses to hunt fugitives down, eliminating trial by jury for the accused, allowing the decision of whether to remove the fugitive to be made by a federal commissioner instead of an ordinary judge, and rewarding the commissioner more if the accused runaway was sent back into slavery instead of released. Throughout the North, people reacted angrily to the Fugitive Slave Act, believing that the South had invaded the sovereignty of the North and had defiled civil liberties and the right to trial by jury. Chicago was part of this general northern reaction. The city council branded the law as "cruel and unjust" and called those free state politicians who had supported and passed it "traitors."[26]

Douglas scurried back to Chicago to douse the embers that threatened to burst into antislavery flames. He needed to return anyway. His real residence had become Washington, D.C., where he spent most of his time, and his wife often remained in North Carolina. Douglas had not been to Illinois for eighteen months, and his reputation and party machinery had fallen into disrepair.

For northern Democrats, the ruckus over the Fugitive Slave Act brought up embarrassing subjects because of the juxtaposition of the rule of law and the sanctity of property. Abolitionists and antislavery persons generally held that slaveholding was a violation of God's law. To be forced by civil law into participating in the capture of runaway slaves was equivalent to being coerced into breaking a commandment of the Lord. There arose from the pulpit and from religiously minded antislavery zealots a howl of protest, and they stated that, given the choice between obedience to God and obedience to the state, they would have to violate civil law.

Douglas confronted these questions in a mass meeting that he called in Chicago at the city hall on October 23. His performance and its results were utterly astounding. This speech has to mark the summit of his power of persuasion in American politics.

Douglas took the podium and addressed a crowd of about four thousand people for two hours. He, of course, justified the measures constituting the Compromise of 1850 and said that neither the North nor the South had won at the expense of the other, and neither side had lost any rights. Douglas asserted that popular sovereignty was a more important principle to have won than the Wilmot Proviso. He added that no Illinoisan should fear that the western territories would produce slave states. Western settlers would mainly hail from free states, and the climate did not favor the great southern staples, so the states arising from the western territories would be free, not slave.

He then turned to the resolutions of the Chicago City Council. He found the language in poor taste and then made an amazing assertion: the Fugitive Slave Act of 1850 was no different than the Fugitive Slave Act of 1793. He carefully went through the provisions and argued that the act of 1850 still had trial by jury, that judicial officers still ruled the fate of alleged runaways, and that the act did not suspend the writ of habeas corpus. What Douglas did—and even today it is difficult to figure out his logic—was show how the mechanics of returning a slave resulted in all the usual procedures protecting civil liberties. His performance was utterly astounding! He argued that the Fugitive Slave Act, though fashioned by irate southerners demanding more stringent provisions, was no different than the law that had been in place for decades! And evidently the people of Chicago bought his explanation. The city council the next night repealed their earlier resolution against the Fugitive Slave Act by a nearly unanimous vote.

Two other themes marked Douglas's oration at Chicago. He had to grapple with an energized clergy. The Compromise of 1850 and the Fugitive Slave Act had brought evangelical ministers out of the pulpit and into the public arena, telling citizens which laws accorded with the will of God and which ones did not. Douglas recognized that the appeal had been made to obey the dictates of conscience rather than the laws of the state. He insisted that all must obey the instructions of the Christian deity: "We should all recognize, respect, and revere the divine law." Then came the qualification: "But we should all bear in mind that the law of God, as revealed to us, is intended to operate on our consciences, and insure the performance of our duties as individuals and Christians. The divine law does not prescribe the form of government under which we shall live, and the character of our political and civil institutions." He warned that if one pushed the idea of divine law too far, then self-government would be sacrificed to priestly rule: "If the Constitution of the United States is to be repudiated upon the ground that it is repugnant to the divine law, where are the friends of freedom and Christianity to look for another and a better? Who is to be the prophet to reveal the will of God and establish a Theocracy for us?" Douglas had just begun a decadelong battle with religious leaders over their influence in public affairs.

In addition, Douglas brought forth the idea of equality—and qualified it. He made it clear that the world was divided into races, and that the races were unequal in their capacities. Indians and Africans were so degraded "as to be utterly incapable of governing themselves," so "they must . . . be governed by others." Indians, Asians, and Africans exhibited nothing but "ignorance, superstition and despotism." Their fate was not governed by divine law but civil law, the law that determined how societies were to function and what rights and duties each class of citizens would have. "These things certainly violate the principle of absolute equality among men," he confessed. "In fact, no government ever existed on earth in which there was a perfect equality in all things among those composing it and governed by it." Thus divine law did not interfere with any civil society that established political gradations among its races.[27]

Douglas enjoyed a spectacular triumph in 1850. He was responsible, as much as any single person, for pushing through the measures of the Compromise of 1850 and avoiding the quagmire of disunion. His political mastery over his constituents was awesome; he convinced them that the Fugitive Slave Act actually did not do what the statute said it did. No other American politician stood at the summit of power the way Stephen Douglas did at the end of 1850. It was hardly any wonder, then, that presidential aspirations began to fire his ambition.

However, if one looked at his behavior and speeches between 1847 and 1850, one saw some strange portents for the Democratic Party. For Douglas in 1850 had turned the corner of commitment. He had been a "thoroughly radical Democrat" who believed in "the rights of people above those of property," "equality," and democracy by majority vote. The democracy of white people remained, but in other ways Douglas began a drift toward conservatism. The radical Democrat of the 1830s and 1840s became the conservative Democrat of the 1850s. This evolution was visible in two areas: the embrace of a doctrine of racial inequality and the acceptance of the sanctity of property rights in slaves. In the Fugitive Slave Act, Douglas agreed that states had the right to designate whatever they wanted as property, and the duty of citizens was to obey the law. The slavery question was distorting the democratic aspirations of both the Democratic Party and Stephen A. Douglas.

The Gordian Knots of Morality and Popular Sovereignty

Democracy as a political system does not easily comport with a heightened notion of morality. Principles or attitudes based on morality derive their strength from some eternal source of truth, be it religious commandment or natural law. In any event, moral commandments, being eternally true, are incapable of being changed by the democratic procedure of majority rule, or at least so say those who advocate moral principles. Humankind must submit to moral truths and obey them, not vote on them. For democratic systems, therefore, moral principles can present a real challenge; for in a democratic polity, the choices of the majority of the citizens rule, not the determinations of a special caste of people who interpret what the moral law says.

Douglas's position on moral principles in a democratic nation has more complexity to it than historians have allowed. Douglas and his party had no hesitation in raising the banner of a superior morality when it served their purposes, but slavery turned out to be a more delicate subject with profound implications for the health of the Union and their organization, the Democratic Party. Moreover, there were apparently two systems of morality operating in the mid-nineteenth century: one was the morality of religious denominations using the Bible, and the other was an Enlightenment morality employing natural rights and natural law. Douglas's morality came from the latter source.

Douglas's religious sentiments are largely a conjecture. He left no pertinent record of religious activity or belief during his early years in Illinois, save an Enlightenment outlook demanding that individuals seek out their religious principles free of state coercion. He accepted, it seems, the religious climate of his country, realizing that he must operate in it to survive politically, writing about the misadventures of one of his supporters, "No party can or ought to be sustained which offends against the moral sense of the religious community."[28] But his disengagement from an active religious life did disturb some friends. One wrote him in 1857, "Permit me to say to you—don't forget that you are *a man*—that you are *mortal*—that you have *a Soul*—that the hour of *death* and the day of *judgment* are *sure to come.*"[29]

Rather, Douglas seemingly came to adopt a Thomas Paine or Thomas Jefferson stand on moral principles: they came from nature. There were things right and wrong in the world—a natural way and an unnatural way—but they were discovered through logic, reason, and discussion, and, in a democracy, by voting. Most people not warped by avarice would choose the correct path. A part of his Paineite/Jeffersonian radicalism was a distrust of the exhorters themselves. Individuals who claimed knowledge of the "divine will" usurped the right of people to make choices for themselves. Instead of reason and logic, the truth came from an oracular voice; instead of discussion, there was dictation. Douglas's bout with religious authority in Chicago in 1850 began his battle against those who claimed to be the voice of God and who by that claim stifled the voice of the citizenry.

But this hardly meant that Douglas and the Democrats refrained from phrases laden with the words "deity," "God," and "moral." Throughout the 1830s, they trumpeted their superior morality in terms of stopping the rich from plundering the poor, the capitalist from grinding the laborer, and the aristocracy from trampling the people. During the election of 1840, Douglas and his fellow Illinois Democrats denounced the Whig campaign style because it brought about the "moral degradation of the intellect of man."[30] At the Maryland State Fair in 1851, he told his audience that "man" had a "religious duty"[31] to leave his land in the condition of abundance in which he had found it, and in his remarks at a banquet honoring the Hungarian Louis Kossuth, Douglas said that American federal democracy was the system most promotive of "the intellectual, moral, and physical condition of the people."[32] Democrats in Illinois had written about all men being endowed "by their Creator with equal political rights,"[33] that the Panic of 1837 was caused by casting aside "duties to God and man [so that] a paper mammon might prevail,"[34] that the American republic prospered and persevered because of the people's "religious spirit and social ethics,"[35] and that parties lost elections because "in politics as well as in morals, the wages of sin is death";[36] in the 1841 address of the State Convention of the Illinois Democratic party was the statement, "This party looks upon man as the image of his Creator, [and] insists on their capacity for self-government."[37]

The Democratic Party of the mid-nineteenth-century United States was no stranger to moral appeals, but on the subject of slavery, they hedged and retreated from an extended discussion. Much of the reason for their evasion was simple politics: the Democratic Party drew much strength from the southern states, and most northern Democrats knew their party would explode if they argued the immorality of slavery in the open—southern Democrats would never tolerate it. And moral evaluations of the peculiar institution endangered the Union itself. Many editors, while listing the evils of slavery, nonetheless at the same time worried for the safety of the Union if moral issues were handled passionately instead of logically. Tucked away in the Douglas papers at the University of Chicago is a newspaper clipping that Douglas evidently cut out: it listed the death toll of the French Revolution—the touchstone of fanaticism—as 1,022,351 killed, 18,603 guillotined, and 900,000 dead in the Vendee including 15,000 women and 22,000 children.[38] Democrats like Douglas feared fanaticism because fanatics failed at the ultimate morality: the sanctity of human life.

Most northern Democrats in the 1850s believed that fanaticism and hyper-moralism would cause either destruction of the freest government on the face of the earth or a civil war, a bloodbath equal to the French Revolution, because southerners would permit no tampering with the peculiar institution. By elevating slavery to the status of a question demanding divine judgment either for or against, the abolitionists were destroying the possibility of compromise, and compromise meant the continuance of the Union without civil war. Southerners would never live in a Union that saw its northern part calling slavery a sin against God. The trap that the moralistic evaluation of slavery placed the Union into was put in nearly perfect form during the battle over the compromise measures, by Mississippi governor and states' rights radical John A. Quitman. Due to their numbers, northerners would soon dominate every branch of the federal government; "What, then, is to be our fate? You say *compromise*. But can we compromise a question of conscience? Can we halve a moral duty? The commandments of the moral law are not discretionary, but imperative: 'Thou *shall*,' or 'thou *shall not*.'"[39] If northern elected officials believed slavery immoral, Quitman summarized, was it not rational for southerners to fear that northerners would carry their prejudices into policy and find ways to attack, weaken, and destroy slavery? The South, to protect slavery, could not let such a sequence of events happen, and therefore would have to leave the Union.

Douglas had a contradictory view of the morality of slavery, and his position is not easy to characterize. He never actually said slavery was not a moral issue. What he said over and over again was that he feared fanaticism, that he rejected zealotry on this issue, and that he would not publicly talk about the evils of slavery. He usually then leaped into a constitutional argument, stating that by the compact of 1788–1789, all had agreed to let the states determine the existence of slavery for themselves, and he was just applying the same rule (local popular sovereignty) now to the territories.

It is not unlikely that Douglas saw two moralities operating on the slavery question. First was the morality of individual treatment. This was the basis of his frequent assertion that Africans "should be allowed to exercise all the rights and privileges which they are capable of enjoying consistent with the welfare of the community in which they reside."[40] Blacks should be treated fairly, should not be abused, and should not be subject to inhumane conditions. In essence, this was the outlook of southern slaveholders: the *treatment* of slaves should follow moral principles. It may have been that Douglas's association with a great North Carolina planter and his personal albeit distant management of a Mississippi plantation dampened a view that black slavery had inherent moral problems. Douglas would not have been the first northerner to allow the experience of slaveholding to change his views on the morality of the peculiar institution.

But then comes the question of the morality of slavery as an economic, social, and political *system*. On that question, Douglas was more evasive and elusive. The question of race twisted the answers given. This distortion revealed itself in numerous ways, two of which are memorable. In 1854, the Democratic editor and promoter of Manifest Destiny, John L. O'Sullivan, wrote Douglas about his position on slavery: "In common with the almost unanimous North, I was opposed to the extension of slavery" because "I used to assume as true without question the old doctrine of the unity of the human race; carrying with it the consequence that the Negro was merely a Black white man." But time and experience and reading proved to him that Africans were a different species; he now believed in the "doctrine of *original diversity of species*" and no longer looked at slavery "as a wrongful oppression."[41] Race twisted the answers to human rights for Africans that an Enlightenment perspective would normally yield. Thus the moral standard for blacks was different than for whites.

The other incident in which racial thinking showed its deep imprint on the question of the morality of slavery as a social system came from Douglas, though in a slightly oblique form. In a debate he had with Jefferson Davis about whether the Mexican system of peonage operated after the American conquest (peonage was a system in which an indebted person had to remain on the land until his debt was paid, and the indebtedness could be a hereditary condition), Davis said yes, partly because this might become a way to establish slavery in California. He then declared, "This is a species of property, and we have no right to interfere with it." Douglas dismissed this argument peremptorily. He objected to peonage because it was not based on race; thus it might be used on white people. Congress, Douglas asserted, should abolish "this revolting system by which white men, our own kindred, may be reduced to a system of slavery."[42]

His response to peonage deserves special comment. His denunciation of peonage for whites appears to have been a moral argument. It would have been instructive if he had said more, had invoked the Creator, natural laws, and perhaps even scripture. But note what was missing in Douglas's abrupt retort to Davis: his position on local government, majority rule, and congressional intervention. When the subject was the rights of Europeans, he did not invoke the right of local communities to make their own laws, to determine the status of whites by majority rule, or to demand nonintervention by Congress on matters relating to domestic regulations. Indeed, his quick response implied that he favored having Congress enact and oversee a national standard for the rights of Europeans, a standard beyond the ability of state or territorial governments to change. For Douglas, peonage was a system of labor that was out of bounds for the white man's republic. No popular sovereignty was to be allowed to operate on the rights of white men.

For blacks, however, a different morality obtained in regard to social and economic systems. In Douglas's estimation, whites deserved free government, democracy, and free labor; Africans did not. He probably believed African slavery an inferior production system, but he may have actually considered it a moral system for blacks. Later in the decade, Douglas argued that slavery was ruled by political economy. Where Africans could work and whites could not, slavery was permissible. This was equivalent to saying that *black* slavery was a moral system under the right economic and geographical conditions. Douglas would let slavery expand if it proved hearty enough, but in the existing climatic and geographical conditions in the western territories, he did not believe it could. Douglas minimized the importance of the morality of slavery because of another attitude about slavery he held: he believed that slavery of Africans posed no danger to white men's liberties or economic opportunities, that slavery of blacks had no economic or political consequences at all for whites. Thus Douglas had a contradictory moral stance on black slavery, sometimes decrying it, sometimes justifying it.

Douglas never solved the Gordian knot of democratic equality involving the subject of morality. One viewpoint he offered did have merit. He rightfully insisted that small groups within the polity could not be allowed to make decisions for the whole polity based on their alleged superior knowledge or wisdom. That indeed would be the prelude to the death of self-government. Likewise, Douglas was also correct in stressing the dangers of fanaticism and unconstrained passionate outbursts; he, as well as many other contemporaries, understood that zealots wrapped up in their own cause were more than willing to sacrifice all of humanity—to commit mass murder—to keep their moral vision unstained. In stressing the Enlightenment virtues of reason, discussion, and logic, he was undoubtedly wise. Yet he failed to recognize that a public investigation of some questions involving moral standards was an inevitable element of a democratic polity. His position on slavery nearly led to an elimination of all discussion whatsoever, not a particularly healthy condition for a democracy.

Douglas, not being a philosopher, desired merely a practical solution to a pressing question, and so he just wanted to eliminate the subject of slavery from national discourse. This was no solution to the Gordian knot involving the handling of moral issues in politics. An irony pervades the matter, however. A debate over slavery emerged anyway, and in fact a national popular sovereignty did operate: by a majority vote, the people—mostly the northern public—did decide the morality of slavery, and in 1860, assuming one can draw such inferences from a vote, they determined that slavery had too many flaws, moral and otherwise, to allow it to expand.

Moral questions in a democratic form of government constituted one in-soluble problem festering in the mid-nineteenth-century United States; the idea of popular sovereignty constituted another dilemma. Douglas placed more and more faith in the doctrine of popular sovereignty to avoid sectional confrontations over the question of slavery's possible expansion into the territories. Imbedded in his formulation were many problems concerning democracy that he never quite owned up to. Popular sovereignty was indeed a democratic doctrine, and Douglas was right when he said that popular sovereignty was one of the great fruits of the American Revolution. But to make the doctrine work in a democratic fashion, someone had to supply definitions. The ones Douglas eventually supplied were marked with exclusions of peoples, not inclusion. And thus the question of democratic equality became a Gordian knot, a highly convoluted problem that required time, patience, and imagination to unravel. Douglas had neither the time nor the patience nor the imagination. He simply cut the knot, applied the doctrine, and took the consequences. The consequences were not benign.

The first definitional problem with popular sovereignty was this: who were the populace? Who were the people who would decide by majority vote the rules by which they would live? Douglas's actual answer to this question was race. He divided the world into Europeans and non-Europeans; democracy only belonged to the European part of the human family. At a time of rising prejudice aimed at immigrants and especially the Irish, Douglas stood forth as a stalwart champion of their inclusion in American politics and economic life. During the debates over territorial government in 1850, Douglas was adamant in granting immigrants in the territories as many rights as given to native-born Americans. In this, Douglas was following a trail that his party had marked out for two decades.

Yet democracy was a system inclusive of people, and Douglas's democracy did not include all people. In essence, he altered the definition of "the people" to create a democracy to his liking. But this maneuver created problems, which his critics quickly pointed out. Slaves were not property but were human beings, and by allowing one race to rule another race, one obtained not democracy but a form of special privilege, a form of aristocracy. Some Americans understood the problem. The brother of a congressman could explain the defects of popular sovereignty thus: "Still, it is not right to give even the semblance of approval to so deceptive and pernicious a doc[trine] as that the majority of the people or a minority have the right to deprive a single human being of his God-given rights, as the doc[trine] of Pop[ular] Sov[ereignt]y clearly assumes to do, and must do, if it is legitimately carried out."[43] Abolitionists also perceived this definitional problem. As the Wisconsin antislavery advocate Edwin Booth wrote, "No man can be a real Democrat and not be an abolitionist at heart. . . . Democracy preserves and protects the rights of all." For this reason, the opponents of popular sovereignty often called it "sham democracy."[44]

Douglas faced more serious limitations with his idea of popular sovereignty because the allegiance of southerners to the democratic principle had its limits. Throughout the nation between 1820 and 1850, the arrival of democratic forms and ideas was highly contested. The reason so much language about states' rights and minority rights emerged was that many people, especially those with property, feared the results of letting everyone vote and participate in politics. Among southerners, there was an additional hesitation because their most important form of property—slaves—was not present in the North, where the bulk of the population resided. Southerners had enormous qualms about letting northern nonslaveholders vote on slavery-related subjects, subjects that could drastically affect the profitability of slavery. The ancient fear of elites toward democracy had always been that the mass of the people, being poor, would seek politically to redistribute the property of the wealthy to themselves. In most ancient and modern formulations, such attempts (back then called "agrarianism") would produce anarchy, dictatorship, or civil war. In any event, civilization would end.

The final problem in Douglas's doctrine of popular sovereignty was less one of definitions and more one of faith in accepting outcomes. Douglas was willing to allow people to settle decisions by popular vote because he optimistically believed that "the people" would choose the morally "right" path. But he actually had one other democratic faith: that the minority would accept the verdict of the majority. Here was a real problem. On the question of property rights in slaves, southerners were not willing to accept the will of the majority, and they said so frequently. Popular sovereignty might work over matters of minor financial importance, but could it truly work on subjects in which the great propertied interests of the nation were involved?

After 1854, Douglas would learn the limits of popular sovereignty as a solution to the nation's sectional ills.

Notes

1. CG, 29-1, 63, 139.
2. CG, 29-1, 559.
3. CG, 30-1, 92.
4. CG, 30-2, 208.
5. CG, 30-1, appendix, 506–7.
6. *Boston Post*, quoted by Detroit *Democratic Free Press*, January 30, 1847.
7. *Cleveland Plain Dealer*, February 8, 1848.
8. *Ill St Reg.*, December 17, 1847.

9. CG, 30-2, 314.

10. *Albany Argus*, October 23, 1848.

11. CG, 28-2, 284.

12. *Washington, D.C., Union*, June 24, 1848.

13. CG, 30-2, appendix, 193, 551, 685.

14. CG, 30-2, 207, 208.

15. James Ferguson to William Allen, November 12, 1848, William Allen Papers, LC.

16. Johannsen, *Douglas*, 251–53.

17. *Ill St Reg*, November 1, 8, 1849.

18. Thomas L. Harris to Charles Lanphier, January 12, 1850, Lanphier Papers, IllStLib.

19. William H. Bissell to Joseph Gillespie, February 12, 1850, Gillespie Papers, IllStLib.

20. SAD to Charles H. Lanphier and George Walker, January 7, 1850, in Douglas, *Letters*, 182.

21. CG, 31-1, 342–43.

22. CG, 31-1, appendix, 364, 365, 368, 369, 370.

23. CG, 31-1, 371, 375.

24. CG, 29-1, 559.

25. Johannsen, *Douglas*, 296.

26. Johannsen, *Douglas*, 300–1.

27. Flint, *Life of Douglas*, "Speech at Chicago," 4, 27–28, 28–29.

28. SAD to Caleb Cushing, February 4, 1852, Douglas, *Letters*, 237.

29. William S. Prentice to SAD, October 23, 1857, Douglas Papers, Uchi, box 3, addenda.

30. *Ill St Reg*, June 12, 1840.

31. November 6, 1851.

32. February 5, 1852.

33. December 7, 1839.

34. June 4, 1841.

35. November 5, 1851.

36. October 29, 1841.

37. December 17, 1841.

38. SAD Papers, Uchi, addenda, clippings.

39. J. F. H. Claiborne, *Life and Correspondence of John A. Quitman* (New York, 1860), 2:260.

40. Johannsen, *Douglas*, 571.

41. O'Sullivan to SAD, February 10, 1854, SAD Papers, Uchi.

42. CG, 31-1, 1143.

43. Edwards Potter to John F. Potter, April 13, 1858, John F. Potter Papers, Wisconsin Historical Society, Madison, Wisconsin.

44. *Milwaukee Daily Democrat*, October 21, 1851.

CHAPTER FOUR

~

The Kansas-Nebraska Act and Its Aftermath, 1851–1856

The years of triumph in Stephen A. Douglas's life had ended; the years of trial and defeat lay ahead. Center stage in the drama of his life was his doctrine of popular sovereignty. Douglas considered it the best compromise formula for avoiding Union-dissolving fights between the nonslaveholding and the slaveholding states: move the debate out of the halls of Congress and let the people of the territories determine whether or not they wanted to have the institution of slavery. His faith in popular sovereignty and the willingness of people to allow matters of exceptional importance to them to be determined simply by a popular vote needed to be tempered with some more realistic assessments about human nature. He failed to curb his enthusiasm, however, and produced a horrendous debacle: the Kansas-Nebraska Act. The consequences of ignoring the complications of the Gordian knots of democratic equality could no longer be evaded.

In Search of the Presidential Nomination

Most northerners were gratified that a reconciliation between the sections had been achieved. This sentiment became apparent in the fall 1850 elections in the North. Not much fanfare surrounded these contests, but when the ballots were counted, the Democrats emerged the big victors. In 1848, Democrats had won 37 congressional seats, Whigs 71, and Free Soilers 9; but in 1850, the tally was 61 congressional victories for the Democrats, 50 for the Whigs, and 6 for the Free Soilers. In Illinois, the Democrats won their usual six of seven congressional seats, and they captured 60,551 votes out of 103,001 cast, or 58.8

percent. Northern politicians should have looked at these numbers as the tea leaves auguring the outcome of the presidential election of 1852.

Douglas at about this time realized that he was a legitimate contender for the 1852 Democratic presidential nomination. He had a national reputation and was one of the acknowledged leaders who had found a way to compromise on the slavery issue and preserve the Union. Between December 1850 and June 1852, Douglas performed at numerous speaking engagements to keep his name before the public. These speeches exhibited his vision of the future.

Douglas engaged in spread-eagle nationalism, one part composed of lambasting the designs of England and the other part of hoisting the banner of Manifest Destiny. During discussion of foreign affairs in Congress in 1852, Douglas cried out against the Clayton-Bulwer Treaty that the United States had signed during Taylor's and Fillmore's presidency (the treaty gave England the right to occupy the Mosquito Coast in South America, while the United States renounced the right to exclusive access to any canal built across the isthmus area). England was a despotic nation bent on extending its evil empire; as a colonial mistress to the United States, England had been a "cruel mother." The United States expanded by honor and consent, while the British expanded by "seizure, violence, and fraud."[1] In 1851, the Hungarian revolutionary Louis Kossuth, hoping to obtain aid, visited the United States and was feted by Congress and various public groups. Douglas delivered some remarks at a congressional banquet held in honor of Kossuth and used the occasion to praise the American system of federalism and local self-government, while denouncing the way Europeans "bullied" smaller nations; aristocrats, he charged, put their "feet upon the necks of the people." He then attacked England, declaring that England "must give up her monarchy, her nobility, her establishment, the whole system of machinery by which she has been able to oppress her own people." And he proclaimed that the crux of future international affairs would be the "great battle between republicanism and despotism."[2]

Douglas wanted a foreign policy looking toward expansion. He thought Central America should be brought within the embrace of American institutions, and he told various groups that he favored annexation of Cuba. He denounced the Fillmore administration for not supporting American adventurers seeking to overthrow the Spanish government in Cuba. Douglas always coupled his expansionist visions with the promise of free government similar to the American system of federalism; "other peoples" would come into the fold of American freedom and republicanism. His "other peoples," however, were usually restricted to Europeans.

Douglas also gave addresses at the state agricultural fairs of Maryland and New York in the fall of 1851 and demonstrated his pride in American growth and technological advance. He boasted about the nation's overflowing agricultural productions and gloried in their victories in the world's markets. As well, he affirmed his faith in modern technology. He told his audiences that farming was now lifted above brute labor because new machines helped farmers produce more.

Railroads truly captured his imagination, and in them he saw the possibility of growth and improvement. The British Historian Asa Briggs called the nineteenth century "the Age of Progress," and Stephen A. Douglas would have heartily concurred.[3] He even equated landed expansion with technological expansion. Douglas's embrace of the railroad was clearly commercial in nature, for the railroad allowed the agricultural products of the Great Lakes to be exchanged with the manufacturing products of the East. He saw the railroad as the technological means of maintaining the Union—a "band of iron to hold the states together."[4] The reasoning behind this was strictly commercial: the more the sections traded with one another, the more dependent they became on one another, and the more the citizens would have to accept that disunion could only result in an economic convulsion that would punish everyone.

Douglas's interest in technology and in America's beginning steps into modern life came out in other ways. He had become a member of the Board of Regents of the Smithsonian Institution. In 1857, he donated some of his Chicago property to assist in the creation of the University of Chicago, Douglas finding that education and scientific advancement marched hand in hand. Given the new vistas opened in business, science, and education, it was no wonder that Douglas talked of the spirit of the age, progress, and change. He wanted to personify in his physical being these forces of change and advancement.

But Douglas's idea of progress and the "spirit of the age" contrasted with others, and his speech at the New York State Fair contained some interesting thoughts about labor and political economy. In 1847, Representative Hannibal Hamlin, a Wilmot Proviso Democrat, explained that he wished to prohibit slavery's expansion because slavery was opposed to the "spirit of the age." The spirit of the age did not mean the same thing to all people. For Hamlin, the spirit of the age was toward individual freedom and liberation for all; for him the future belonged to free labor. According to Hamlin and antislavery spokespeople, free labor was a system that permitted individuals to use their talents fully and to earn fair rewards for their labor; it stimulated intelligence in production and unleashed people's inventive capacities.[5] Antislavery politicians feared that slave labor, when brought into competition with free labor, took away all these wholesome outcomes by ruining the character of free labor and by reducing the wage rate so that rewards for good work disappeared—slave labor, in short, destroyed the incentives in free labor for productive work.

Debates in Congress, on the stump, and in newspaper editorials endlessly paraded the question of free labor versus slave labor, but Douglas never responded to it. In fact, except for two occasions later in the decade, he never used the phrase "free labor." One can find a belief about free labor in several of his addresses, and the historian can also deduce that Douglas's "spirit of the age" harbored suspicions about the merits of slavery. Yet Douglas never directly replied to the northern apprehension that slave labor was a threat to northern free labor society. His spirit of the age had no room for an antislavery passion.

In his agricultural fair address at Rochester, Douglas demonstrated a belief in free labor without ever using the term. He lavished praise upon farmers—not a novel activity for a vote-seeking politician at an agricultural fair—and rejoiced that the farmers of the land were "a far more intelligent, energetic and independent yeomanry, than any other [in the world]." American farmers owned their own land, and by establishing in the United States a vast system of "independent farming," the nation had "restored agricultural labor to that natural dignity, of which the feudal systems of the old world had deprived it." Thanks to technology and the application of science and education to farming, agriculture had become in America "a highly respectable, and, at the same time, a most attractive pursuit"—that is, it was financially rewarding.[6] During the election of 1860, he praised the work ethic by complimenting a Vermont audience that "you inculcate virtue, you educate your children, you train them to habits of industry—you *teach them the necessity of labor*."[7] Douglas used the analysis of free labor advocates even though he never mentioned the term. He never applied the analysis to the slavery controversy, and he simply avoided the free labor arguments of his antislavery opponents—most famously those of Abraham Lincoln.

His time in Congress between the Compromise of 1850 and the election of 1852 was uninspiring. He took time to praise the compromise, and he explained how the measures came to be adopted and his role in promoting them. As well, he insisted that northerners live up to the compromise and return fugitive slaves, and he deprecated the sensational cases in which northerners helped runaways escape from slave catchers and federal marshals. Another facet of political life was becoming visible: the withering away of the traditional issues of the tariff, internal improvements, national banks, and western land use. During the battle over slavery extension, these issues got lost, and after 1850 they were not immediately found.

Douglas developed his Chicago property but basically stayed in Washington, D.C. He bought property around New Jersey Avenue and I Street North to build a more spacious home for his wife. His family—growing with a second son born in November 1850–did not travel with him to Illinois, and this circumstance upset him. Interestingly, given his New England upbringing, his home in Washington became a center for parties and hard drink–it was called "Mount Julep" in reference to the voluminous consumption of alcoholic beverages. In these days, the only darkness in his private life was the ill health of his wife, Martha.

Douglas moved steadily toward his goal of earning the Democratic nomination at Baltimore in 1852, but he miscalculated. For a few years, a brief movement swelled in the North called "Young America," a movement of boisterous nationalism, expansion, and youth. Young America wanted the nation to take the lead among nations and to trumpet its power and economic growth. Young America remains something of a mysterious political development, loud in its exhortations, but small–even minuscule–in its numbers. Its adherents did not exalt the agrarian ethos of the Jacksonians of the 1830s but rather furiously thundered for expansion, commercial development, and market growth. They were impatient of impediments to economic dynamism and were bored with the agrarian preoccupations of their Democratic elders. They wanted youth and vigor in Democratic politics and economic policy. They wanted the thirty-nine-year-old Stephen A. Douglas.

In 1851, the *United States and Democratic Review* came under the editorship of an unstable person, George Nicholas Sanders. Sanders belonged to Young America, and he championed Douglas for the presidency. He unfortunately wrote articles that were personal attacks on other candidates, articles that Douglas had to disown. Moreover, as it became clear that Douglas was openly seeking the nomination early in the game, he aroused the ire of other stalwarts in the party who felt no need to surrender to Young America. Douglas's open desire for the nomination looked unseemly to others and broke with the unwritten tradition that the nomination was bestowed upon a person and was not conspicuously sought after.

At Baltimore, Douglas's overt desire for the nomination, and the blunders of his followers, thwarted his chances. His most important rival was James Buchanan of Pennsylvania, and though Douglas obtained a plurality of the votes of the delegates, he never achieved a majority. After two days of balloting, party leaders looked for a dark horse and found one in the person of New Hampshire's Franklin Pierce. On the third day of the convention, Pierce earned the nomination.

Of course Douglas was disappointed, but as a good party man, he suppressed his frustrations and did yeoman work to ensure a Democratic victory. He spoke at numerous northern cities, and in his speeches he expounded on the themes of Manifest Destiny, federalism, the compromise measures, and popular sovereignty. At New York, he told Democrats that the Whigs were doomed because they "don't understand the doctrine of progress,"[8] and at the capital city, he declared that Whigs "lack that sympathy with the masses of our population, that confidence in the virtue of the people, which should pervade every branch and department of a free government."[9]

About the fate of the Whigs, Douglas proved a good prognosticator. Pierce won 254 electoral votes to Whig candidate Winfield Scott's 42; the actual vote was 1,601,117 to 1,385,453 (John P. Hale, the Free Soil candidate, got 155,825 votes). In Illinois, the tally was 80,597 for Pierce, 64,935 for Scott, and 9,966 for Hale. Thus, in the presidential race in Illinois, the Democrats obtained 51.8 percent of the vote, the Whigs 41.8 percent, and the Free Soilers 6.4 percent. But in the congressional races, the Democrats of Illinois did not fare as well as they had in the 1840s. A new census had been taken, and the nation's representatives had been reallotted. The Illinois delegation grew from seven members to nine. But the migration into Illinois was now decidedly from New England and the mid-Atlantic states. These individuals began voting against the Democratic Party. The Whigs won four seats, and the Democrats only five, a lackluster performance when compared to their previous victories.

Somewhere in the nation, the Whigs might have rejoiced over their showing in Illinois, but their voices were drowned out by the wails of defeat. One correspondent to Douglas wrote that he felt the Whigs were "virtually defunct,"[10] while some Whigs even admitted, "We are extinct."[11] Not only did the Democrats win the presidency, but they controlled Congress in commanding fashion. The elections of 1852 (and then 1853) gave the Democrats 158 members compared to 76 for the Whigs, and the Senate remained reliably Democratic. The Democrats should have sailed through 1853 and 1854 easily, passing their program and solidifying their position over the Whigs. But the problem that would dash the Democratic Party was already brewing. Two years earlier, Stephen A. Douglas had stood before the Senate and presented a petition from settlers asking for the formation of Nebraska Territory so that settlers there could begin the journey of self-government. The West was demanding attention.

The Kansas-Nebraska Act

Douglas deserved some relaxation after the tumultuous experiences of the Compromise of 1850 and the presidential election of 1852. He only obtained grief. His wife died in Washington, D.C., after delivering a third child, a daughter. Compounding the loss was the death of the infant a few days later. The effects of this loss on his life are difficult to assess. As a widower for the next three years, he fell back into old habits of slovenly dress, tobacco chewing, and overindulgence in alcoholic spirits. He often appeared unkempt. Whether the death of his wife also clouded his political judgment is more difficult to tell, but for several years he certainly fell into one miscalculation after another.

Partly owing to his wife's passing, Douglas determined to tour Europe in 1853 after Congress adjourned. His friends arranged his passage and itinerary, and he left in May. A European visit was becoming common for important American political figures, individuals who wanted to acquaint themselves more with the cultures and institutions of the nations with whom they were having more trade and diplomatic relations. Often it was seen as a chance to compare American republican institutions with European aristocratic ones. Douglas engaged in this comparison, noting how modern and advanced the United States was compared to the nearly feudalistic societies of Europe and how degraded their common people looked. He thrilled people back home when news arrived that he had not been received by Queen Victoria of Great Britain because he refused to appear in proper attire; Douglas insisted that clothes good enough to wear to visit an American president were good enough for a crowned head of Europe. The Americans loved the story. He visited England, France, Italy, Greece, Turkey, Russia, and Prussia, among other places. One piece of information that he tucked away was the performance of the German Zollverein, a free trade association of German states. The Zollverein was working well in producing prosperity, and Douglas saw in it a possible way to band countries into a North American free trade empire without having to absorb them into the Union. Douglas returned to the United States at the end of October full of ideas and in good health. Some of the grief at the loss of his wife had been dissipated.

As Douglas settled in for the next round of lawmaking in the Thirty-third Congress, the subjects of expansion, abolitionism, and administration policy dominated his thinking. He found his distaste for the abolitionists growing. Antislavery zealots, especially of the political variety, were not "honest." He did "not believe that they really dislike slavery *per se*. On the contrary, I am frank to confess that they appear to me more and more every day as the covert, sly enemies to white man's liberties, far more than they are friends to [the] negro's freedom."[12] In his reduction of the antislavery movement and its spokespeople to emotionally disturbed monomaniacs and religious zealots, Douglas was not unlike his southern contemporaries. But this analysis—which has served many a historian for nearly a century—had major flaws. The political antislavery movement in the North did have its hypermoralists, but it also exhibited a fear of concentrated power in the hands of the planter class (the Slave Power) and a dread of bringing the cheap cost of slave labor into competition with free white northern labor. Douglas never grappled with these fears, and neither did southern statesmen. All the apprehensions of northerners about slavery were left to grow unhindered, because no one was frontally attacking the arguments of the antislavery spokespeople.

Douglas now embraced popular sovereignty as *the* cure for the nation's sectional ills concerning slavery's expansion. The Missouri Compromise line of 36°30' had lost its charm. It had failed to placate legislators during the fight over the compromise measures in 1850, and Douglas began to accept the southern claim that it violated the spirit of the Constitution by introducing an inequality among the states. In November of 1852, he wrote, "I am now for its repeal."[13] Caution, however, marked Douglas's actions toward the compromise line, and he understood the potential public outcry that repeal might provoke if not properly done.

A third consideration weighed heavily on Douglas. He had set himself as the guardian of the western territories in the Senate. Fostering territorial government for the lands west of Iowa and Missouri, however, ran into problems. Sectional bitterness over slavery's expansion continued to cause problems, but Douglas also faced the commitment made to Indian tribes during Jackson's presidency. Jackson had uprooted the eastern tribes between 1830 and 1840 and had put them into Indian Territory (now Oklahoma) and the plains area, promising them that there they could develop their civilizations without interference from Euro-Americans. In a mere thirteen years, those promises thwarted the desires of many U.S. citizens to seize those lands and develop them commercially.

Douglas chafed at the promises made to the Indian tribes. Those treaties were stopping the creation of territorial government and were blocking the eastern portion of the country from communicating and having commercial relations with the far western portion. No, an Indian civilization could not be allowed to have "perpetual occupancy" of the land west of Iowa and Missouri, for it would be a "barbarian wall against the extension of our institutions, and the admission of new states." The Euro-Americans would not live under the dictate, "Christianity, civilization, and Democracy 'thus far mayest thou go, and no farther.'" "The Indian barrier," he proclaimed, "must be removed."[14]

Since 1846, Douglas had sponsored bills establishing territorial government for the Nebraska country. In the short session of December 1852 to March 1853, the situation grew more serious for him for several reasons. The nation slowly lumbered toward building a transcontinental railroad, and the leading routes for such a project were in the South. Douglas wanted Illinois to participate in such a venture, especially his new hometown of Chicago; he wanted a northern route. But a northern route had to go through unorganized territory, and that meant those lands had no government, no law, and no white population. One could not build a railroad under these conditions. Thus, organization of lands west of Missouri and Iowa was vital if a northern transcontinental railroad were ever to be built. Beyond the railroad consideration, however, Douglas wanted to organize these areas into territories because it was part of his vision of Manifest Destiny.

Attempts to frame a government for the Nebraska area ran afoul of continued sectional bitterness and perhaps even personal rivalry. In Missouri, two Democratic senators battled for party supremacy: the free soil advocate Thomas Hart Benton, and the proslavery agitator David R. Atchison. Atchison, who had first favored organization of Nebraska, turned away from it to curry favor among proslavery Missouri voters. At the end of the session, he declared that he would not favor organization until the Missouri Compromise line had been repealed and the slave states and free states were placed upon an equal footing in regard to expansion. This view rallied southerners to defeat the bill to organize Nebraska.

So, at the opening of the first session of the Thirty-third Congress, Douglas tried again. On January 4, 1854, Douglas reported out of the Committee on Territories a bill to establish territorial government for Nebraska. In the proposed legislation, Douglas did not offer an outright repeal of the Missouri Compromise line, only stipulating in a nebulous fashion that the principles of the Compromise of 1850 would prevail. When the bill came up for discussion on January 16, Archibald Dixon, a Kentucky Whig, offered an amendment explicitly repealing the Missouri Compromise. Discussion of the bill, however, was scheduled to come a week later, and Douglas then took the bill back to committee and tried to refashion it so it could pass southern muster.

In the frenzy of activity that occurred between January 16 and 23, Douglas moved quite warily, knowing that repeal of the Missouri Compromise line might cause a ruckus in the North. The area between Missouri and the Rocky Mountains had been pledged to the free states by the Missouri Compromise of 1820–1821 through the application of the 36°30' line; according to the compromise, slavery was forbidden in all land above the line but permitted below it. The land making up Nebraska Territory was entirely above 36°30'. Over the years, the compromise had acquired a sacred place in the northern political conscience, and to disturb it, as Douglas himself had said in 1849, was to invite massive voter retribution. Northerners assumed that those lands had been guaranteed a nonslave future; any repeal of the compromise was tantamount to admitting that slavery could migrate into that area. In the northern view, popular sovereignty did not count there because the land had already been granted a nonslave status; at best, popular sovereignty was to be used on other territories where compromise had not been reached.

Douglas worked with southerners, Democrats, and the Pierce administration to get sanction for a change in the Missouri Compromise. A group of southern senators who ate together at a boarding house (the "F Street Mess"), composed of Robert Hunter (Virginia), James Mason (Virginia), Atchison, and Andrew Butler (South Carolina), pressured Douglas to repeal the Missouri Compromise line. Douglas worked with his committee members, he sought out Dixon for a full discussion, and then he consulted on Sunday with President Pierce and some members of his cabinet about repeal. Pierce reluctantly agreed, and it was a measure of Douglas's understanding of the gravity of the step he was taking that he demanded that Pierce put on paper his approval of the proposed repeal. Douglas then hurriedly rewrote the legislation.

On Monday, January 23, 1854, Douglas introduced an entirely new bill to the Senate. It divided Nebraska into two territories, Kansas and Nebraska, it enshrined the principle of popular sovereignty that permitted the people in the territories to determine the question of slavery's establishment, and it declared that the Missouri Compromise line was now "inoperative." Because the bill was such a change from the first proposal, several senators asked for a week's grace to study it before debate began, and Douglas agreed to the postponement.

The storm broke. A clique of antislavery congressmen—nearly abolitionists—concocted a diatribe against the repeal of the Missouri Compromise, entitled "Appeal of the Independent Democrats in Congress to the People of the United States," and published it in the antislavery newspaper *The National Era* on January 24. The appeal powerfully castigated the proposed Nebraska legislation and raised the antislavery themes that had been prominent during the fight over the Wilmot Proviso. Repeal of the Missouri Compromise was called a "monstrous wrong" that was destructive of a grand compromise that had pledged areas of the West to freedom, and those areas included both Kansas and Nebraska. Behind the repeal was the Slave Power, seeking aggressively to expand its dominion. According to the appeal, southerners had wrought all they could from the Compromise of 1820, and now the Slave Power coveted land west of Missouri. The authors then asked what the consequences would be of slavery's westward expansion. Northern prosperity and economic growth would not occur, because slavery created land monopoly and lackadaisical work habits. Free labor would not move west: "Freemen, unless pressed by a hard and cruel necessity, will not, and should not, work beside slaves. Labor cannot be respected where any class of laborers is held in abject bondage." They then wrote that the South intended to bottle up the free states and overwhelm the government with slave states; the Union was in peril because the Slave Power wanted to take over the federal government and undermine justice and the blessings of liberty. Democrats had to live up to the Democratic maxim of "EQUAL RIGHTS AND EXACT JUSTICE FOR ALL MEN."[15]

Douglas was livid with rage at the perfidy of these men, and when he took the Senate floor on January 30, he lashed out at them in vituperative language. Then came the defense of his bill. The Missouri Compromise line had been rejected during the debates of 1846–1850; he had tried with others to get the line accepted, but the North refused to accede to an extension of the line to the Pacific. That experience had taught him that the Missouri Compromise was dead. The new principle for settling the question of slavery in the territories was popular sovereignty, as written in the organization of the New Mexico and Utah territories in the Compromise of 1850; nonintervention by Congress was the doctrine that all were to obey. Douglas further explained once again that the will of Congress did not in truth have any importance for the slavery issue—only climate did. Using once again the example of Illinois, Douglas argued that the history of his state proved that the will of Congress could be disobeyed and slavery smuggled into a land regardless of congressional prohibition. But if climate did not allow slavery to be profitable, then slavery would not take root. And Douglas implied that the climate of the West militated against slavery's expansion there. He ended by declaring his principle of nonintervention to be right and constitutionally sound. In his speech was no mention of the Slave Power or the fate of free labor.

In this senatorial debate, Douglas proved his unmatched mettle at handling detractors and critics. Some felt it was his finest moment, as he easily pulled from memory countless facts to disembowel the propositions of his opponents. Foremost in this duel with Douglas were the opposition members William H. Seward (New York), Salmon P. Chase (Ohio), Benjamin Franklin Wade (Ohio), and Charles Sumner (Massachusetts). In the cockpit of the Senate floor, Douglas employed sarcasm and outrage to describe the actions of those who betrayed him in order to publish the "Appeal of the Independent Democrats" before debate began; he shredded the insinuations that he wavered from his duty or that he had made bargains to place slavery in Kansas. And he rejected the claim that the Missouri Compromise had a sacred quality, showing that in 1821 a majority of the northern states had voted against it. Senator Seward simply gave up his attempt to make Douglas admit his mistake (or, among the opposition, his perfidy). So, on the Senate floor Douglas looked triumphant.

The problem was that the Senate floor did not determine the outcome in northern voting booths. In the Senate, Douglas defended himself ably and never retreated from his position that the Compromise of 1820 had no sacredness to it and was immediately violated by northern states. It was a hollow victory. The Compromise of 1820 had become sacred in the North over time, a fact that Douglas in 1854 would not recognize and that no one could make him recognize, although he had testified to it in 1849. Thus his ability to withstand the intense questioning of the opposition had a quixotic quality to it; he won a victory over a windmill but did not win the hearts and minds of voters. This time, Douglas's reliance on facts to obfuscate a generalization—the importance of the Missouri Compromise to northerners—utterly failed.

Debate over the Kansas-Nebraska Act then consumed the attention of Congress and the North—but not so much the South—until its passage in May 1854. Northerners railed at the repeal of the Missouri Compromise and took from its passage the lesson that, as Richard Yates of Illinois put it in 1856, "The day of compromize [sic] is gone forever." Before, southerners had demanded that northerners live up to the compromises of the Constitution, but now with the trampling of the Missouri Compromise, "who in the North, retaining one particle of manhood, will ask for another compromize to be broken again when ever the South in her Sovereign pleasure may see proper to break it[?]"[16] Fear of the Slave Power and a dread that free labor might be ousted from its territorial inheritance filled opposition speeches and editorials. No one accepted Douglas's claim that the Compromise of 1850 had superseded the Compromise of 1820, and most commentators were vexed that at a time of sectional peace the explosive issue of slavery had been reintroduced into Congress. And Douglas's depiction of the opposition as ranting abolitionists did not go uncontested. One Indiana Democrat wrote a congressman that Douglas's "wholesale denunciation of the opponents of this bill as 'abolitionists' and 'nigger' sympathizers will avail him but little. People are not to be frightened from their propriety by such epithets now-a-days, whatever may have been their effect a few years since."[17]

Southerners stood by the measure, believing that they were obtaining equality of rights among the states. By removing the Missouri prohibition, all citizens were free to migrate to the territories with their property. The property aspect of the southern argument became unmistakable. Lawrence Keitt rebutted northern assertions that property in slaves was only a state regulation: "You deny that there is property in the slave. Your denial shakes the very foundation of property,"[18] and, "As a southern man, sir, I demand that this Government shall protect, constitutionally, our slave property." Several southerners also saw that the definition of popular sovereignty was too loose, because they distinctly demanded that slave property be allowed in the territories prior to the creation of a state constitution; only when a territory passed to the blissful stage of sovereignty and statehood could slavery be prohibited. Many southerners, however, did not press the issue and were content with the repeal of what they believed was an obnoxious and unconstitutional statute concerning slavery.

Northern Democrats struggled with the Kansas-Nebraska Act and had to be pulled into line. Many of them did espouse the doctrine of popular sovereignty, and they took their cue from Douglas that it was a founding principle of the Revolution: people in a community had the right of self-government. Popular sovereignty upheld *"the fundamental principle of self-government,"* and the "first gun of the Revolution sounded the note of popular sovereignty; the last one, at the gates of Mexico, reechoed the principle," said his Democratic colleagues.[19] But many northern Democrats testified against the repeal of the Missouri Compromise and wanted it left alone. Advice to Democratic congressmen was inconsistent; some said the bill was having no effect on party followers, while others warned of dangers. Even in Douglas's former hometown of Jacksonville, Murray McConnel warned that "from the signs of the times we are going to have trouble over [the Nebraska question]."[20]

Douglas furiously worked to keep Democrats true to the party line, going so far as to make voting for his measure a party test, meaning that those who did not support the bill would be punished. Party fidelity—one of the themes of Douglas's life—had to be maintained. "The principle of this Bill will form the test of Parties, & the only alternative is either to stand with the Democracy or to rally under Seward, John Van Buren & co."[21] He wrote to the editor of a New Hampshire newspaper that no one should doubt the appropriateness of the Nebraska bill: it "proposes to carry into effect, the great fundamental principle of self-government upon which our republican institutions are predicated." He added as well that if white people can legislate for themselves, they surely could "legislate for the black man."[22] The administration applied patronage pressure while Douglas twisted arms. The Kansas-Nebraska Act passed the Senate on March 4, gained approval from the House of Representatives on May 22 by a vote of 113 to 100, and was signed by the president on May 30.

Douglas should have foreseen the firestorm he was creating. Contemporary analysis of the vote on the Kansas-Nebraska Act showed that in the House of Representatives the bill split the northern Democrats almost in twain, with forty-three voting for the legislation and forty-five against. The opposition press had more than its usual share of nasty comments, a few insinuating that Douglas had concocted the Kansas-Nebraska Act to increase the value of the family's slaves in Mississippi. One Wisconsin paper called him the "arch-traitor of Illinois."[23] Douglas, however, seemed to receive comforting letters about his constitutional doctrines and about how *"Popular Sovereignty* will win, if it is thoroughly & properly discussed & understood."[24] Nonetheless, a powerful and active opposition existed, and Douglas knew it. Even though he was sent a congratulatory letter on a speech from the old Whig warhorse Robert Winthrop of Massachusetts, Winthrop did mention, "The effigy-burners do not seem to have consumed you as yet."[25] Aroused citizens in the North found Douglas's Kansas bill deplorable.

Regardless of the opponents' charges against him, Douglas had at this time no desire to see slavery spread, for he had a low opinion of the peculiar institution. He told the son of his friend Murray McConnel, "I am not pro-slavery. . . . I think it a curse beyond computation, to both white and black." He most feared, however, that northern meddling in slavery would produce dissolution and civil war; to him, the "integrity of this political Union . . . [was] worth more to humanity than the whole black race."[26] Yet Douglas never explained what about slavery was such a "curse." Whatever curse he found in slavery, he certainly believed southern slavery had no capacity to distort the free market economy of the North.

Douglas also failed to discover any meaningful political drawbacks to having slave states in the Union. Antislavery speeches were brimming with references to the Slave Power and to its aggressiveness. As in the debates of 1846–1850, Douglas never made a response to the charge that the material interests of slavery injured the politics of freedom, that southern power was concentrated in a few hands, and that the Slave Power wanted domination of the federal government and the suppression of northern freedoms. Douglas never conceived of slaveholders and the South in this manner. Most likely he considered slavery simply a material interest—like the textile interest, the wheat interest, or the iron interest—and the slave interest had no more damaging effects upon republican institutions than did those other interests.

One challenge to the act he did not ignore. Edward Everett of Massachusetts on March 14 stood before the Senate to submit a petition signed by 3,050 New England clergymen—about 80 percent of all of New England's clergy—that solemnly protested "in the name of Almighty God" the Kansas-Nebraska Act and sought its modification or repeal, for the Kansas-Nebraska Act was "a great moral wrong" and a "breach of faith."[27] Later, in May, many Chicago clergymen also petitioned Congress against the legislation, using the same wording as the New Englanders, except leaving out the phrase "in the name of Almighty God." Douglas would not let this challenge to his moral purity go uncontested. And his point of attack was exact: the role of ministers in passing moral judgment on congressional laws. His Paineite/Jeffersonian religious disposition had just been activated.

His response was a reaffirmation of his unyielding faith in the democratic process as the only true and just means of settling political disputes. "I differ with you widely, radically, and fundamentally," he wrote to the Chicago ministers, "in respect to the nature and extent of your rights, duties, and powers, as ministers of the Gospel." A democracy, he argued, could not permit any single group to claim possession of greater wisdom and intelligence to resolve political issues than other citizens. That was the principle of aristocracy: the people could not be allowed to solve their own problems by reflection and voting, but instead had to follow the inclinations of a select few, who were supposedly wiser than all the rest. He wrote, "Your claims for the supremacy of this divinely-appointed institution are subversive of the fundamental principles upon which our whole republican system rests. What the necessity of a Congress, if you can supervise and direct its conduct?"[28] Within the Democratic Party, Douglas's arguments struck a common chord of distaste for clerical interference in the affairs of state. Democrats also sensed something they did not like: the religious leaders of the North were mobilizing against them.

Of all the arguments for or against the Kansas-Nebraska Act, the one that, seemingly, most penetrated the consciousness of Stephen A. Douglas and many southerners was the moral argument against slavery. In congressional debates, the moral attack on slavery was actually weak compared to the free labor and Slave Power charges. Douglas wanted to avoid assessing the moral character of slavery, as it would only injure either the northern Democrats or the southern Democrats; moreover, it worked against compromise solutions. Thus, attacking the antislavery position by attacking the self-righteousness of its spokespeople was an easy choice for Douglas, and it was the one he pursued for the remainder of his career. Yet the desire to attack the self-righteousness of moralizers was as much a political tactic to obtain votes as an exercise in analyzing the forces at work in the extension controversy. What was lost in this strategy of blaming sectional ill will on moralistic posturing was the necessity of directly assuaging the free labor and Slave Power apprehensions of the northern public. Northern Democrats under Douglas's guidance were destined to war against the assumed power of northern moral sensibilities instead of northern material and political trepidations.

The Elections of 1854

In the first half of 1854, concerns other than the Kansas-Nebraska Act captured the attention of Douglas and the nation. Congress passed a homestead act, and Dorothea Dix obtained from Congress some federal aid to build insane asylums, but both measures were then vetoed by President Pierce. Douglas still struggled with the problem of adequate funding to make permanent improvements on the Great Lakes harbors. Outside of Congress, the nation witnessed some spectacular collisions over runaway slaves, the most notable being the case of Anthony Burns in Boston. In foreign affairs, Manifest Destiny still captivated many adventurers, and the Pierce administration was involved in an unsuccessful attempt to purchase Cuba—the episode involving the writing of a document, the Ostend Manifesto, which was a declaration by three American foreign ministers that Spain either had to sell Cuba to the United States or the Americans would seize it. At various times, these subjects grabbed Douglas's attention, but the center of his universe was the Kansas-Nebraska Act and its doctrine of popular sovereignty.

In the congressional struggle over the passage of the legislation, Douglas isolated himself somewhat from the state of public opinion. Even the remonstrances of the clergy did not alert him to the looming battle. Perhaps Douglas, knowing that repeal of the Missouri Compromise was the only way to get Manifest Destiny rolling again and to create new states, convinced himself that popular sovereignty was such a sound doctrine that the northern public would immediately agree with it. Others recognized a growing problem. In Pennsylvania, the Democrat Francis J. Grund wrote former Senator Simon Cameron that the Kansas-Nebraska Act required "too much explanation, and too much argument" to be understood. "Judge Douglas," he decided, "is completely absorbed, and has rather been too quick on the trigger, I believe."[29]

As the session closed, Douglas became more aware of northern anger. In August, Congress adjourned, and Douglas traveled back to Chicago. As he did so, protests against him mushroomed, and he was burnt in effigy all along the line back to the Windy City; he wrote, "I could travel from Boston to Chicago by the light of my own effigy."[30] To start the campaign for the elections of 1854, Douglas decided to justify the principle of popular sovereignty to the people of Chicago on the evening of September 1. All his life, Douglas had swayed crowds with his oratory. He had convinced the people of Chicago in 1850 that the Fugitive Slave Act was not a revision of the old law at all, and they had swallowed it. He expected to triumph once again.

But, for the only time in his life, Douglas had totally miscalculated public sentiment. Whenever he tried to talk, he was hooted down by a crowd of thousands (estimated at ten thousand by some). He would begin speaking, and from the assemblage would issue hisses and groans. He lost his temper, hurled epithets at the crowd, and shook his fists, but the crowd outlasted him. For four hours, Douglas tried to speak, and for four hours the crowd denied him the opportunity. Finally, it was reported, Douglas roared out, "Abolitionists of Chicago! It is now Sunday Morning. I will go to church while you go to the devil in your own way."[31] He stormed off the stage and retreated to his room at the Tremont House.

Douglas was shaken by the experience. Between citizen and politician was a strange bond. Douglas had always perceived it in a singular way: he would explain the democratic truth to the masses, and they would follow. He had never before experienced a revolt of the masses against their leaders, to be on the wrong side of the people. An important element of a thriving democracy is for the people, or members of them, to tell their leaders their concerns and expect and even demand concessions. Douglas's political life with the people had pretty much been a one-way street prior to 1854: he explained; they obeyed. In 1854, the people demanded, and now Douglas had to take their complaints into account.

And this moment revealed the fiber of his character. Some politicians quailed at an outraged public and backtracked, but not Stephen A. Douglas. He may have been hurt; he may have been offended—but he was right! Popular sovereignty was right! The people required an intensive tutoring session to bring them away from their emotional, unfounded fears about slavery's expansion and into the light and truth of popular sovereignty. And the congressional elections of 1854 would constitute the first tutoring session.

The congressional elections of 1854 were largely held in the North, and in them the Kansas-Nebraska Act reigned as the dominating issue, but confusion emerged in all the races, state as well as national. The nation had received over four million immigrants between 1840 and 1854, about one-third of them from Ireland, another third from Germany, and the remainder from the British Isles. Both the German and Irish migrations brought Catholicism to the United States and made the Catholic Church for the first time a strong presence in American religious life. Thus was engendered a cultural conflict between Protestants and Catholics, the Protestants believing that only their religion was fit for a republic; the Catholics, Protestants thought, were too used to taking orders from a hierarchy. Also added to the mix was an undiluted ethnic hostility: the Irish were seen by many of English descent as lowly, unintelligent, and even criminal. Reaction to this great wave of immigration produced a political movement called the American Party, or Know-Nothings, and it emerged just at the time when many northerners were upset with the Kansas-Nebraska Act. Adding to the mix of movements in 1854 was a prohibition crusade. Because the Democratic Party befriended immigrants, promoted them within the party ranks, disliked antidrinking laws that seemed to regulate private morality, and repealed the Missouri Compromise line to give slavery a chance to spread, the party became the enemy of all kinds of popular movements.

Temperance and reform parties operated openly, and all could see and assess them, but in 1854, Democratic and Whig politicians barely discerned the activities of the Know-Nothings, for the American Party was a secret society that had established lodges throughout much of the United States. The Know-Nothings were strongest along the East coast—in states like New York, Pennsylvania, Maryland, Massachusetts, and Rhode Island—but their presence was distinctly felt in the Great Lakes states as well. Increasingly, politicians became concerned about the strength of the Know-Nothings. By the end of the elections, Douglas's good friend William A. Richardson wrote, "The Know Nothings are more numerous than any one anticipated. We know of seventeen lodges in this District & the smallest No. of dem[ocrats] in either of them is twenty which makes changes enough to affect our maj[ority] and loose [sic] the District."[32] The Know-Nothings did dampen the efforts of the Democrats, but their emergence was even more fatal to the Whig Party.

In fact, those opposed to the Democrats in 1854 were disorganized. The Whigs continued to operate, but only feebly, having been mortally injured by the Kansas-Nebraska Act and the connection of the party with proslavery southerners; Know-Nothings and Temperance Party advocates jumped into the election with their own organizations. People who harbored antislavery sentiments and who detested the Kansas-Nebraska Act represented another group contesting the supremacy of the Democrats. In Michigan and Wisconsin, antislavery elements created a new political entity, the Republican Party, but elsewhere the opponents of the Democrats lacked a central organization. In some states, the opposition called itself the "People's Party," and in most localities, the anti–Democratic Party contingent referred to itself as the "fusion" or the "opposition." In Illinois, the Republicans would not become the primary vehicle of opposition to the Democrats until 1856, a circumstance that proved to be true nationally as well.

Disorganized as politics were in 1854, Stephen A. Douglas battled the opposition leaders who denounced him, he argued for popular sovereignty, and he justified the repeal of the Missouri Compromise. Though he recognized how powerfully temperance and nativism worked on the public, he viewed the election as a means to vindicate his legislation for Kansas and his principle of popular sovereignty. He arranged an extensive speaking tour throughout the state and defended popular sovereignty and the repeal of the Missouri Compromise line. As usual, he spoke about two hours per place, and, also as usual, opposition papers called his claims "total lies," "fabrications," and "sophistry,"[33] while Democratic papers wrote, "Never, we say, was truth more triumphantly vindicated."[34]

The opposition in the Illinois congressional elections of 1854 made use of fears about the Slave Power and the status of free labor, but in dealing with Douglas they had to explain the errors in popular sovereignty; why could people in the territories not decide the question of slavery for themselves? Douglas hammered this theme home. Popular sovereignty was the gift of the American revolutionaries, and the nation was founded on the idea of the consent of the governed. If one had an optimistic view of the people, as Douglas did, then one should have known that the people would prohibit, not establish, slavery. Douglas knew his Illinois audience had to be told that slavery would not claim any new land in the West, and he assured them that popular sovereignty would have the result of creating free states.

Abraham Lincoln came out of political retirement to do battle with Douglas and his theory of popular sovereignty. Lincoln believed that restricting slavery to its present boundaries would produce its eventual death, and he was upset that Douglas's Kansas-Nebraska Act allowed slavery to keep expanding and surviving. Most of the time, Lincoln used the standard opposition attacks on slavery: dread of the Slave Power, fear for the prosperity of free labor, and the immorality of the institution. He had trouble, however, when it came to explaining why popular sovereignty should not operate on the slavery expansion issue. "The sacred right of self-government, rightly understood, no one appreciated more than himself," he explained at Bloomington, but the Nebraska act "was the grossest violation of it." The error of popular sovereignty, Lincoln believed, was that it denied the humanity of African Americans: "But if the negro, upon soil where slavery is not legalized by law and sanctioned by custom, *is* a man, then there is not even the shadow of popular sovereignty in allowing the first settlers . . . to decide whether it shall be right in all future time to hold men in bondage there."[35] Lincoln used this line of thinking several times, always stressing that the humanity of blacks removed them from being an object for voting to operate on. Even so, Lincoln fumbled quite a bit in finding the direct way to contradict popular sovereignty.

Lincoln gave a version of his objections to popular sovereignty in Springfield on October 4, and Douglas was in the audience. As soon as Lincoln finished, Douglas sprang up, took the podium, and went through Lincoln's criticisms one by one and offered his refutation. According to Charles Lanphier, "Never have we seen such a deep, heartfelt and heart-reaching concurrence in the sentiments of a public speaker,"[36] and the historian George Fort Milton wrote that Douglas obliterated Lincoln's argument.[37] But the truth was that in 1854 there was an unbridgeable gap between Lincoln and Douglas, and it involved the status of black Americans. Douglas consigned blacks to a position of some humanity, but who obtained only the rights that white people would confer on them. Lincoln and others argued that the natural rights of blacks were equal to the natural rights of whites, rights that no government should ever be allowed to assail. Logically speaking, this was the only way the opposition could undermine popular sovereignty; if anti-Democratic leaders did not make the claim of humanity for black people, they had no refutation of popular sovereignty at all.

The northern congressional elections came in two waves in 1854. Citizens in Ohio, Pennsylvania, and Indiana voted in October: the results were "astonish[ing]"; the Pierce administration was "annihilated."[38] New York and some eastern states followed in November, and a Democratic paper in Wisconsin summarized the returns by writing, "It certainly is, as the good natured little lawyer in 'The Attorney,' says—'bad, very bad. I think I may venture to say, d—d bad!'"[39] The extent of the disaster was almost unbelievable and represented one of the great upheavals in American political history. The northern Democrats had elected in 1852 seventy-nine congressmen; in 1854, they elected twenty-four. Previously, the Indiana Democrats had ten of eleven congressional seats; in 1854, that fell to two seats out of eleven. Ohio was even worse: in 1852, the Democrats held twelve districts to the Whigs' seven and the Free Soilers' two; in 1854, the Democrats won no congressional seats at all.

Illinois fared a little better. Democrats in 1852 grabbed five of the nine congressional seats; in 1854 they took four—and in one of those districts (seventh), the Democrat, James Allen, won by one vote, 8,452 to 8,451! But what worried politicians like Douglas was the anemic Democratic vote. The Democratic vote had shrunk from its 1852 presidential totals. In that year, the Democrats earned a total of 77,433 suffrages in the congressional races, and, discounting the unanimous vote that obtained in one of those districts, they still managed to get 65,333. In 1854, the total votes cast for Democrats in all nine congressional districts was a paltry 59,391.

In the Great Lakes states, it was obvious that the opposition managed to fuse all discordant anti-Democratic groups together—Free Soilers, political abolitionists, nativists, Whigs, temperance advocates, and others. Many were calling themselves Republican, although the opposition party had yet to fully coalesce, and in the eastern states, the Republicans hardly existed as an organization.

The numbers must have galled Douglas. Now he had to rebuild the Democratic Party of Illinois and refurbish its reputation. He took some steps by setting up a new newspaper in Chicago, the *Chicago Daily Times*, that would more faithfully mirror his opinions, and he obtained the services of James Sheahan, a Washington, D.C., reporter, to edit it. Yet the fate of Kansas cast a dark shadow over the future. One correspondent told Douglas that the key to the Democratic Party's prospects was to bring Kansas in as a free state and prove to northerners the worth of popular sovereignty; "*But*, should Kansas be brought in as a slave state I predict troubles to meet that we have never yet saw."[40]

Democrats did not assign all their woes to the passage of the Kansas-Nebraska Act, though many cited it as a prime cause. Rather, most agreed that some unholy fusion of the opposition was responsible, "a conglomeration of antagonisms, [such as] were never before heard of in any political canvass."[41] Prominent among that fusion was the Know-Nothings, or the American Party, whose activities had been undertaken in secrecy and whose members bitterly denounced immigrants and Catholics. Here was an enemy that Douglas could sink his teeth into, and one that could also provide him with an easy rationale for the 1854 election debacle. He wrote to Lanphier in December, as the next session of Congress started, that the Nebraska agitation was over, and Know-Nothingism "has taken its place as the chief issue in the future."[42]

He fully expressed his opinion in the short session of Congress between December 1854 and March 1855. Senators and representatives went about the government's business in a desultory way, and as usual, sectional issues wormed their way into appropriation bills, into comments on the president's annual message, and into bills originating from various committees. Douglas took one occasion to offer an analysis about the elections of 1854, and his views were indeed remarkable. The election of 1854 had nothing at all to do with the Kansas-Nebraska Act; the elections instead confirmed the wisdom of popular sovereignty. What had happened was the rise of a new opponent, the secretive Know-Nothings, who spread lodges throughout the North, and "every lodge was under the control of Abolition leaders."[43] Nativism had produced the 1854 electoral debacle; if the issue had been merely Nebraska, the Democratic Party would have rung up huge majorities! Stephen A. Douglas had more audacity than all those in Congress put together.

Kansas Explodes

One of the last details Douglas had to attend to in 1854 and early 1855 was making sure the Illinois legislature chose the correct person to be his colleague in the United States Senate. The elections of 1854 had produced a new legislature filled with fusionists. Douglas counseled Democrats to stick with James Shields, the current senator whose term was expiring, because he, being a Catholic, would also fit the new stress the party would put on nativism as the latest issue confronting the nation. In the battle to elect a senator, the fusionists lacked cohesion, partially because a portion of their group hailed from the old Whig party—now virtually eliminated from politics—and another portion came from the Democrats. Abraham Lincoln played a stellar role in the election of 1854 and was the stalwart that many fusionists wanted to send to the U.S. Senate, and he led in the early balloting. However, he never obtained a majority, and it looked as if the legislators might opt for a regular, pro-Kansas-Nebraska Democrat. Lincoln told his supporters to back Lyman Trumbull, a Democrat who was anti-Kansas-Nebraska and who was working with the opposition. Trumbull won election to the Senate, Shields was denied another term, and Lincoln slumped down in despondency. Douglas was not happy with Trumbull's selection, and the two men would clash frequently in the Senate.

Meanwhile, migrants to Kansas tested the democratic theory behind popular sovereignty. Residents from Missouri, Iowa, Illinois, and other states pushed into Kansas Territory. A sectional edge to the migration was introduced by an agency, the Massachusetts Emigrant Aid Society, which had been created to transport New Englanders to Kansas to insure that it became a free state. Few New Englanders actually journeyed to Kansas, but the publicity surrounding the company stirred southerners, who believed that a "natural" migration to Kansas would be undercut by a purposeful political agency. Southerners, especially Missourians, took it upon themselves to make sure that Kansas was not stolen from the slaveholding column. Most of the settlement occurred just to the west of northwest Missouri, along the Kansas River. Southerners and Missourians settled near present-day Kansas City, whereas those from the free states established towns upriver at Topeka and Lawrence.

Kansas Territory's first governor, Andrew H. Reeder, came to the land in October, conducted a census, and called for elections. They were held on March 30, 1855, and the first problem with popular sovereignty became clear. Missourians crossed the border in great numbers and voted fraudulently. The result was a territorial legislature filled with proslavery men, and they proceeded to write laws establishing slavery in Kansas, making it a capital offense to assist runaway slaves and a felony to question the right to hold slaves. Moreover, this legislature expelled free soil legislators under the guise of contested elections. This action in turn made antislavery settlers believe that the democratic process in Kansas was meaningless, and they proceeded to construct their own legislature, which convened in January 1856 at Topeka. President Pierce replaced Reeder with Wilson Shannon because Reeder made public his sympathies for the free state settlers.

Although most migrants went to Kansas Territory to obtain land, slavery seemed to be driving its politics. A proslavery man killed a free state man over a land claim, and that then led immediately to the question of which rival government would actually administer the law. The proslavery government, now at Lecompton, released the proslavery man; free staters, acting for the Topeka government, ran the proslavery person off his land and burned his cabin. A deputy sought to arrest the free state men responsible, assembled an army of nearly one thousand men, then added to it a large force of Missourians known as Border Ruffians, and moved on Lawrence, Kansas. Governor Shannon intercepted them and argued them out of their attack. This incident was called the Wakarusa War. It foretold what was eventually to happen in Kansas—civil war.

Many things in Douglas's life in 1855 did not bode well for his political future. He received a letter from Andrew Reeder indicating that deciding issues by majority vote would not satisfy Kansas settlers, especially southerners. Southerners attacked any who did not hold proslavery doctrines: "The doctrine they assert is that it is a constitutional right of Mo. to have Kansas a slave State, there is no difference between a free State man and an abolitionist." They had no concern for the rights of free speech, and they "openly cross" the border to "disfranchise" free staters.[44] This was not the way popular sovereignty was meant to operate.

Know-Nothings were supposed to provide Douglas with an easy political target, one that avoided raising the question of slavery in any of its guises. In the middle of 1855, Douglas started losing his target, for the Know-Nothings split on the slavery issue. The American Party had indeed made a strong appearance in the state elections of 1854, capturing most of New England while running strong in Pennsylvania and New York. They also made a striking showing in the Border South and in New Orleans. For a moment, it indeed looked like the American Party might replace the Whigs and become the chief opposition to the Democrats. Northern Know-Nothings were largely antislavery, however, and they distinctly wanted the reimposition of the Missouri Compromise line, while southern Know-Nothings were essentially Whigs who desperately sought acceptance of the Kansas-Nebraska Act. To survive in southern electoral politics, southern Know-Nothings simply had to present themselves as favorable to the expansion of slavery.

The leaders of the Know-Nothings sought to create a national party and arranged a national convention in Philadelphia in June. A fight broke out over the twelfth section of the platform, which called for all laws on the books to be seen as a final settlement of the slavery issue—in effect, a Know-Nothing acceptance of the Kansas-Nebraska Act. A large contingent of northerners refused, and the convention suffered a sectional split. The Know-Nothings fell prey to the slavery issue. For Douglas, this meant that his hoped-for enemy would disappear from the political landscape before he got the chance to campaign against it.

Douglas made a tour of Illinois and surrounding states in mid- and late 1855 to revivify the Democrats and prepare them for the 1856 presidential contest, and perhaps lay claim to the presidential nomination. He stressed popular sovereignty and the evils of fanaticism. He ventured into Lexington, Kentucky, to help the election there and to assist his friend John C. Breckinridge. At the Lexington meeting, Douglas formulated a set of resolutions that he hoped the Democratic Party in all states of Union would agree to, proving that the Democrats had a single set of principles for both free states and slave states. The resolutions warned against centralization by the federal government, praised states' rights, asserted federal nonintervention in the matter of slavery in the territories, offered a purposefully ambiguous reference as to when people in a territory could vote on slavery's establishment, and demanded obedience to the Fugitive Slave Act and the Kansas-Nebraska Act in order to promote sectional calm.

Douglas probably figured that many Democrats would be returning to the party in 1856 after their momentary absence in 1854. He had reason to be optimistic. The elections of 1855 were largely in the South, and there the Democrats scored victories against the Know-Nothings, although the latter did surprisingly well in the states of Kentucky, Maryland, and Tennessee. In the northern state races, when such races were held, the results were more mixed. Know-Nothings continued to be strong in New York, but they were ousted in Pennsylvania. The New England states of Massachusetts, Rhode Island, and New Hampshire remained true to nativism. In other states, the small Republican Party began to claim a large following; the Republicans took the states of Vermont, Maine, Connecticut, and Ohio. The Know-Nothings were losing strength because they failed to cement the various groups in their coalition into a unified whole. Douglas observed that problem with the American Party in Illinois, where the fusion had been disintegrating throughout 1855.

One of Douglas's failed predictions was a withering away of the slavery extension issue. He had no way of knowing that Kansas would explode and breathe new life into the matter, and he misperceived the growing strength of the infant Republican Party. As for his own presidential aspirations, he misjudged how others would hold him responsible for the 1854 debacle of the Democratic Party. One of the strong Democratic leaders in Indiana, Joseph A. Wright, understood quite well that the path to the nomination had been closed to Douglas but cleared for James Buchanan. Buchanan had been ambassador to England during the passage of the Kansas-Nebraska Act and had thus escaped connection with it; whoever the future Democratic candidate might be, Wright wrote, that person could not be connected "in any way with the measures of Pierce's administration," a direct reference to the Kansas-Nebraska Act.[45]

Douglas was doing well in rallying the Democratic troops in 1855 when in October his voice failed him and he was wracked with coughing fits. His heath had deteriorated seriously. He eventually journeyed to Cleveland where a doctor performed surgery on his throat to improve his condition. The surgery worked, and by January he was beginning to feel vigorous once again. However, he did not arrive in Washington, D.C., until early February, and even then he spent several days resting before participating in the Thirty-fourth Congress. Health problems started ominously recurring, a fact that he should have taken more seriously.

When Congress convened in December 1855, the national legislature immediately underwent a spasm of anarchy. Due to the elections of 1854, the House no longer had a Democratic majority, but the northern opposition elements did not have one either. It took the House nearly two months before it organized itself by electing a speaker, the Massachusetts Know-Nothing Nathaniel P. Banks. During this time, the Senate engaged in desultory activities, which for Douglas was a blessing, as his throat was still healing and he was regaining his strength.

Two essential chores faced the Senate when business could finally be conducted. One was to dispose of various presidential messages, and the other was to prepare a bill enabling Kansas to write its state constitution. The first involved the Wakarusa War and the administration's explanation of it. Pierce sent a message to Congress giving his interpretation and accompanying documents. This material was then sent to the Senate Committee on Territories, which was to report on the president's findings. Douglas took over the task and blamed all difficulties in Kansas on the abolitionists, particularly the Emigrant Aid Society; he insisted that Missouri transgressions at the ballot box were minor. The new Illinois senator, Lyman Trumbull, then engaged Douglas in a debate on the meaning of abolitionism, Know-Nothingism, Democratic loyalty, and the results of the election of 1854. Douglas's slashing counterattack indicated that he intended to pin the labels of "fanatic," "abolitionist," and "black Republican" on his opposition.

On March 17, Douglas read a bill to allow Kansas to form a constitution and enter the Union. The sectional fireworks began. Most of the usual insults and complaints were hurled at one another about the Slave Power, free labor, northern aggression, and southern property rights, but there were some different and interesting moments for Douglas. For one, he became more explicit about race in senatorial debate. He taunted Seward, whom many believed the likely opposition presidential nominee, about being pro-Negro; in Illinois, Douglas said, the state constitution "was made by white men for the benefit of white men." On the same day, Douglas responded to those who accused him of name-calling because of his labeling of opposition leaders as "black Republicans." For the second time in his life, it would seem, Douglas mentioned the "Slave Power." He countered the complaint about name-calling with the truth, in his view, that the "watchword of the party with which he [Jacob Collamer of Vermont] acts is opposition to '*the dictation and aggressions of the* SLAVE POWER!'" and that he called the northern Democrats "doughfaces and tools of the slave power!"[46] But no analysis followed. It was as though Douglas knew the term but thought it a meaningless epithet used by opponents for political advantage. To Douglas, the charge was so silly and void of substance, it seems, that it did not merit his attention.

Later on, Trumbull examined the open wound in Douglas's doctrine of popular sovereignty that would eventually pit southern Democrats against northern Democrats. From the beginning, Calhoun had called the idea "squatter sovereignty" because it allowed the first settlers to vote on slavery, thereby possibly deciding the question for all later arrivals. The southern position had generally been to disallow territorial governments from outlawing slavery and only to permit territories to decide the question of the existence of slavery at the moment they wrote their state constitutions. Douglas affirmed his belief that territorial governments could write laws hostile to slavery. At this point, both Albert Gallatin Brown of Mississippi and Benjamin Fitzpatrick of Alabama disagreed; it was their understanding that a territorial legislature could not disallow slavery. This breach over definition had never been resolved, and Kansas was about to transform it from a breach into a chasm, from a theoretical question into a crushing problem.

Then came the incident that earned this session of Congress its notoriety. Ablaze with the wrath of the righteous, abolitionist politician Senator Charles Sumner rose on May 19 to deliver his well-prepared speech, "The Crime against Kansas." He not only blasted away at the Slave Power, Border Ruffians, and the ignominies of slavery, but he delivered a personal attack on Douglas and two southerners, Andrew Butler of South Carolina and James Mason of Virginia. Whatever the provocation, Sumner let his antislavery zealotry get the best of him as he dealt out one insult after another. Douglas was disgusted with the performance and replied to Sumner that he would "not imitate you, sir," by resorting to calumnies. But others did not so easily dismiss Sumner's words.[47] Sumner went so far as to intimate sexual relations between Butler and his slaves. Representative Preston Brooks, a relative of Butler's, sought revenge and obtained it in the early afternoon of May 22 when he confronted Sumner at this senate desk and beat him senseless with a gold-tipped cane. Douglas was in the antechamber of the Senate talking to others when the attack occurred, and because of his earlier confrontation with Sumner, he thought it best not to rush in for fear that his actions might be mistaken and make matters worse. The Sumner-Brooks affair inflamed public opinion North and South and turned the nation full tilt back into sectional acrimony. It undoubtedly helped augment the numbers of the Republican Party while diminishing the lure of the Know-Nothings.

Only a day before Sumner's beating on the Senate floor, Kansas exploded into national consciousness once again. Not content with letting the free staters live unmolested in Lawrence, a proslavery vigilante group organized by a local sheriff entered Lawrence, ruined the newspaper office, and burned down a hotel. Outraged northerners called this the "Sack of Lawrence." An extreme abolitionist who believed in physical retribution went berserk at the news. John Brown led seven free state militiamen to the Pottawatomie Creek area and there took five men from their cabins, split open their skulls with broadswords, and dismembered them. Abolitionist John Brown had just created the "Pottawatomie Massacre," and Kansas now verged on civil war.

Here was the situation Douglas inherited, and it did not make his doctrine of popular sovereignty a beacon of hope to those weary of sectional strife. But Douglas would not bow. In a speech to the Senate on June 9, he reiterated that the only way peace could ever be restored to Kansas was to let the people there handle their own affairs. All the violence was the fruit of "foreign interference." He praised the Democratic Party for being the "law-abiding, constitution-loving conservative party" that held that "all true liberty is to be found under the protection of the Constitution and the laws."[48] What Douglas did not acknowledge was a fundamental requirement for democracy to work: if the majority rules one way, the minority must accept the verdict. If no one is willing to lose, a democracy is impossible. And who in Kansas in 1856 was willing to lose?

The Election of 1856

Douglas abhorred sectional animosities, for they could ruin his vision of an expanding United States that would grow into the greatest nation in the world. In political terms, he wished for the political parties to be nonsectional; he wanted to avoid having one of the parties become entirely sectional in its voter support and platform. For that reason, he hoped that the American Party would replace the northern free soil organizations; moreover, Douglas felt that the Democrats could triumph over the nativists if sectional issues were removed from politics. Unfortunately for Douglas, the American Party would not cooperate, and it, too, split asunder due to the slavery extension controversy. The American Party divided into two camps over the Kansas-Nebraska Act during a convention in mid-February 1856, one group becoming the North Americans, and the other retaining the claim to being the national party; the latter nominated Millard Fillmore for president and Andrew J. Donelson for vice president. The North Americans were to hold their convention in mid-June in New York City, only a few days before the Republicans held their convention in Philadelphia. Bleeding Kansas had kept the slavery extension issue alive and growing.

Democrats were to assemble in Cincinnati on June 2 for their national convention. Douglas had tried to act aloof from the presidential nomination this time, as opposed to his very public actions in 1852, but through his chosen supporters, David Disney of Ohio and James W. Singleton of Illinois, he let his interest in the presidency be known. He should have been a better judge of his chances. President Pierce sought backing for the nomination, but the Kansas problems had so tarnished him that he had little chance. The same circumstance undercut Douglas's bid, though he refused to acknowledge it. Perhaps his hopes were buoyed by the lack of strong Democratic challengers that year. James Buchanan of Pennsylvania was one of the few who had a strong political machine and extensive contacts. Many rallied to him.

Douglas believed he could get the nomination by having the Great Lakes Democratic Party stand unified behind him, and he thought much of the South would also back his nomination because of his work in eliminating the Missouri Compromise line. But the Great Lakes states did not remain unified on Douglas. The Indiana delegation, controlled by the state's political boss, Senator Jesse Bright, swung to Buchanan—Bright did not want the power of his region in the hands of a political rival. Buchanan also had other powerful senators working for him, most notably John Slidell, and they appeared at the convention to marshal delegates for his nomination. The Pennsylvanian led the balloting from the start, and on the sixteenth ballot, the Douglas supporters capitulated and made the choice of Buchanan unanimous, the vice presidential selection then going to John C. Breckinridge. At least Douglas obtained the satisfaction of having a platform that mirrored his political views: popular sovereignty, states' rights and strict construction of the Constitution, further Manifest Destiny in Central America, a low tariff, the construction of a Pacific railroad, and denunciation of religious proscription. The endorsement of the Kansas-Nebraska Act and popular sovereignty were kept ambiguous once again, thereby avoiding a war over definitions between northerners and southerners.

About two weeks after the Democratic Convention, the North Americans and the Republicans met to determine their platforms and candidates. On the state level, the Republicans had been growing because of the continuous battle over Kansas, and the Know-Nothings found Kansas tearing their political operation apart. It was widely believed that some sort of accord between the parties would occur, but the Republicans utterly outmaneuvered the North Americans and absorbed them without having to alter their antislavery creed. The North Americans nominated Nathaniel P. Banks of Massachusetts for the presidency; a day or two later, the Republicans nominated John C. Frémont. Discussions between leaders of both parties led some to believe that a fusion was in the offing, whereby the Republicans would have the presidential nomination and the Americans the vice presidential nomination. Instead, Banks stunned the North Americans by withdrawing his name and announcing his full membership in the Republican Party. Most North Americans sullenly joined him. The remainder of the North Americans proceeded to accept the earlier nomination of Millard Fillmore for their presidential nominee.

The Republican Party now had a solid base in the North and had brought together major portions of the anti-Democratic elements into one party. Only the Fillmore supporters—a vital group—remained beyond the Republican grasp. And the Republican Party was clear about its principles: no extension of slavery and no recognition of polygamy in Utah, the "twin relics of barbarism." Republicans also made a few statements about a homestead act and a Pacific railroad, but theirs was a short platform devoted to the slavery issue. The Republican Party was the first major party in American history that was entirely sectional in its support, for it had almost no following in the South, and its strength came entirely from the nonslaveholding states. That strength increased the further north one went.

At the close of the congressional session in August, the battle for electoral victory in the 1856 election began. Douglas came back to find problems in the Illinois Democratic Party. The 1856 election in Illinois was also a gubernatorial election year, and both the Democrats and the Republicans nominated popular men: the Democrats chose William A. Richardson, Douglas's close friend, while the Republicans selected William H. Bissell, former congressman and Democrat. Moreover, the Republicans had in the early part of the year made great strides in organizing their party and bringing in the warring factions under one standard. What made the prospects somewhat gloomy for the Democrats was a shift in population. The northern counties grew tremendously and started to overwhelm the southern counties; and in Illinois, the strength of the Democratic Party had always been in the southern counties. An additional problem for Douglas was the financial difficulty that the *Chicago Daily Times*, edited by James Sheahan and partly owned by Isaac Cook, found itself in; the two men became engaged in a bitter feud. Douglas arranged to buy out Cook's share of the paper, but not to Cook's satisfaction; Cook then became a bitter foe of Douglas. Sheahan was unhappy as well but continued to support Douglas.

As usual, Douglas performed Herculean oratorical feats for the Illinois Democrats. He campaigned extensively throughout the state in September and October. Though he felt sure that Illinois would not vote for the radical antislavery party and would be safe for conservatism on sectional matters, he feared for the election of Richardson. He was correct. Bissell won the governorship by receiving 111,375 votes to Richardson's 105,643 (the American Party candidate obtained 19,241). In the presidential race, Illinois cast 105,348 suffrages for Buchanan, 96,189 for Fremont, and 37,444 for Fillmore. Overall, the Democratic Party did quite well; they retained control of both houses of the legislature (though in the House the American Party had the balance of power), and they returned to strength in the congressional elections, winning five of the nine districts. In percentage terms, the Democrats received 44.7 percent of the votes cast in the gubernatorial race, 48.3 percent in the congressional contests, and 44.1 percent in the presidential election. These were marked advances over the pathetic showing of the Illinois Democrats in the congressional elections of 1854, when the party only obtained 42.6 percent.

For both the Republicans and the Democrats in Illinois, the path to victory was clear: obtaining the allegiance of American Party followers. If the percentages that the American Party obtained in Illinois in the presidential election (15.7 percent) and in the gubernatorial election (8.1 percent) were added to the Democratic column, the Democrats would have an overwhelming majority. Of course, the reverse was also true: if added to the Republican column, the Republicans would have an overwhelming majority. Douglas recognized this fact, and to draw the American Party to the Democrats, he fashioned a strategy based on appealing to the nationalism of the Fillmore men. He believed that the American Party followers, many of them former Whigs, would respond to a national call for conservatism and would avoid any party that appeared fanatical on the slavery issue.

The end of 1856 saw life brighten for Douglas. The political situation had improved with a Democratic resurgence in the North, and the Republican onslaught had been halted. And his personal prospects had improved immensely. He had fallen in love with Adele Cutts, daughter of a Washington clerk. The family had Maryland roots and was Catholic, a fact of some importance given the Know-Nothing agitation of the day. Adele was only twenty-one but beautiful, vivacious, and a darling of Washington society, even though the family lived in modest circumstances. The forty-three-year-old Douglas married her on November 20. After the marriage and honeymoon, Adele reshaped the Little Giant's behavior and dress, making him more presentable to the public. Douglas built a new mansion in Washington, and in it Adele conducted parties making the Douglas home one of the liveliest in the capital. Financial prudence was not one of Douglas's hallmarks in the 1850s; he lived lavishly.

Douglas's future looked promising. All that was required was a quietus on the slavery issue and for popular sovereignty to return the correct result in the territories, and he would again rule Illinois politics. But the Gordian knot of democratic equality knew no slumber.

Notes

1. Johannsen, *Douglas*, 326.
2. *Ill St Reg*, February 5, 1852.
3. Asa Briggs, *The Age of Progress* (London, 1965).
4. *Washington D.C. Union*, January 11, 1852.
5. CG, 29-2, 195.
6. *Rochester Advertiser*, September 20, 1851.

7. Johannsen, "Stephen A. Douglas' New England Campaign," *New England Quarterly* 35 (June 1962): 175.

8. *New York Herald*, September 3, 1852.

9. *Washington D.C. Union*, June 11, 1852.

10. W. H. Russell to SAD, January 1, 185[3], in Douglas Papers, IllStLib.

11. E. J. Terry to Richard W. Thompson, November 13, 1852, R. W. Thompson Papers, IndStLib.

12. SAD to Parmenas Taylor Turnley, November 30, 1852, in Douglas, *Letters*, 255–56.

13. SAD to Parmenas Taylor Turnley, November 30, 1852, in Douglas, *Letters*, 255–56.

14. SAD to J. H. Crane, D. M. Johnson, and L. J. Eastin, December 17, 1853, in Douglas, *Letters*, 269–70.

15. *Appeal of the Independent Democrats in Congress to the People of the United States* (1854), 3, 6, 7.

16. Richard Yates, 1856 speech, folder marked 1856, Yates Papers, IllStLib.

17. J. Bohannon to William English, February 8, 1854, English Papers, IndHS.

18. CG, 33-1, appendix, 456–66.

19. CG, 33-1, appendix, 887, 460.

20. M. McConnel to SAD, January 28, 1854, Douglas Papers, Uchi.

21. SAD to Charles Lanphier, February 13, 1854.

22. SAD to the editor of the *Concord (N.H.) State Capitol Recorder*, February 16, 1854, in Douglas, *Letters*, 283, 284, 290–98, 300.

23. *Milwaukee Daily Sentinel*, May 29, 1854.

24. P. M. Johnston to SAD, March 24, 1854, Douglas Papers, Uchi.

25. Robert Winthrop to SAD, April 17, 1854, Douglas Papers, Uchi.

26. Johannsen, *Douglas*, 419.

27. CG, 33-1, 617, 653–54.

28. Stephen A. Douglas, *Letter of Senator Douglas Vindicating His Character and His Position on the Nebraska Bill Against the Assaults Contained in the Proceedings of a Public Meeting Composed of Twenty-five Clergymen of Chicago* (Washington, D.C., 1854), 8, 9.

29. Francis J. Grund to Simon Cameron, April 23, 1854, Cameron Papers, Historical Society of Dauphin County, Harrisburg, Pennsylvania.

30. Johannsen, *Douglas*, 451.

31. Flint, *Life of Douglas*, "Douglas at Chicago," 67.

32. William Richardson to SAD, November 5, 1854, Douglas Papers, Uchi.

33. *Chicago Daily Tribune*, September 15, 19, 23, 1854.

34. *Ill St Reg*, September 28, 30, October 3, 4, 5, 1854.

35. Basler, ed., *Collected Works of Lincoln*, 2:239.

36. *Ill St Reg*, October 6, 1854.

37. Milton, *Eve of Conflict*, 179–82.

38. *National Era*, October 19, 1854.

39. *Madison (Wisc.) Argus and Democrat*, November 10, 1854.

40. Elder Benj. Bradbury to SAD, December 12, 1854, Douglas Papers, Uchi.

41. E. B. Sugg to William H. English, January 1, 1854 [1855], English Papers, IndHS.

42. SAD to Charles H. Lanphier, December 18, 1854, in Douglas, *Letters*, 331.

43. CG, 33-2, appendix, 214–17.

44. A. H. Reeder to SAD, February 12, 1855, Douglas Papers, Uchi.

45. Joseph A. Wright to James Buchanan, November 14, 1854, Buchanan Papers.

46. CG, 34-1, appendix, 361–62, 358.

47. Johannsen, *Douglas*, 501–5.

48. CG, 34-1, 1369, 1370, 1371.

Head and shoulders portrait of Stephen Arnold Douglas, c. 1844–1860.
Courtesy of Library of Congress
(reproduction number LC-USZ62-110141 DLC).

Photograph of Stephen A. Douglas, c. 1860,
Chicago Daily News photograph. Courtesy of Chicago Historical Society
(reproduction of glass negative, DN-0060391).

Oval photograph of Stephen A. Douglas, c. 1860,
Chicago Daily News photograph. Courtesy of Chicago Historical Society
(reproduction of glass negative, DN-0060391).

Monument to Stephen A. Douglas in Douglas Monument Park,
Chicago. Courtesy of Chicago Historical Society
(reproduction of glass negative, DN-0086536).

Here a log cabin and hard cider barrels ought to
follow, but not being able to obtain such a representation, we sustitute a *man in a cider-barrel*.
which we suppose will answer every purpose.
Here he is.]

Democratic Party cartoon lampooning the Whigs during the 1840
"Log Cabin and Hard Cider" presidential election.
From Springfield, Illinois, *State Register*, May 22, 1840.

The
princi-
ples of the
good old DEM-
OCRATIC party,
secure to man social
and political Equality—
they elevate the masses—
they secure the greatest good
to the greatest possible number
—they protect man in the pursuit
of LIFE, LIBERTY & HAPPINESS—
they spread the Empire of Human
Freedom--they dethrone Kings and Tyrants—break the fetters imposed by petty
despots—they laugh wickedness to scorn,
and spurn the intrenchments of Iniquity—
hey are the Cloud by day, and the Pillar of
Fire by night.guiding the nation through all
perils to the glorious consummation that
Destiny has in store for it—they are the
spear of Ithuriel, detecting Falsehood—the thread of D a n d a l u s,
guiding through the labyrinth
of Cunning. To preserve
and perpetuate these glo-
r i o u s principles,
VOTE FOR

GENERAL LEWIS CASS, OF MICHIGAN!
the Soldier, Statesman,—and his Compatriot,
GEN. WM. O. BUTLER. OF KENTUCKY.

Freemen! cheer the Hickory Tree,
In storms its boughs have sheltered thee;
O'er Freedom's Soil its branches wave—
'Twas planted on the Lion's Grave!

The principles of the Democratic Party—emphasizing equality—arranged in a
hickory tree, a reference to Andrew Jackson who was known as Old Hickory.
From Fort Wayne, Indiana, *Sentinel*, October 28, 1848.

~

CHAPTER FIVE

Popular Sovereignty Fails:
The Lecompton Constitution Battle,
1857–1859

A relentless battle for political supremacy in Kansas produced the moment of personal crisis for Stephen A. Douglas. His solution to the sectional controversy over slavery's expansion was popular sovereignty. Behind the doctrine, however, was a deep commitment to democracy as the appropriate form of government. The Douglas version of democracy demanded a constitutional framework and an agreement on rights and duties, but then the central mechanism was to let the people rule by popular vote. Since 1850, his enemies had largely been, at least in his mind, the fanatics of the North and their insistence on the primacy of the slavery issue and the inadequacy of popular sovereignty to handle such a weighty matter correctly. Northern antislavery leaders until 1857 had said that the decision about slavery should be formulated by Congress, not by settlers. After 1857, the new enemies of popular sovereignty chewed at the doctrine with sharper teeth. Southern radicals insisted that property rights were above popular majorities and that democracy could easily descend into the tyranny of the majority. Douglas could not accept such notions without revealing himself a complete fraud. He broke with southerners and the Buchanan administration and became for the first time in his life a party renegade. The press of the Gordian knot of democratic equality evoked by the slavery question refused to wither and go away.

The Buchanan Administration Takes Over

Douglas made it through the short session of the Thirty-fourth Congress in fairly good shape. The usual sniping over the president's message occurred, and

Congress still had the unity to pass appropriations bills and keep the government running. The major issue during that session was the tariff. Federal revenues in the 1850s had produced budget surpluses, and the Democrats wanted no politician to feel tempted to use such money for new federal projects. So Congress sought to reduce revenues by lowering the tariff. Overall, the Tariff of 1857 was a triumph for the free trade portion of the Democratic Party, as it lowered tariff duties even below those set by the Tariff of 1816. Douglas did not participate in this debate, but he voted for the bill.

During a discussion about statehood for Minnesota Territory, Douglas finally acknowledged the free labor argument of his Republican opposition, but he interestingly incorporated it into his vision of Manifest Destiny. Sectionalism arose when John B. Thompson of Kentucky said that he was not sure he wanted to add another free state. Douglas replied that he had never voted against the admission of a slave state when settlers decided in favor of slavery, so now southerners should return the favor and never vote against a free state because its citizens voted against slavery. He further explained that attempts to equalize free and slave states were useless because the tide of immigration favored the free states. The fate of the nation was to gain more free states because the territory acquired by the founders was more susceptible to "free labor than to slave labor." Expansion and Manifest Destiny ruled the policy of the country: "We must have new Territories from time to time for the benefit of our own children, and I am willing that those children should follow the example of the bee, and swarm from time to time, and seek new hives in order to leave room for the old people to live and die in happiness while they are here."[1] In this rare instance when Douglas used the phrase "free labor," he indicated that the health of his free labor nation depended on imperial conquest, again not an adequate or final solution to the Gordian knot of democratic equality.

James Buchanan was sworn in as the fifteenth president of the United States on March 4, 1857, and in his inaugural, devoted to avoiding sectional animosities, Buchanan said he hoped that soon the Supreme Court might lay down some rules to end the bickering over the question of slavery and the territories. He had advance word, obtained by corresponding with Justices John Catron and Robert C. Grier, that such a case was before the Court. On March 6, Chief Justice Roger B. Taney delivered a long decision in the case *Dred Scott v. Sanford* in which he offered his opinions about slavery in the territories, even though the case was technically about the status of a slave when taken into nonslave jurisdictions. Four points governed his decision: one, Africans were not citizens and never were; two, slaves were property by law, not people; three, the federal government had to protect property rights in the territories; and four, by virtue of the previous determinations, the Missouri Compromise line was unconstitutional.

Taney's opinion stirred up a hornet's nest of excitement, but much of it was short-lived. Republicans denounced the decision because it made their party illegal by denying Congress the ability to stop the spread of slavery into the territories. Southerners hailed it as justification of their position. Douglas salvaged what he could by asserting that the decision was wise and contained nothing to upset his doctrine of popular sovereignty. He insisted that property rights were only made practical through local legislation, a subject not addressed by the Supreme Court. Douglas, and the Democrats generally, praised Taney's decision because it made the inferior status of African Americans the law of the land. The long-term power of the decision, however, was the declaration that slaves were property in the eyes of federal law. That determination frightened northerners, like Abraham Lincoln, who thought Taney had "nationalized" slavery—had even allowed it to expand into the northern states.

A second problem emerged in August 1857, and it, too, would take some time before its political effects were visible. The American economy had been on a fragile footing, buffeted by inflation caused by California gold and disruptions in trade due to the Crimean War. By 1856, the Crimean War ended, and the United States and Europe returned to more normal trade patterns, which meant a diminution in wheat and hog exports from the United States to Europe. During 1857, the readjustment of the world economy caught up with the American financial sector: on August 24, the Ohio Life Insurance and Trust Company in New York City went bankrupt, sending a shock wave through the banking system. Weakened by the determination of depositors to withdraw their money, the banks finally declared specie suspension on October 14.

The suspension lasted little more than a month, but the economic effects of the Panic of 1857 rippled through the economy for the next two years. The middle states endured a sharp recession, and the Great Lakes states faltered, especially in railroad construction and grain shipments. The South was hardly touched, and soon King Cotton was delirious with prosperity. Politically, however, the Panic of 1857 had brought economic issues back into the national arena. Douglas was so absorbed in Kansas affairs that he barely noticed the Panic of 1857, except as it affected his personal finances, but its effects would strongly diminish his appeal to northern voters in 1860.

And then arose again the problem of Kansas Territory. Just after his election in November 1856, James Buchanan received the usual congratulations for his victory, and some of his letters were prophetic. One person from Bloomsburg, Pennsylvania, wrote the new President, "If we . . . shall bring Kansas in as a free State and thereby falsify all the prophecies, predictions, and prognostications of the Opposition, our hold on the administration is as firm yet more firm than at any former period of our history." But if Kansas came in as a slave state, he predicted fusion between antislavery and Republican leaders, making 1860 a dubious year for Democratic victory.[2] The writer proved quite prescient.

The Lecompton Constitution Battle

Kansas refused to remain quietly in the background. Pierce had replaced territorial governor Wilson Shannon with John W. Geary, who, like his predecessors, had little effect in pacifying Kansas. When Buchanan took office, he appointed Robert J. Walker to be territorial governor to replace Geary and bring Kansas to statehood. Walker found that the free staters vastly outnumbered the proslavery faction, but he thought Kansas could be enticed into the Democratic column, so he openly courted the people around Lawrence and Topeka. But the free state contingent continued to boycott elections, and in June 1857, they failed to vote for delegates to a state constitutional convention, permitting the proslavery element to have a majority. In a legislative election in October 1857, the proslavery group won a majority again through massive fraud; Walker overturned those results, and for the first time the free state contingent had control of the legislature. The proslavery members of the constitutional convention that met at Lecompton then made a desperate bid to make Kansas a slave state. They wrote a constitution that allowed citizens to pass judgment only on whether Kansas would permit future importations of slaves, but not to vote on the constitution as a whole. Various parts of the document had objectionable elements to it, such as forbidding the legislature to emancipate any slaves already residing in Kansas. The free state group boycotted this election on the Lecompton Constitution, and on December 21, it passed with 6,266 voting for the constitution with slavery, and 569 voting for the constitution without slavery. Walker departed Kansas to argue against the constitution's legitimacy to Buchanan, and in his stead, the acting governor, Frederick Stanton, let the legislature enact another election law permitting an information vote on the whole constitution, even though the vote had no legal validity and was only done to obtain the true sentiment of the citizens; it was held on January 4, 1858, and produced a vote of 10,226 against the constitution entirely to only 138 for it with slavery and 24 for it without slavery. Taking the two votes together, the free staters outnumbered the proslavers by about 11,000 to 6,000.

President Buchanan had a distinctly southern orientation to his thinking and tended to agree with the southern interpretation of events. He acknowledged that it would have been better had the people of Kansas been allowed to vote on the whole constitution, yet the basic form of popular sovereignty had been followed. Southerners in his cabinet—especially Secretary of the Treasury Howell Cobb and Secretary of War John B. Floyd—pressured him to accept the verdict of the December vote on the Lecompton Constitution and back a bill in Congress that admitted Kansas as a slave state under the Lecompton Constitution.

Douglas kept abreast of Kansas affairs and did not like a constitution that had not been submitted to a vote of the residents. He had written to Walker in July, calling for such a procedure. In November, he inked a letter to McClernand, stating that he wanted the "will of the people [to be] freely & fairly expressed."[3] Matters about Kansas were not helped any because Douglas and Buchanan distrusted each other. Buchanan had many advisers, notably senators Slidell and Bright, who now openly disliked Douglas.

Douglas moved warily on the question of the Lecompton Constitution because he was a loyal party man. His entire career had been marked by devotion to party; he had been foremost in demanding loyalty from those who called themselves Democrats and in ousting those from the party who refused to live up to its standards. Now, however, he felt the same pangs of conscience that other Democrats had experienced: to follow his own convictions or to follow the party line. Pressuring him to fight acceptance of the Lecompton Constitution were his public pronouncements for nearly eight years: he had staked his reputation on popular sovereignty, and to preserve his integrity he had to object to a fraudulent vote. Popular sovereignty was an extension of the original impulse to extend democracy and equal rights to all white men; Douglas had pursued that goal all his life and would not abandon it now. In terms of the health of the party, he realized the obvious: one more massive shock from the slavery extension issue, and the northern Democratic Party was dead. To preserve the northern Democratic Party, he had to reject the Lecompton Constitution. By late November, it was generally known that Douglas would fight the admission of Kansas under the Lecompton Constitution.

When Douglas arrived in Washington, he soon arranged an audience with the president. He had been warned by Walker that Buchanan had already decided to accept the Lecompton Constitution and to make Kansas's admission a chief measure of his administration. Insulted that the president had not the grace to consult with him on a matter concerning the territories, Douglas confronted Buchanan about the Lecompton Constitution, and the meeting then became one of the legends in American political history. Buchanan told Douglas that the admission of Kansas as a state under the Lecompton Constitution was to be the principal measure of his administration and that Douglas needed to fall in line; he threatened destruction to those Democrats who would not follow him, reminding Douglas of what happened to those who had crossed the will of Andrew Jackson. Douglas fired back, "Mr. President, I wish you to remember that Gen. Jackson is dead."[4] The battle had begun.

The struggle over the Lecompton Constitution had two faces, one in the formal congressional operations and the other in backroom political maneuvering. Douglas made clear his opposition as soon as Buchanan's annual message arrived, and he elaborated on his criticisms in a long speech on December 9. He then faced the hostility of the administration Democrats, who bypassed him in the Committee on Territories, selecting James Green of Missouri to write a report in February approving the admission of Kansas. Douglas, the chair of the committee, was reduced to writing a report in opposition.

Most of the debate over the Lecompton Constitution covered well-worn grounds. Southern Democrats cried for the sanctity of equality of states within the Union and for their personal right to go into the territories with their slave property. Northerners, they charged, by opposing the admission of Kansas under the Lecompton Constitution, proved that they would never admit any more slave states to the Union. Republicans responded with their usual strident cries that free labor was being ousted by slave labor and that the North was suffering the blows of the Slave Power. Douglas and the anti-Lecompton Democrats generally avoided these arguments, staying on the theme of how democracy in Kansas had been perverted by fraud and violence.

Within these debates, though, was a withering assessment of popular sovereignty, even if Douglas refused to recognize it. For southerners, the question was increasingly becoming one of their property rights being jeopardized by the democratic process—a Gordian knot of democratic equality. Trying to maintain democratic forms in the midst of highly unequal property accumulations, the propertied group feared seizure of their wealth by the multitudinous rabble in the name of equality. In debate, Clement C. Clay of Alabama affirmed that "protection in the enjoyment of equal rights and privileges, in equal security of person and of property, is the political bond of our Union," and he declared that the purpose of the Constitution was to remove property from the touch of popular majorities.[5] This attack was continued by others, such as by Virginia representative Muscoe R. H. Garnett, who said of majority rule that when "unlimited and unrestrained, it is as truly a despotism as can be the government of one man."[6] Property, in short, was more important than democracy.

Republicans were drawn quickly into this property argument because the proslavery writers of the Lecompton Constitution placed it in that document. Maine's representative Israel Washburn quoted the objectionable portion: "The right of property *is before and higher than any constitutional sanction, and the right of the owner of a slave to such slave and its increase is the same, and as inviolable, as the right of the owner of any property whatever.*"[7] That section elicited from Mason W. Tappan of New Hampshire the exclamation, "Never before, to my knowledge, has the attempt been made, by express terms in a written constitution, to put property in man upon the same ground of natural right as that by which other property is held."[8]

The discussion about property rights, democracy, and popular sovereignty ensnared Douglas. The Gordian knot had to be confronted. The administration newspaper, the *Union*, had written that slaves as property were sacrosanct and above legislative tinkering, hinting that northern emancipation had been an *"outrage on the rights of property."* Douglas stepped in with a forthright declaration in good Jacksonian fashion that human rights were above property rights: "I recognize the right of the slaveholding States to regulate their local institutions," he said, "but I do not admit, and I do not think they are safe in asserting, that their right of property in slaves is higher than and above constitutional obligations, is independent of constitutional obligations." He had been read out of the party by the administration Democrats for "disputing this higher law . . . that slavery, the right to slave property, does not depend upon human law nor constitutional sanction, but is above and beyond and before all constitutional sanctions and obligations!" As a Democrat, he had to "repudiate and rebuke this doctrine."[9] The sectional crisis had pushed the stands on the slavery issue to the point of deciding between democracy and property rights, of going beyond the furthest boundary in which popular sovereignty could reasonably be expected to operate. Douglas decided that democracy was primary and property rights secondary, and so he redeemed the northern Democratic Party of subserviency to proslavery. In so choosing, Douglas was nearly admitting that this Gordian knot was unsolvable.

Border state senators John Bell and John J. Crittenden then addressed what many must have realized: as a practical mode of settling sectional disputes over slavery in the territories, popular sovereignty did not work. Crittenden admitted that the Lecompton Constitution was fraudulent and that the people of Kansas did not want it. He then mourned the repeal of the Missouri Compromise line. Bell of Tennessee agreed; the Kansas-Nebraska Act had been foolish: "The pulpit was converted into an engine of anti-slavery propagandism," and hundreds of thousands of conservatives came to fear southern designs on the future.[10] And what they needed to say, but did not, was that democracy was no cure for this kind of problem. Douglas had not yet reached this conclusion.

Politics and maneuvering for future electoral victory was the other face of the Lecompton struggle. That Stephen A. Douglas, the leading northern Democrat, was in open revolt against the Buchanan administration and its southern supporters induced some strategic thinking on the part of a few eastern Republicans. Twice in the past, rifts in the Democratic Party had built up an antislavery party: the Barnburner revolt of 1848 and the Kansas-Nebraska rebellion of

1854. One more split in the Democratic Party could possibly reduce it to impotence in northern electoral politics and elevate the Republicans to supremacy. This was the thinking of New York senator Seward, leading contender for the Republican presidential nomination in 1860; with him in his plotting was his chief lieutenant, Albany editor Thurlow Weed, and Horace Greeley, editor of the most-read newspaper in America, the *New York Tribune*.

Some Republicans met with Douglas at his house in Washington, D.C., to determine the depths of his opposition. Schuyler Colfax of Indiana and Anson Burlingame of Massachusetts interviewed Douglas on December 14. Colfax wrote that Douglas would stick to his principles and "was convinced that Jeff. Davis & others of the Southrons were really for Disunion, wished an opportunity to break up the Union." According to Colfax, Douglas agreed that he would not pursue proslavery measures except for the acquisition of Cuba, and on that subject he would not support any actions that had a dishonorable character.[11]

Republican infatuation with a Douglas defection from the Democratic Party was far-fetched, but many were hopeful. Seward therefore made his move. In a major speech on the ultimate triumph of free labor over slave labor, he applauded Douglas and agreed that congressional prohibition was no longer necessary to preserve the West for freedom: popular sovereignty was all that was needed. He even went so far as to say that he now accepted the climate theory of labor division between whites and blacks. Through their newspaper columns, an eastern clique of Republicans called for the inclusion of Douglas into the Republican Party. As Douglas's term was to expire at the end of 1858 and the Illinois legislature was either to reelect Douglas or choose another, the Sewardites called for the Illinois Republicans not to contest Douglas's reelection.

What had happened among the Republicans in terms of the ideas of popular sovereignty, however, needs to be precisely understood. Popular sovereignty was not acceptable to them because they thought people should vote on the establishment of slavery; it was acceptable because it guaranteed that free labor principles would win. In other words, the only reason some Republicans came to embrace popular sovereignty was because they expected to win on the issue of slavery extension; they came to realize that Douglas's predictions of victory for nonslave states in the West for eight years had been correct. On the other hand, southerners moved quickly to the other conclusion: popular sovereignty had to be repudiated because by it southerners would always lose. In 1858, popular sovereignty was on its last legs as a possible compromise solution. When neither side is willing to risk losing, compromise is impossible; another Gordian knot about democracy had been reached.

Douglas refused to jettison popular sovereignty, because that doctrine seemed to him the only means of uniting the Democratic Party and preserving the Union. He had no intention of joining the Republican Party, preferring only to retain them as allies to defeat the Lecompton Constitution. Some of his correspondence indicated some of the differences between him and the Republicans. One writer called himself a "rank freesoiler" and could not understand "how any democrat could be any thing else." And then the correspondent added a free labor observation that Douglas would have never used or admitted: the "Irish . . . have a silly fear of the competition of negro labor[,] failing to see that *slave* labor is the great evil against which they have to contend."[12] Douglas never used this argument and indeed used the one the writer called silly: Douglas told audiences to fear an emancipation that would release freed blacks to come North to reduce the wage rate.

Douglas received a stunning avalanche of mail due to his fight against the administration. The tenor of these missives was simple: popular sovereignty was a foundational principle of the United States and had to be maintained, and if the northern Democrats caved in on Lecompton, "the result would be an absolute dissolution of the democratic party."[13] Within the Douglas correspondence, however, lay some surprises. First, slavery as an institution was almost never mentioned or examined. Writers discussed almost solely popular sovereignty, and what seemingly frightened them was not the introduction of slavery into the territories but the subversion of democracy, of the right to vote. Democrats feared that they were losing the essence of their ideals. Second, though some correspondents attacked the South and nearly came to a Slave Power interpretation of southern behavior, the most common trait they shared was that Lecompton was a personal fight between the honorable Stephen A. Douglas and the deranged president. Douglas's correspondents blamed Buchanan—"poor imbecile old man!"—rather than southerners; Lecompton was an error of judgment on Buchanan's part.[14]

A final aspect of Douglas's correspondence deserves mention. The appeals for printed copies of his speeches were absolutely overwhelming—there were hundreds of such requests. The reason for these demands for offprints of his speeches goes far to explain the role of oratory in antebellum politics. Communication had improved, but nonetheless people still did not have access to analysis of political issues. Important statesmen supplied that analysis in their speeches, and then they sent their printed speeches through the mail to editors and to people of importance so that the ideas could circulate. Thus was the party position established. The demand for copies was explained in the remarks that one correspondent made: "We wish to circulate the correct Democratic doctrines."[15] Oratory may have fallen flat in the twentieth century, but in the mid-nineteenth century, it was the means of instruction, persuasion, and unification of party adherents. It was not an ornament; it was indispensable to party cohesion.

Southerners had a mixed reaction to Douglas's revolt. Many feared the impact his desertion would have on the Democratic Party. Others, like the Mississippi senators, Jefferson Davis and Albert Gallatin Brown, howled at Douglas's failure to obey the party line. In North Carolina, John A. Gilmer wrote that if Kansas did not become a slave state, it would be "no great loss to the South," but there were those who would "try to make the South believe that they have lost a great thing."[16] Southern congressmen and senators voted in favor of Lecompton, regardless of their misgivings about actual events in Kansas or whether slavery would be too feeble a plant to survive the Kansas climate.

The Senate had no problem passing the bill to admit Kansas under the Lecompton Constitution, but it failed in the House of Representatives. Douglas, who was quite ill during most of the session, worked with Thomas L. Harris of Illinois to defeat the measure and return the constitution back to Kansas so the citizens could vote to accept or reject the entire document, not merely one provision about slavery. On April 1, the House defeated the admission of Kansas under the Lecompton Constitution, to the wild cheering of Republicans. However, a compromise solution was forged so that the administration could save some dignity. William H. English of Indiana offered a compromise by which the people of Kansas were to be given millions of acres of additional land if they voted for the Lecompton Constitution, but no extra acreage if they voted it down. This compromise passed the House and Senate, but Douglas ending up voting against it. The Lecompton Constitution went back to Kansas, where it was soundly defeated by a vote of 11,300 to 1,788; Kansas would enter the Union in 1861 and become the most Republican state in the Union.

Debating Lincoln

Douglas faced reelection by the state legislature in 1858, and he had to fight to retain his position. Due to the complications of the Lecompton controversy, the political situation in Illinois was muddied. Most Illinois Democrats stood by Douglas and proved their fidelity in a state convention in late April when Douglas followers ran the meeting and presented the resolutions. But a group of discontented Democrats, especially from Chicago, created a schism. These dissidents, led by Isaac Cook, who still rankled at his fight with Sheahan and Douglas over the *Chicago Daily Times*, created a faction supporting Buchanan, sometimes dubbed the "Buchaneers." A divided party never boded well for victory at the polls. Because Douglas and Buchanan could not be reconciled, the administration moved to assist Cook by using its patronage powers. Douglas faced a monumental task because not only did he have to battle administration efforts to defeat him, but he also confronted a Republican opponent of merit.

Illinois Republicans found their situation frustrating due to the machinations of Seward, Greeley, and Weed. On the one hand, Republicans loved the split in the Democratic Party, both in terms of electoral possibilities and in advertising the antislavery point of view. Illinois Republicans were less pleased that some national leaders were courting Douglas and wanted his reelection to the Senate to be uncontested. John Wentworth, radical antislavery Democrat and Chicago editor, informed Lincoln, "I fear, Lincoln, that you are sold for the Senate by men who are drinking the wine of Douglas at Washington."[17] Lyman Trumbull commented, "Some of our friends here act like fools in running after & flattering Douglas."[18]

Illinois Republicans rejected the advice of their eastern counterparts and waged war on Douglas. They held a state convention at Springfield on June 16 and, for the first time in the nation's history, announced whom they would elect to the Senate if they won control of the Illinois legislature—Abraham Lincoln. Lincoln then delivered one of his more famous speeches, the "House Divided" speech. The first paragraph was theoretical: taking a line from the Bible, he warned, "'A house divided against itself cannot stand.' I believe this government cannot endure, permanently, half *slave* and half *free*." He did not foresee dissolution but did predict a final end to the struggle between freedom and slavery in the United States. After that memorable introduction, he then plunged into the nuts and bolts of politics and offered a conspiracy theory of how certain individuals—Stephen A. Douglas, Roger B. Taney, Franklin Pierce, and James Buchanan—had plotted to destroy the fabric of freedom and transform the United States into a slaveholding despotism. "We cannot absolutely know," ominously intoned Lincoln, "that all these exact adaptations are the result of preconcert. But when we see a lot of framed timbers, different portions of which we know have been gotten out at different times and places by different workmen—Stephen, Franklin, Roger and James, for instance . . . we find it impossible not to believe that Stephen and Franklin and Roger and James all understood one another from the beginning, and all worked upon a common plan." Lincoln emphasized the *Dred Scott* decision and its implications; scored Douglas for not caring whether slavery "'be voted down or voted up'"; and warned that if the movement were not arrested, Illinois would soon be a slave state. Douglas was up to his neck in this transformation of America from a land of liberty into a land of slavery; "He has done all in his power to reduce the whole question of slavery to one of a mere right of property."[19]

Douglas started campaigning in his usual vigorous way, planning to make speeches around the state and making certain that Democrats were elected to the state legislature. He began with a speech in Chicago on July 9 justifying his past actions. In the audience was Lincoln, who on the next day made a rebuttal. Douglas then made plans to visit dozens of Illinois towns, published his itinerary, and began exhorting the crowds to endorse the Democratic Party. As he did so, he found that he had a shadow: Lincoln followed him and spoke immediately afterward. This was not the most pleasing of all worlds, and though he felt that all the advantages of a series of debates fell to Lincoln, who did not possess a national reputation as he did, Douglas wanted to bring the shadow into the light where under cross-examination it could be shriveled into nothingness.

At the end of July, Lincoln and Douglas agreed to a series of seven debates. Lincoln and the Republicans originally wanted the two to debate throughout the state; Douglas suggested only seven times, and the Republicans accepted. The seven debates were to be held at Ottawa (August 21), Freeport (August 27), Jonesboro (September 15), Charleston (September 18), Galesburg (October 7), Quincy (October 13), and Alton (October 15). They were only part of a massive speaking tour undertaken by both candidates. Lincoln traveled four thousand miles and gave sixty-three major addresses; Douglas journeyed nearly five thousand miles and gave fifty-nine speeches. The joint debates, however, attracted national attention and earned Lincoln a national reputation.

First-time readers of the debates are often surprised at the extent of repetition in them—indeed, at the amount of repetition in all political activity. Candidates repeated themselves for a particular reason: they could not assume that the different audiences they addressed knew the issues, the logic of the politician's stand, or the defects in their opponents'. Not everyone read the papers or conversed constantly about politics. The only safe route was endless repetition. Except for a few interesting deviations, the seven debates illustrated this facet of American electioneering.

Douglas knew that electoral victory in Illinois hinged on the party that conservatives—old-line Whigs, some Know-Nothings, and unionists of various stripes—would call home. In 1856, they had been with the Democrats and so had elected James Buchanan president. Douglas's strategy was to keep these people in the Democratic camp by portraying the Democratic Party as the party of conservatism and sectional compromise. This was the reason he endlessly referred to the patriotism of Henry Clay. At the same time, he painted the Republicans—especially Lincoln and Trumbull—as abolitionists, fanatics, and zealots. Both of these men had ruined Henry Clay's Whig Party and its Union-loving proclivities in order to build the abolitionist, Black Republican

Party. On the question of abolitionism, Douglas then paired abolitionism with social equality between blacks and whites. Lincoln's speech at Chicago on July 10 helped Douglas mightily here. Lincoln had proclaimed that the constant belittling of blacks and the division of people into races was undercutting the equality spoken of in the Declaration of Independence. To this, Douglas charged that Lincoln believed in the social and political equality of blacks with whites, and in every appearance he made, he had one standard refrain: "For one, I am opposed to negro citizenship in any and every form. I believe this Government was made on the white basis. I believe it was made by white men, for the benefit of white men and their posterity for ever, and I am in favor of confining citizenship to white men, men of European birth and descent, instead of conferring it upon negroes, Indians, and other inferior races."[20]

He, of course, would justify his course as senator by stressing the doctrine of popular sovereignty and its connection to the hallowed principles of the American Revolution. He defined the power of a local community as he had so often in the past: "The great principle is the right of every community to judge and decide for itself, whether a thing is right or wrong, whether it would be good or evil for them to adopt it; and the right of free action, the right of free thought, the right of free judgment upon the question is dearer to every true American than any other under a free government." Republican belief in prohibiting territories from establishing slavery took away a community's freedom of action. The justification for local rule was diversity in the soil, climate, and conditions of life. Douglas asserted that people knew what was best for them and would judge correctly and fairly. Lincoln's rejection of popular sovereignty, Douglas declared, was an attempt to foster a uniformity among all the states, to build up a grand central government, and to destroy popular government. Douglas never hesitated to use some exaggeration when battling opponents.[21]

In the debates, he provided a vital perspective on how he joined popular sovereignty to the imperative of landed expansion. Douglas had lost none of his exuberance for adding territory to the United States; he was still an advocate of Manifest Destiny. He believed the mechanism for successfully adding new lands to the republic to be the granting of local autonomy in domestic relations and economic affairs to the smaller political units—that is, popular sovereignty. His understanding of the difference between the federal principle of the American "empire" as opposed to older empires, such as the Roman Empire, was the granting of local control to the administrative districts (states) and avoiding the imposition of rules from the imperial center. In Douglas's view, it was popular sovereignty that enabled Manifest Destiny to operate successfully. Moreover, territorial expansion was necessary to keep the American experiment in self-government alive—his solution to a Gordian knot of democratic equality—be-

cause population pressure, now abetted   .ed
available land and ruined prospects for p   his
argument often in the debates, but he no  'er-
eignty, Manifest Destiny, and democracy'   ıke
a close-fitting ideological suit for the spo

> We must bear in mind that we are yet a young nation, growing with a rapidity
> unequaled in the history of the world, that our national increase is great, and
> that the emigration from the old world is increasing, requiring us to expand and
> acquire new territory from time to time, in order to give our people land to live
> upon. If we live upon the principle of State rights and State sovereignty, each
> State regulating its own affairs and minding its own business, we can go on and
> extend indefinitely, just as fast and as far as we need the territory.[22]

And Douglas had an awesome vision of future expansion: when the time
came, the United States would have to absorb Cuba, Mexico, and Canada,
and even then American expansion would not cease. His objection to the
slavery controversy was that it interfered with the acquisition of new lands. If
Americans kept to the principle of popular sovereignty, that interference would
disappear.

Lincoln blasted away at Douglas on several fronts. He pursued his idea that
freedom in the United States was dying because of the expansion of slavery,
and that Douglas was playing a major role in this ongoing deterioration of freedom. He constantly blistered Douglas about the *Dred Scott* decision, arguing
that the Supreme Court had utterly gutted the doctrine of popular sovereignty
by ruling that territories had to allow slave property throughout the territorial
stage. He went into detail about the passage of the Kansas-Nebraska Act, asking why Douglas had not supported the Chase amendment, which would have
directly given the Kansas territorial government the ability to prohibit slavery.
Lincoln tried to undermine Douglas's public standing as a champion of democracy by showing that he approved the Toombs bill, which did not provide
for a popular vote on the Kansas constitution. Later in the campaign, Lincoln
stressed more heavily the question of the morality of slavery and its corrosive
effect on American freedom.

The debates were a great spectacle, and huge crowds between fifteen to
thirty thousand people turned out to hear Illinois' two famous stump speakers. Douglas and Lincoln had jousted before on the public platform. The long,
thin, and somewhat morose Lincoln made a contrast with the short, stubby,
heavy-shouldered, and large-faced Douglas. In debate, both gesticulated forcibly, and there were flashes of temper and base appeals. Douglas made the
most of the appearance of Frederick Douglass, the black abolitionist orator, sit-

ting in a carriage with a white woman: "All I have to say of it is this, . . . if you . . . think that the negro ought to be on a social equality with your wives and daughters, and ride in a carriage with your wife, . . . you have a perfect right to do so." At Freeport, Douglas was angry at a portion of the crowd for chanting "white, white" when he called the Republicans the Black Republican Party; he also became upset at hecklers at Galesburg.[23]

For his part, Lincoln found the tactics of Douglas infuriating. Douglas tried to take the most extreme statements of Republicans and make Lincoln wear that brand. During the debate at Charl congressman Orlando Ficklin, sitting on the s him before the audience to rebut a charge Do havior during the Mexican War. And Douglas was mightily perturbed by Douglas's descripti at Freeport, where Lincoln had been carried Douglas said of the ending of that meeting, Li depiction that irked Lincoln and which he said man Douglas exactly."[24]

Certain elements of the debates stood out in bold relief. The first was the handling of the *Dred Scott* decision by Douglas. Lincoln formulated a question for Douglas based on how popular sovereignty was to have any substance since the Supreme Court had ruled that slaves, being property, must be permitted to enter all territories of the United States. Douglas's answer became known as the Freeport Doctrine. Slavery could not exist in any territory, Douglas said, unless it had accompanying "local police regulations." "Those police regulations," he insisted, "can only be established by the local legislature."[25] Thus, popular sovereignty still worked because Douglas had just gone from theory to practice: the *right* to property might exist in law, but without the *practical protection* by a police power, the right was meaningless. This pronouncement of Douglas's received wide circulation in the nation, and it further invalidated the doctrine of popular sovereignty in the eyes of southerners. To southerners, the *Dred Scott* decision was a victory for their position that territorial legislatures could not outlaw slavery; but in the Freeport Doctrine, Douglas found a new way for a territory to exclude slavery. Thus Douglas practically invalidated the triumph that southerners thought they had obtained from the Supreme Court.

The second striking element in the debates was the centrality of race. Racial commentary actually stemmed from two distinct sources. First, Douglas intended to ride the Republicans and Lincoln as hard as possible on being racial egalitarians because he expected a visceral response from a racist white public in favor of him and the Democratic Party. In this, Douglas was openly distorting the truth: egalitarians were abolitionists like William Lloyd Garrison, Wendell Phillips, and Theodore Weld; Republicans were not abolitionists. Douglas wanted the Illinois audience to equate Republicans with abolitionists because the abolitionists were the most despised white political minority in the nation.

Lincoln clearly feared the race issue and knew h[...] insisted that the Declaration of Independence covered that they had the same rights as Euro-Americans, but h[...] were probably inferior and did not have the capacity to the extent that white people did. In addition, he indicated separation of the races and favored colonization as a long-term of his descent into racism came quickly, however: "I agree with he [black man] is not my equal in many respects. . . . But in the r[...] bread, without the leave of anybody else, which his own hand ear[...] *equal and the equal of Judge Douglas, and the equal of every living man.*"26

On the question of race, there was a palpable difference between the two men. Lincoln started by giving equal rights and then backtracked when faced with the racism of his day: he started on the high ground and retreated to the low ground. Douglas went the other way. He started out proclaiming that blacks had no rights whatsoever, and then he moved upward. Just because blacks were inferior did not mean that they were to be treated as objects: "On the contrary, I hold that humanity and Christianity both require that the negro shall have and enjoy every right, every privilege, and every immunity consistent with the safety of the society in which he lives."27 The ending point of both Lincoln and Douglas appeared to be about the same: white superiority mixed with a recognition of humanity and some rights for black people. But the ending place during these debates disguised the dynamic. Given the chance, Lincoln returned to the high ground, while Douglas retreated to the lowlands.

The second reason that race figured so heavily in the debates stemmed from Lincoln's tactical situation. To dethrone Douglas, one simply had to attack popular sovereignty. No other strategy made much sense, because it was on popular sovereignty alone that Douglas held his position among northern Democrats and conservatives. How to discredit the idea was a problem, because, as Lincoln had acknowledged, popular sovereignty was the gift of the revolutionary forefathers and was true in itself. The answer for Lincoln was one of definition. If black men were men, then they should be added to the decision makers in popular sovereignty and not be the objects of popular sovereignty. This was the basic error of Douglas's position. In Lincoln's understanding, Douglas refused to acknowledge the natural rights of blacks the way he acknowledged them for whites. This was the source of Lincoln's constant moralizing during the debates. As he put it, "The other way is for us to surrender and let Judge Douglas and his friends have their way and plant slavery over all the States—cease speaking of it as in any way a wrong—regard slavery as one of the common matters of property, and speak of negroes as we do of our horses and cattle." But to do this, Lincoln had to make the case that blacks were humans with rights, and such a strategy invoked the racial consideration. He was constantly warned against appearing to favor "Negro equality."[28]

A third theme worthy of remark about the Lincoln-Douglas debates is the absence, not the presence, of some subjects. The debates were warped by Douglas's stature and the importance of popular sov~~~~~~~ ~~ his career. This was not the case elsewhere. In Pennsylvania, New Y issues, especially the tariff, roared back into p vania, orators talked of little but the tariff. Ir Slave Power and the free labor ideal constituted not popular sovereignty. One of the strange qu debates is the lack of extensive discussion of free la Lincoln-Douglas debates were disconnected with the . campaigns in the other northern states.

It is commonly said that Lincoln and Douglas were more alike in their positions than they were different. But they held radically opposite views of the future. Lincoln saw slavery distorting and reshaping the United States into a despotism; Douglas saw only a continuation of a glorious past. Lincoln's vision was gloomy and troubled: either slavery would be restricted to its present limits and put on the path of eventual extinction, "or its advocates will push it forward, till it shall become alike lawful in all the States, old as well as new—North as well as South." To this, Douglas had an eloquent rejoinder:

> Why cannot this Government endure divided into free and slave States, as our fathers made it? When this Government was established by Washington, Jefferson, Madison, Jay, Hamilton, Franklin, and the other sages and patriots of that day, it was composed of free States and slave States, bound together by one common Constitution. We have existed and prospered from that day to this thus divided, and have increased with a rapidity never before equaled in wealth, the extension of territory, and all the elements of power and greatness, until we have become the first nation on the face of the globe. Why can we not thus continue to prosper?[29]

Indeed, why not? For Douglas, slavery was just another property arrangement—like horses, cows, real estate, or machinery. Slavery had no more connection with control of government than the textile interest. Why would slavery thus endanger freedoms any more than, say, the iron interest? Understanding why these two men came up with such different answers concerning the effect

of slavery on the major institution   usive; no
definitive answer exists.

The question naturally arises as   glas won
reelection, one could simply skip this question as irrelevant, but the query does
reveal something about Douglas's power and stature. Ultimately, one would
have to conclude that Douglas emerged the victor over Lincoln. On certain
crucial subjects, and on the main theses that each opponent propounded,
Douglas did better. First, Douglas made Lincoln retreat on the subject of race;
he said he would make Lincoln squirm over the race issue in southern Illinois,
and Lincoln did indeed squirm. Second, Douglas never retreated from his use
of popular sovereignty or from justifying it. On trying to brand Lincoln an
abolitionist and making Illinoisans believe his brand of political history—that
Lincoln and Trumbull actively sought the destruction of the Whigs in order to
give birth to the Republicans—Douglas probably lost, although he never quit
the allegation.

Lincoln lost on some of his major points. He started with an overtly conspiratorial view of the Slave Power, Stephen A. Douglas being one of the ar-
chitects. That did not last long. Lincoln had to give up his effort to prove that
Douglas was part of a conspiracy against freedom, a charge that was somewhat
ludicrous to begin with. Toward the end of the debates, Lincoln was on more
solid ground when, without having to resort to personalities, he stressed the
direction of the country toward the nationalization of slavery, toward favorable outcomes for slavery. In debate tactics, Lincoln also failed in his attempt
at infighting with Douglas over the minutia of the Kansas-Nebraska Act, the
Lecompton Constitution, and the Toombs bill. Simply stated, Douglas was at
his best—most ferocious—when an argument turned to small facts. Douglas did
not fare so well on more general, theoretical grounds. It was at the end that
Lincoln started scoring his victories, and his victories were largely on the question of slavery's morality. Despite what Douglas said, slavery was a moral issue,
and nearly everyone realized it. But the overall assessment of the two men's
performance as debaters probably has to give the edge to Douglas.

Douglas had some triumphs in the numbers as well, although the totals
showed that Republicans edged out the Democrats. The election came on November 2. In the vote for the legislature, some 250,566 votes were cast; Republicans took 49.8 percent, the Democrats 48.4 percent, and the Buchaneers 1.9
percent. Yet the Illinois legislature was Democratic in both the House and the
Senate, and on January 6, 1859, the Democrats proceeded to reelect Douglas
for another term as United States senator. Illinois managed this feat because
the population swell in the northern counties had not been taken into account
by redrawing election districts. Thus one obtained huge Republican majorities

in the ——————— he smaller Democratic majorities in
the sou ——————— d circumstance that Republicans had
a majc ——————— majority of victories in the electoral
district

While the numbers might indicate that the Republicans were cheated out of a victory because of a lack of redistricting, another story resides in the outcome. Illinois Democrats won 48.4 percent of the total vote for the state legislature, and in the congressional races, they won 49.3 percent. When compared to 1854 and 1856, Illinois Democrats were distinctly rebounding. In the congressional race of 1854, the Democrats only received 42.6 percent; in 1856, they recovered to 48.3 percent; and in 1858, they obtained 49.3 percent.

Douglas was proud of the showing of the Illinois Democratic Party in 1858 and had reason to be. Given the direction of the results, he could hope that the Democrats might again be the majority party in the state in 1860. He basked in the commentary of the nation, for he had bested both the Republican Party and the administration. Indeed, given his correspondence in the summer and fall of 1858, it appears that his friends were more concerned with administration patronage and party manipulations than they were with Lincoln. The editor of the *New York Times* was "astounded" at the result and remarked that the victory proved that northerners could rally around Douglas and preclude the introduction of any more slave states.[30]

Another player had entered the game, and it is not clear that Douglas recognized that fact in the rejoicings over the victory of the Illinois Democratic Party in November of 1858. Most of the elections in New England and the Great Lakes states went as they had in 1856; the anti-Lecompton revolt actually produced few surprises. This was emphatically not the case in Pennsylvania and New York. Pennsylvania in 1856 had sent fourteen Democrats to Congress, the opposition eleven; in 1858, the Democrats only elected four members to Congress, whereas the opposition (called the People's Party) won twenty-one districts. New York's delegation of thirty-three congressmen had twelve Democrats in 1856; in 1858, they only numbered four. Here was an electoral disaster for the national Democratic Party, for the Democrats lost the "Keystone State," the one state most essential to presidential victories. If Pennsylvania and New Jersey had voted Republican in 1856, Frémont would have been elected president instead of Buchanan. And in 1858, the most precious of the northern Democratic states revolted against the Buchanan administration and the Democratic Party. While New York had mostly internal strife causing its reversals, in Pennsylvania economic issues carried the day. The issue was the tariff.

Douglas had presidential aspirations for 1860, and this time he did not intend to be denied. He had watched the withering of the northern Democratic

Party at the hands of the slavery issue and needed to arrest and reverse the flow of popular approval to the Republican Party. Although the North seemed ready to accept popular sovereignty—they now knew that the North and free labor would win—he had other problems crowding in on him. The first and most obvious was the reaction of the South. Here the inherent problem of democracy—a Gordian knot—reared its head: in order for democracy to work, the losing side in an electoral contest must accept the verdict of the people. Was the South ready to lose the territorial issue? Douglas already knew that for southern radicals the answer was no. His second problem was one peculiar to the Democratic Party. The presidential year of 1860 would see a revival of the economic issues that had powered the Whig-Democrat party system and which had been absent for a decade. In 1858, these issues returned to the political arena. But this time, the Democrats were on the losing side.

Popular Sovereignty and Property Rights, 1859

Douglas faced enormous political problems in the Democratic Party after his 1858 senatorial campaign. The president and his cabinet had shown a hostility toward him that likely would not cease. Just as important, he needed to rescue the northern Democratic Party from oblivion. During the Lecompton fight, the remnants of the northern Democratic Party became restive over southern control of the party. Increasingly, northern Democrats were saying things about southern power that sounded very much like Republican protests about the Slave Power. As the northern Democrats' distemper at the actions of southerners grew, southerners began deserting Douglas. Douglas's Freeport Doctrine finally brought out in the open the two very different interpretations about popular sovereignty. Most southerners insisted that the doctrine only applied at the moment when a state formulated its constitution, whereas Douglas and the North maintained that the territorial legislature from the beginning could ban or establish slavery. This divergence between northern and southern Democrats over popular sovereignty was well known but was overlooked because it had no practical application until the verdict of the *Dred Scott* decision and the Lecompton Constitution battle.

One other vision of the political future emerged. Some held that the slavery extension issue died with the Lecompton Constitution. After Kansans turned down the Lecompton Constitution, where else in the West was the problem of slavery in the territories to arise? For some commentators, there was no visible controversy left, because no one could see over the next twenty years any territory that would have the problems with slavery that Kansas had encountered. So some, like the Philadelphia *North American and United States Gazette*, pronounced the slavery issue dead, although kept alive by partisan agitators. Here was the kernel of a historical interpretation about the sectional conflict over slavery: the rending of the Union and inauguration of civil war was brought about by agitators because the issue they ostensibly battled over had disappeared; demagogues took control of the politics of the nation, raised tempers to a fever pitch, and brought about the catastrophe of the Civil War. This interpretation still hangs over the time period, and it is the one that Douglas would eventually come to adopt.

Douglas left Illinois in late November 1858 and did not resume his seat in the Senate until January 10, enjoying a long trip to New Orleans and then traveling by ship to New York City. His absence and the slow arrival of many senators and representatives to the second session of the Thirty-fifth Congress gave his enemies a chance to attack. Douglas had revolted against party discipline over Lecompton, defied the administration, and infuriated southern states' rights ideologues with the Freeport Doctrine. Douglas needed to be disciplined, according to some high Democratic Party officials. Leaders in the move to punish Douglas were Slidell, Bright, Graham Fitch, and Jefferson Davis, with the connivance of administration officials like Howell Cobb and Jacob Thompson. At a Democratic Senate caucus on December 9, the radicals made their move and stripped Douglas of his chairmanship of the Committee on Territories, giving it instead to Missourian James Green. The action caused its own divisions within the Democratic Party, as a number of senators and representatives denounced it—Robert Toombs, for example—and stormed out of the caucus after the vote.

The action of the caucus shocked Douglas, but he quickly determined not to engage in petty squabbling over his fate, which would give his enemies a chance to further aggravate the situation. Instead, he conducted himself as a conscientious Democrat, attended caucus meetings, and avoided discussion of the Freeport Doctrine, which was exactly what southern fire-eaters wanted to tear into. However, the anti-Lecompton Democrats read the action as "the declaration of war upon all Douglas men," and so any chance of mending the rift in the Democratic Party between Douglas and the administration was gone. Somewhat interestingly, few of Douglas's correspondents mentioned Davis or other southerners as the instigators of the removal, but instead they blamed it all on the "President and his tools."[31] Republicans, by contrast, would have had no trouble understanding who consummated the deed—the "Slave Power." But Douglas Democrats did not think that way and most often refused to generalize about southern behavior in those terms; they saw Douglas's problems as linked to his personal duel with Buchanan.

His activity in the congressional session was quite limited, seeking as he did to avoid ideological confrontations, except for one poignant moment.

New Hampshire's impish provocateur, John Hale, offered an amendment to a bill on Kansas that reignited sectional animosities. The one-day debate turned on the Gordian knot of the relation of property rights to a democratic form of government and the reaction of a disaffected group when its members found their property in jeopardy from the majority. Southerners seized the opportunity to belittle the Freeport Doctrine as a violation of the *Dred Scott* decision and to argue for federal protection of slavery during the territorial stage of government. Mississippi's Albert Gallatin Brown took center stage and gave his argument about property rights. His basic point was that a right to hold property without actually enforcing the ability to hold property meant nothing; individual property could not exist without the power to coerce others to recognize the right. Inanimate objects took a certain amount of law to provide protection, Brown lectured, but "animate" property took more; more law was required to protect property rights in a horse than in a wagon. He next extended the analysis to slavery: "Then, if you superadd to the animate property the power of reason, your law again must be adapted to that kind of property. Now, the slave partakes of all of these qualities, the inanimate, the animate, and, adding the power of reason, your law must be adapted to the nature of the thing." Because the Supreme Court had decided that slaves were property in the territories, and property must be protected by the Constitution, the territorial government either must protect that form of property, or the federal government would have to assume the chore. Thus Douglas's Freeport Doctrine was heresy.[32]

Of course Douglas could not let this assertion go unchallenged, and he drove to the core problem in the entire debate: *someone* had to define and protect property rights. For Douglas, the most obvious agency to do so was local government, territorial government; for Republicans, the agency was the federal government; and for southerners until the Kansas episode, no one enforced property rights in slaves because the decision could not be handed down until a state constitution was made (although the radicals insisted from the start that it was the duty of the territorial government to protect all forms of property that had been sanctioned by the states). After the Lecompton battle, radical southerners saw that reliance on territorial government or on simple social consensus would not work, and they, like the Republicans, called for the federal government to intervene—but intervention in order to oversee protection of property rights in slaves, not to extinguish it. Between 1846 and 1858, most southerners feared establishing such a federal obligation because such power also gave the federal government the right not to protect property rights in slaves.

Douglas denounced Brown's position as a violation of the Democratic Party's Cincinnati platform of 1856, which posited congressional nonintervention in the territories. He offered a mature version about the property rights dilemma. All citizens could take their property into the territories, because there was no congressional discrimination placed on any type of property. But the enforcement of property rights depended on the actions of the territorial legislature. A territorial legislature has "the same power to legislate in respect to slaves, that it has in regard to any other property, to the same extent and no further." If the territorial legislature does not protect slavery, then the slaveholder loses, and "it is the misfortune of those who own that species of property." Later in the debate, Douglas refuted the charge that legislatures could not discriminate against various kinds of property. He used the example of cattle, which were taxed and regulated differently by the states. He then noted that in the states, schools and libraries were exempt from taxation: "I do not know a State in this Union that does not discriminate between different species of property in taxes." He then laid down his law about the territories, states' rights, and the definition of property:

> When a man goes into the Territory of Kansas from Mississippi, he is no longer a Mississippian; he is a citizen of Kansas, and then he has acquired the right to vote, to make his own law. The people of Mississippi are not to be governed by his law, nor is he to be governed by them; but you say that he and his associates make such laws as you do not like in Mississippi. Who cares whether you like them or not in Mississippi? They were not made for you; they were made for the people of Kansas.[33]

This one-day debate over Hale's amendment brought other remarkable sentiments to the surface. Jefferson Davis told Douglas that he offered a bad rendering of the Constitution, and then Davis gave a reading that, in modern parlance, was entirely off the wall. Davis said the people in a territory are "tenants for the States who own the territory" until the territory reached statehood. Ohio's George Pugh, recently elected popular sovereignty Democrat, joined the discussion and called all the constitutional doctrines of southerners a "vast piece of special pleading, eked out by the fictions of history." Asking where the doctrines of the South tended, he came to a Republican conclusion: they propelled slavery into northern states, and slavery became a national institution. The Ohioan insisted that he would give the South equality of rights but not suffer northerners to endure an inequality: "You shall not carry the laws of your State into the territories, unless you allow me to carry the laws of my State there."[34]

This debate on February 23, 1859, presaged the division of the Democratic Party into sectional fragments. Out in the open was the southern position of a territorial slave code enforced by the federal government. The northern position was Douglas's: congressional nonintervention in the territories and determination of the existence of slavery by popular sovereignty.

Much activity during the session involved finding a new platform for the Democratic Party to appeal to the public. Democrats looked to the acquisition of Cuba, and a proposal was made by Slidell to give President Buchanan $30 million to purchase the island from Spain. Douglas favored the idea and loved the prospect of a resurrection of Manifest Destiny. He supported Slidell in a Democratic Party caucus and even went so far as to suggest that the best way for acquisition was to find some incident that could provoke the use of force on the part of the United States. Douglas's musings on how to obtain Cuba certainly call into question all those statements Democrats made about acquiring land "only if by honorable means."[35] The Cuba scheme got nowhere, but it was decidedly popular in the Democratic newspaper columns. Under different circumstances, Manifest Destiny might indeed have roared again.

Another issue emerged before Congress, and its attempted resolution badly mauled the Democrats. Politically conscious observers knew that the horrid results of the 1858 congressional races for the Democrats stemmed from the debacle in New York and especially in Pennsylvania, and the disaster in Pennsylvania had more to do with cries for a higher tariff than with the Lecompton struggle. The president understood his state well and recommended a higher tariff in his annual message. Of all the economic issues that fired southern rage, the tariff was the most potent. Virginia senator Robert M. T. Hunter killed Buchanan's recommendation in Democratic Party caucuses, creating immense consternation and anger among the Pennsylvanians.

No change in the tariff came out of this session, squelched as it was by southern Senate Democrats. In Pennsylvania, bitter resentment grew among Democrats, and those frustrations began producing comments similar to the ones made by Republicans about the Slave Power. While this anger festered and grew, the truth was that the Pennsylvanians were backed by few of their Democratic peers in other states. Most northern Democrats did not believe in a higher tariff and did not champion Pennsylvania's cause. Their inability to handle the issue adroitly, however, augured poorly for them in the election of 1860. For Democrats to seize victory, Pennsylvania was the most significant northern state, the tariff was the key to Pennsylvania, and the Democratic Party—Douglas very much included—refused to acknowledge the need to respond to the economic demands of the Keystone State.

When the session ended, disgruntlement filled the ranks of the Democratic Party. The rift between popular sovereignty Democrats and administration Democrats—soon to be slave code Democrats—only widened. The tariff Democrats of Pennsylvania abused their brethren in the South and were suspicious of their colleagues in the North. To top it off, James Buchanan disappointed many northerners, like Douglas, by vetoing a bill to improve the St. Clair Flats and a bill to support agricultural colleges in the states by the sale of public lands. Congress could not obtain majorities to seek the acquisition of Cuba, to establish a homestead (free land) policy in the West, or to determine a route for a Pacific railroad. The pitiful condition of the Democratic Party, just a year before a presidential contest, was marked by many observers. It was often ascribed to personality contests instead of issues. Wrote future director of the census Joseph C. G. Kennedy to Virginian Alexander H. H. Stuart, "The Democracy seem to view as of more importance the slaughter of each other, than union against their foes, they certainly are pursuing a course calculated to weaken themselves."[36]

Douglas was quite aware of the condition of his party, and he also probably knew he had lost some southern support. As one person wrote to Indiana's John G. Davis, Douglas's stock is "at a discount, but can hardly be called entirely flat." On the other hand, "The Brown & Davis platform has many advocates, but seems, after all to have but a slight hold on the popular sentiment even of the extremists of the South."[37] Douglas had his supporters in the South, but increasingly there were those who spoke of the "heresies of Judge Douglas,"[38] and he received mail from southerners arguing that the right of property in slaves could not be abridged by a territorial legislature—southerners had "a *constitutional* right of property" in slaves in the territories.[39]

Southerners displayed a heightened emotional attachment to the abstract idea of equal treatment within the Union, a sentiment that undercut a widespread recognition that for the foreseeable future, the nation did not have any territories that might provoke a controversy over slavery. Alexander H. Stephens of Georgia, retiring from Congress, admitted in a farewell address that slavery in the territories was now an "abstract question" because no application of it could be made for several decades. He added, though, that the principle was just as important as the actual admission of new slave states: "Nations which submit to abstract questions of wrong will not long maintain their independence."[40] When Georgia senator Alfred Iverson explained his advocacy of secession, he said that the South rode on the horns of a political dilemma. On the one hand, the Republicans kept gaining in the North; on the other hand, the northern Democrats continuously grew weaker—"We cannot close our eyes to the fact, according to our notions of soundness, at least upon this Territorial question, the Northern Democrats who may be relied on, 'like angel's visits, are few and far between.'"[41]

Douglas must have operated under the assumption that a powerful argument could convert the bulk of the Democrats to his point of view. Oratory had been his chief weapon all his political life. He was in no mood to abandon popular sovereignty but was even more convinced that he needed to press its righteousness upon the Democratic Party. When the congressional session ended, he did not return to Illinois but stayed with his young wife at their home in Washington, D.C. He decided to write a history of popular sovereignty, showing that the founders had applied the principle to the territories from the very beginning, and that to understand the break between the colonies and Great Britain, an understanding of popular sovereignty was essential. Using resources in the Library of Congress and obtaining assistance from historian and fellow Democrat George Bancroft, Douglas produced an article for *Harper's Monthly Magazine*, which, unusual for most politicians, he copyrighted. The article was entitled "The Dividing Line between Federal and Local Authority: Popular Sovereignty in the Territories," and it fell into readers' hands in September. Douglas provided a few twists to his doctrine but basically covered old ground. The article provoked responses in the South and from President James Buchanan, who had the attorney general, Jeremiah S. Black, write a rebuttal. The exchange illuminated nothing, Douglas and his opponents assuming positions they had always taken and offering no concessions whatsoever.

In the fall of 1859, Douglas had been invited to speak in various cities in Ohio to assist the Democrats in state elections. He did so, stressing popular sovereignty and the foulness of the Buchanan administration. Ohio Republicans thought this would be a good moment to pit Douglas against his old Illinois nemesis, Abraham Lincoln, so they asked Lincoln to canvass Ohio as well. Douglas continued to press his arguments for popular sovereignty on the public, and just as earnestly, Lincoln sought to discredit these arguments. Lincoln was perhaps still worried that the Republican Party might adopt popular sovereignty instead of standing foursquare against the expansion of slavery. Douglas must have wondered what he had to do to get rid of this lanky doppelganger who constantly intruded on his public speaking tours.

The Lecompton battle and the struggle over Kansas revealed a Gordian knot about democracy that Douglas did not want to confront: the failure of people to live by the will of the majority. He had ducked this possibility, as had many northerners, because somehow or other he (and they) refused to grapple with the material and social strength of the peculiar institution. But the problem was general in any system of governance, perhaps more poignantly so with democracy. Some understanding of the limits of obedience to the law had to be acknowledged, and no one took the time to be so enlightened. And so this Gordian knot was not solved but was allowed to grow larger, tighter, and more ominous.

Notes

1. CG, 34-3, 852.
2. J. G. Freze to James Buchanan, November 15, 1856, Buchanan Papers.
3. SAD to McClernand, November 23, 1857, in Douglas, *Letters*, 386, 403.
4. Johannsen, *Douglas*, 586.
5. CG, 35-1, appendix, 146, 148.
6. CG, 35-1, 1243.
7. CG, 35-1, 235.
8. CG, 35-1, appendix, 329.
9. CG, 35-1, appendix, 199–200.
10. CG, 35-1, appendix, 137.
11. Memorandum of Interview of Burlingame and Colfax with Douglas, at his residence, December 14, 1857, Schuyler Colfax Papers, IndHS.
12. A. S. Johnson to SAD, March 26, 1858, Douglas Papers, Uchi.
13. O. S. A. Peck to SAD, December 9, 1857, Douglas Papers, Uchi.
14. H. B. Payne to SAD, April 9, 1858, Douglas Papers, Uchi.
15. William W. Cable to SAD, April 10, 1856, Douglas Papers, Uchi.
16. John A. Gilmer to W. A. Graham, February 23, 1858, in *The Papers of William Alexander Graham*, ed. J. G. DeRoulhac Hamilton, 5 vols. (Raleigh, NC, 1961–1973), 5:37–38.
17. John Wentworth to Lincoln, April 19, 1858, Lincoln Papers, LC.
18. Lyman Trumbull to Lincoln, January 3, 1858, Trumbull Papers, LC.
19. Johannsen, *Lincoln-Douglas Debates*, 14, 18, 19, 20.
20. Johannsen, *Lincoln-Douglas Debates*, 45.
21. Johannsen, *Lincoln-Douglas Debates*, 27, 130.
22. Johannsen, *Lincoln-Douglas Debates*, 130.
23. Johannsen, *Lincoln-Douglas Debates*, 92, 95, 100.
24. Johannsen, *Lincoln-Douglas Debates*, 151, 201–2.
25. Johannsen, *Lincoln-Douglas Debates*, 88.
26. Johannsen, *Lincoln-Douglas Debates*, 53.
27. Johannsen, *Lincoln-Douglas Debates*, 46.
28. Johannsen, *Lincoln-Douglas Debates*, 200.
29. Johannsen, *Lincoln-Douglas Debates*, 14, 197.
30. *New York Times*, November 6, 7, 1858.
31. Ben Blackmore to John G. Davis, December 25, 1858, Davis Papers, State Historical Society of Wisconsin.
32. CG, 35-2, 1242, 1243.
33. CG, 35-2, 1244, 1246–47, 1258, 1259.
34. Pugh, CG, 35-2, 1247, 1251.
35. Johannsen, *Douglas*, 692–93.
36. Joseph C. G. Kennedy to Alexander H. H. Stuart, September 28, 1859, Stuart-Baldwin Family Letters, University of Virginia Library, Charlottesville, Virginia.

37. S. G. Dodge to John G. Davis, July 13, 1859, John G. Davis Papers, State Historical Society of Wisconsin.

38. *Jackson Semi-Weekly Mississippian*, September 27, 1859.

39. George W. Thompson to SAD, February 11, 1859, Douglas Papers, Uchi.

40. *New York Herald*, July 11, 1859.

41. (Milledgeville, Ga.) *Southern Recorder*, October 4, 1859.

CHAPTER SIX

~

The Election of 1860

The northern Democratic Party was dying, and Stephen A. Douglas knew it. He also knew the disease: the issue of slavery. At one time, the party bestrode the nation, conquering all, and now it looked like a withered old man. With his victory over Lincoln and the near resurrection of the Illinois Democratic Party, Douglas felt reinvigorated and hopeful; he decided to return the national party to its glory years, and to do that, his interpretation of popular sovereignty had to triumph in the councils of the party. To accomplish the feat, he needed to obtain the presidential nomination in 1860. The Gordian knot of democratic equality that he faced, however, was minority acquiescence to majority rule. Douglas had struggled with the issue in the controversy over Kansas; now he confronted it in the Charleston Democratic Convention.

The Speakership Fight, 1859–1860

Both Douglas and his wife, Adele, struggled with sickness in the fall of 1859, just when the nation encountered one of its most wrenching events. The abolitionist John Brown gathered a small troop of men, momentarily seized the federal arsenal at Harpers Ferry, Virginia, and issued a call for the slaves to revolt. John Brown had always been an abolitionist and a religious zealot, his seething rage at slavery fueled by his experiences in Bleeding Kansas in 1856. His attack on the armory was poorly planned and even more poorly executed. No slaves revolted. In a few days, he was taken prisoner, and in a few more weeks, he was tried for treason by a Virginia court, was found guilty, and was then hanged on December 2.

Shortly thereafter, the first session of the Thirty-sixth Congress convened, and southerners were outraged at the Brown invasion. A panic swept over the South as inhabitants sought out abolitionists and insurrectionists. For southerners, the Brown invasion changed the nature of the quarrel over slavery; no longer was it merely about the hypothetical existence of slavery in the territories; now it was about whether northern fanatics would inflict on the slaveholding states one insurrectionary attack after another. If such were the case, of what value was the Union? The purpose of Union, according to the preamble of the Constitution, was domestic security; living under constant fear of invasion by northern zealots was anything but domestic security.

Douglas was unable to respond immediately to the event because of his battle with Attorney General Black, and then sickness, but his ultimate reaction was entirely predictable. Brown was a religious fanatic, and his fanaticism had been fed by Republicans and abolitionists who had continuously given the public horror stories about slavery and the foulness of southern civilization. Religious passion filled their speeches, and that passion led to outrageous attacks on southerners. At first the blows had been verbal; with John Brown, the attacks had become physical. Douglas and all Democrats North and South found John Brown to be the logical result of Republican doctrines. They pointed out the folly of religious extremism and the need to understand the dilemmas of slaveholders.

Brown's raid and the results of the elections of 1858 made the start of Congress vexing and dangerous. Because of the Republican sweep in 1858, the numbers of northern Republicans and Democrats were almost even, the balance of power being held by a few border state opposition leaders. Thus the election of a speaker of the House became difficult. Douglas worked to get a Democrat elected speaker, but he and his followers were viewed suspiciously by everyone else. Southern Democrats thought the Douglasites no better than Republicans, and the Republicans looked contemptuously upon Douglas for not breaking with the Democrats. Eventually William Pennington of New Jersey was elected speaker on February 1, 1860, and the organizational agony of the House was over.

Preparing for the Charleston Convention

A presidential contest loomed in 1860, and Douglas intended to make sure he was the Democratic nominee. Twice he had been thwarted in his quest for the nomination, and he wanted no repeat of the mistakes he had made earlier. To ensure victory, he started early by creating a committee to promote his candidacy. The committee, headed by Virginia-born newspaperman A. D. Banks, opened an office in New York City and attracted helpers to send out

Douglas speeches and maintain correspondence with important Democrats. A campaign biography of Douglas, to be written by James Sheahan, was to be ready for the public by 1860.

In the midst of this activity, Douglas worked to make sure popular sovereignty became the leading platform of northern state Democratic conventions, especially in the Great Lakes area. The conventions that met between December 1859 and March 1860 followed his wishes. The Douglas machine also had success in New England and managed to obtain satisfaction from the tricky, faction-ridden convention of New York. Pennsylvania was more problematic, as it was Buchanan's home state, but even there some pro-Douglas movement was evident.

Southern Democrats gave Douglas a difficult problem. Because of his opposition to the Lecompton Constitution and his subsequent formulation of the Freeport Doctrine, Douglas had lost much popularity in the South and had inspired a fierce opposition among radicals because of his supposed abandonment of southern rights. Southern fire-eaters now demanded a slave code for the territories, by which the federal government was committed to protect property rights in slavery. Jefferson Davis and Albert G. Brown created resolutions to this effect and refined them sufficiently to present them to the Senate in early March; they were labeled the Davis resolutions. The Davis resolutions may have subtly permitted the Freeport Doctrine to operate, but the subtlety was wasted on Douglas and most northern Democrats. What the Davis resolutions represented for northerners was a direct repudiation of popular sovereignty.

The Alabama State Democratic Convention committed a grievous folly. Under the direction of fire-eater William L. Yancey, the delegates adopted a platform that mirrored the ideas in the territorial slave code, but then they went on to threaten that if such ideas were not put into the national party platform, the Alabama delegates would withdraw from the convention. Throughout the South, the action became known as the Alabama platform. Other Democratic state conventions also called for the territorial slave code, although not threatening withdrawal. And so the two forces kept building, with northerners demanding popular sovereignty, and southerners insisting on a territorial slave code.

A few southern individuals and editors supported a Douglas nomination, but the general sentiment was that Douglas was not acceptable to the South. "The South is united, to a man against him," wrote Ethel Barksdale to Jefferson Davis.[1] But no southerner matched the prominence of Douglas as a potential presidential nominee. Virginia's Robert Hunter was frequently mentioned as a candidate, it was known that Howell Cobb harbored presidential ambitions, and Kentucky endorsed former secretary of the treasury James Guthrie. None of them really had national credentials, leaving southerners without a viable alternative to Douglas.

Some individuals wanted to crush Douglas's political career: the Indiana senators Bright and Graham Fitch, the Louisianan Slidell, Secretary of the Treasury Cobb, Secretary of War Floyd, and probably President Buchanan. Once again, the Buchanan administration rolled out the patronage power in an effort to undercut Douglas. The Buchanan-Douglas feud continued to be an open wound in the Democratic Party.

Nonetheless, the personal animosities that came to dominate the Democratic Party in 1860 had a basis in a deep division over the slavery issue. That question and all its implications inflamed personal hatreds and loyalties. True, certain southerners admitted that no territory currently owned by the United States threatened to evoke the slavery question again; the issue had become an "abstraction." Yet behind the southern stand was the belief that the ultimate fate of slavery was at stake; the subject of slavery in the territories foreshadowed how northerners in the future would treat the peculiar institution when in control of the federal government. In this respect, the doctrine of popular sovereignty worked as injuriously to the slaveholder as did the Republican platform of outright prohibition. With the whole North turning against them, southerners demanded some sign that sanctity of property rights in slaves would be observed, and the territorial slave code controversy was entirely about the sanctity of property rights.

On the part of northern Democrats, and especially those of the Old Northwest (Great Lakes states), popular sovereignty became a doctrine that Democrats could not forgo and still call themselves Democrats. As his father-in-law, James Madison Cutts, wrote Douglas, popular sovereignty "is one of those eternal truths which must prevail. It lays at the very foundation of our government. It is the foundation itself."[2] The notion that people ruled by voting in elections and that the majority should rule was the heart of the Democratic Party; it was the equality among citizens that Democrats strove for in the 1830s. For several decades, northern Democrats had surrendered to southerners on one ideal after another about slavery until they were left with but one: fundamental, primitive democracy. To abandon the ideas of equality of citizens, voting, and majority rule was almost equivalent to abandoning the purpose of democracy. During the campaign, Douglas's correspondents over and over stressed not the issue of slavery in the territories, but holding true to the principle of democracy.

The Charleston Convention

In April 1860, delegates to the Democratic National Convention converged on Charleston, South Carolina, the city that was to play host to their meeting. A malignant fate could not have chosen a worse place for the Democrats to gather. Hot and humid, the city's climate only exacerbated tensions. And Charleston was home to the people who held the most extreme form of states' rights doctrines.

The convention started on Monday, April 23, and then suddenly found itself listless for nearly a week. After the opening-day ceremonies, the delegates voted to let the platform committee finish its task first, then have the delegates vote on a platform, and then turn to the selection of presidential and vice presidential nominees. But the platform committee deadlocked over the doctrines to bring forth. One group favored a territorial slave code—the southerners on the committee. Another desired a confirmation of the Cincinnati resolutions of 1856, plus an additional plank affirming the faith of the party in the *Dred Scott* decision—the view of Douglas's supporters. The third position was simply to readopt the Cincinnati platform. Efforts at alternative wording or ambiguous phrasing failed.

The Old Northwest Democrats held firm in their support of Douglas and popular sovereignty, but in the first few days of the Charleston meeting, they were unsettled by the hostility surrounding them. Douglas's managers wrote and telegraphed him almost daily about the passage of events. Just before the opening day, Murray McConnel told Douglas, "I am surprised at the bitterness of some of our Southern opponents."[3] As the first speeches were delivered, Douglas managers felt that the "ultras," if not given their demands, would disrupt the party: "There is much feeling & many reckless assertions made by our Southern extremists."[4]

During the convention, prominent congressional politicians visited to promote their favorites or to denigrate Douglas; chief among the latter was John Slidell, supposedly the mouth of Buchanan at the convention. Slidell wanted Douglas defeated, and when he saw that he could not crack Douglas's support in the northern Democratic Party, he encouraged the southern states to act on their pledge of secession if they did not obtain a territorial slave code provision in the platform. Evidently Slidell thought the northerners would then cave in, compromise their position, and ask the seceding states to rejoin the convention. How much his personal animosity toward Douglas determined events is impossible to gauge, but its presence was noted.

The platform committee finally admitted their inability to resolve the differences dividing them. On Friday, April 27, the committee submitted three reports to the delegates to vote on: the majority report containing a territorial slave code, the minority report embracing popular sovereignty, and a second minority report calling for readoption of the Cincinnati platform. Northern and southern representatives clashed over the merits of the majority and minority reports, the climax coming in an exchange between Yancey and Ohio senator George Pugh. Yancey stressed the need for northerners to give southerners new guarantees about the security of slavery and then lectured the northern Democrats that their great error was to have ever admitted that slavery was morally wrong. Pugh countered vehemently that the North was not going to bow to southern dictation: "you mistake us—you mistake us—we will not do it."[5]

On Monday, April 30, the showdown finally arrived. By this time, many of the delegates were simply angry and stubborn. This was especially true of the Douglas delegates, who had formed an indissoluble bloc. The second minority report by Ben Butler was eliminated by a vote of 105 to 198. Then the numerically superior northerners took the prize by voting for adoption of the minority report—the popular sovereignty platform—by a vote of 165 to 138. Representatives of the Cotton South sullenly watched proceedings thereafter and refused to vote. Former Michigan senator Charles Stuart tried to offer an olive branch to them by adding some material to the platform, but he ended up by declaring that he "could never consent to yield his honor, as was demanded of him by the South."[6] Yancey made a brief retort, and then Mr. Walker of the Alabama delegation read a message announcing the withdrawal of the Alabama representatives; he was followed by the chairmen of the delegations from Mississippi, Louisiana, South Carolina, Florida, and Texas. The next morning, Georgia did likewise.[7]

Slidell and administration supporters hoped that the withdrawal of the southerners from the convention proceedings would bring the northern Democrats back to their subservient position, but the Douglas supporters did not flinch. Indeed, not only were the Douglas Democrats mad, but they also calculated that the loss of the Deep South was not so important after all. So far as the majority report was concerned, the Douglas delegates saw it as instant political death: "The addoption [sic] of the majority Report would absolutely annihilate the Democratic party, & the nomination of any man but Douglas would do the same."[8] Another pointed out the electoral reality about the cotton states of the South: Congress in 1860 contained 236 representatives; the southern states that left the convention only had 33; New York by itself had 33. Thus, wrote a New Yorker, if all the Gulf states were lost to Douglas in the election, it only amounted to "30 to 35 electoral votes, or fully made up by the almost certain gain of New York, Pennsylvania, and Ohio."[9]

The Great Lakes Democrats turned their backs on the Deep South and tried to nominate Douglas. However, various northern delegates and Border South delegates found the split in the party too ominous and refused to back Douglas; the Little Giant did not obtain the necessary two-thirds majority to win the nomination. May 2 saw twenty-three fruitless ballots, and the realization settled in among all the delegates that this convention lacked the capability of making a nomination. On May 3, they agreed to postpone the nomination until June 18, when the Democratic Convention would reconvene in Baltimore.

Back in Washington, D.C., the news of the blowup at Charleston shocked Douglas, and he promptly resorted to some strong doses of alcohol to ease the stress. Somewhat interestingly, his correspondents blamed Buchanan and his agents for the fiasco. Missing in their views was the Republican notion of the Slave Power. Individual southerners worked against Douglas, and certain southerners were fanatics in the same fashion that abolitionists were fanatics, but none testified to the existence of a broad, organized conspiracy among slaveholders to rule the party. Douglas Democrats saw individuals when they looked at the South, not a collectivity.

Certainly miscalculations ruled the day in Charleston—all sorts of convention wire-pullers were betting that people would react to their threats and actions in certain ways. But many understood that beneath the surface of personal dislike ran a strong current of division over basic issues. As Robert Toombs wrote Alexander Stephens, "I am fully aware that personal hostilities and personal advantages are at the bottom of the strife; but there is a right and a wrong to the controversy for all that."[10] Toombs correctly pointed to an unresolvable controversy between the Douglas Democrats and the Deep South. The Deep South wanted guarantees that property rights in slavery would take precedence over all other facets of American political life. Douglas's southern correspondents revealed this. One writer from Augusta, Georgia, explained that the power of a territorial legislature had to be defined "so that it cannot destroy or *injure* the property of the slaveholder," and "the doctrine of popular sovereignty does not intend to give the people of the Territory *absolute* power—they cannot destroy property & as to injuring[,] neither God or man has the right to do this."[11] But Douglas did see popular sovereignty as giving the territorial legislature the power to determine property rights. The issue was the right of the people to define all the laws of their existence by majority voting—that is, democracy—versus the right of an individual to hold property regardless of majority voting, the Gordian knot of democratic control over a propertied minority. When the amount of property involved was substantial, the issue of property rights versus democratic procedures was indeed a perilous question, and the Gordian knot only grew tighter and more complex.

The Baltimore Convention

As the Democrats scrambled to piece together their broken party after May 3, 1860, two other national nominating conventions met. On May 9 in Baltimore, persons forming a new party calling itself the Constitutional Union

Party assembled, adopted the U.S. Constitution for its platform, called for an end to the slavery issue, and nominated John Bell of Tennessee for president and Edward Everett of Massachusetts for vice president. The Constitutional Union Party was an agglomeration of border state conservatives who dreaded the fanaticism of both sections and the drift of the country to separation. But the party lacked organization at the state and local levels, and its candidates failed to inspire the public. The Douglas people were not overly concerned.

More important to the Democrats North and South was the action of the Republican nominating convention. That gathering commenced on May 16 in Chicago, and the delegates proceeded to write a lengthy platform that testified to their awareness of how to win the presidency. They kept their standard anti-slavery issues but then added a slew of issues made popular in the North by the Panic of 1857: they called for a homestead act, a revenue tariff with more pro-tective features to it, a transcontinental railroad, and appropriations for river and harbor improvements. Republicans understood that to win the election they had to win the northern states that voted for Buchanan in 1856: Illinois, Indiana, Pennsylvania, New Jersey, and California. Of these, Pennsylvania and New Jersey were most susceptible to a tariff plea, and so the Republicans made one.

Many Democrats counted on the Republicans to make a strategic mistake by nominating Seward for the presidency. Seward had actually moderated consider-ably since 1856, but his record put him in the advanced antislavery camp. He constantly made phrases that seemed extreme: in 1850 he announced the idea of a "higher law" than the Constitution, and in 1858 he labeled the struggle between the free labor and slave labor states "an irrepressible conflict," thereby seeming to predict future civil war. Against an opponent with this record, Demo-crats figured they would have a strong chance to win the nation's moderates and conservatives. But the Republicans were too wily to turn Democratic dreams into reality. On May 18, they rejected Seward as their nominee and turned to Abraham Lincoln, a person with a less antagonistic record on sectional affairs, and one who had a distinct appeal to moderates and conservatives based on his law-abiding constitutionalism.

Lincoln's view of Douglas was somewhat dark, for he in many ways consid-ered Douglas to be something of a demagogue, and one who had consistently beaten him for political office since the mid-1830s. Douglas, however, praised Lincoln for his debating skills and honesty. Some felt that the unknown Lin-coln would be easy prey for Douglas in the national canvass, but others believed it would be a bitterly fought and close contest.

During the Constitutional Union and Republican conventions, the Senate commenced debate on the Davis resolutions on federal protection of slavery in the territories. Douglas, enfeebled by illness, delivered a response on May 15 and 16. He gave his standard speech on the wisdom of congressional non-intervention in the territories. This oration was not of his usual quality, but two important points came out strongly. First, he raised the question of fundamental democratic rule: "Can you preserve the [Democratic] party by allowing a minority to overrule and dictate to the majority? Is the party to be preserved by abandoning the fundamental articles of its creed. . . . Shall the majority surrender to the minority?"[12] Here was the Gordian knot and Douglas's recognition of it: what extreme southerners demanded was that the Democratic Party sacrifice democracy, and on this demand Douglas would countenance no concession. The second point was electoral politics pure and simple. Prior to the slavery issue, the North had been the land of Democratic victories: "[W]hen we had a non-intervention platform . . . the North was Democratic." Surveying the political landscape in 1860, Douglas told his peers to look at the dismaying results the party had suffered because of the slavery extension issue; the Democrats had lost "New Hampshire, Rhode Island, Connecticut, New York, Pennsylvania, and Ohio." "I should like to know," he queried, "how many States will be 'certain,' if you repudiate the Cincinnati platform . . . [and adopt] up this new one, this Yancey flag of intervention by Congress for slavery in the Territories in all cases where the people do not want it."[13]

Davis's resolutions passed the Senate on May 24, and the debates added no new ideas. Congress then careened to a conclusion in June. No new tariff was passed, much to the anguish of Pennsylvania and New Jersey Democrats, and again a transcontinental railroad required a different Congress for action. A homestead bill was passed and then vetoed by President Buchanan. He had earlier vetoed a bill for deepening the St. Clair Flats in the Detroit area. When all of his vetoes were put into a list, and when one adds to that list the failure of Congress to enact tariff revisions and a plan for a transcontinental railroad, the inevitable conclusion is that the Buchanan administration was a total failure in economic policy. Here were the issues that might have enticed northern conservatives and moderates into the Democratic Party, but Buchanan and the South said almost in a collective voice, "Go elsewhere." And so they did: the conservatives and moderates migrated to the Republican Party and Abraham Lincoln. A wiser perspective on economic issues might have had a powerful effect on the outcome of the election of 1860.

Before the Democratic convention reconvened in Baltimore, Democrats in the South fought over the legitimacy of the delegates who seceded. Many southern Democrats wanted to elect new slates. In most of the cotton states, the Douglas operatives organized new conventions and elected different individuals to attend the Baltimore gathering. The appearance of new southern delegations altered the strategy of the Charleston seceders and forced them to attend the national meeting as well.

The Democratic Party finally broke into sectional fragments in June. The Charleston seceders met as planned in Richmond, Virginia, on June 11, and promptly decided to go to Baltimore to see if proceedings there might permit their reinstallation as delegates; South Carolinians refused to attend; and Floridians only went as observers. On Monday, June 18, the second half of the 1860 Democratic Convention commenced in Baltimore. The northwest delegation remained firmly in control and was determined not to recognize the seceders. Among the northern delegates was the general feeling that the South had too long dictated the fortunes of the party and that the northern Democrats had borne too much popular disfavor for obeying southern commands. As one writer expressed the situation to Douglas, "If our former co-partnership can be no longer maintained unless by dishonorable concession and base servility, 'let the union slide.'"[14]

The great fight at Baltimore was in the credentials committee. For four days, the committee tried to resolve which slate of delegates would be allowed to sit, the Charleston seceders or the newly elected delegations. The committee produced a majority and a minority report; the minority report favored seating the Charleston seceders, while the majority report, reflecting the views of the Douglas managers, recognized the newly elected state delegations. Actually, much compromising did go into the majority report, as various previously elected individual delegates were readmitted, as well as some entire state delegations. On the fate of Alabama's seceders, however, the Douglas managers would not budge: under no circumstance were Yancey and his colleagues to regain accreditation.

Douglas now reassessed his claims to the presidential nomination. On Tuesday, he wrote to his manager at Baltimore, William A. Richardson, to withdraw his name for the nomination, but only if the platform adopted nonintervention in the territories. Richardson showed the letter to no one; he wanted the showdown. A frustrated Douglas then sent the same letter on Thursday to his lieutenant in the New York delegation, Dean Richmond. But Richmond let Douglas know that the time had passed when such tactics could solve the crisis. A showdown over control of the party and its standards had to come to a head.

On Friday, June 22, the North-South breach of the Democratic Party became complete. The seceders were not allowed back into the convention. Before nominations were taken up, a Virginia delegate announced the withdrawal of his state's delegation. He was then followed by the rest of the Border South; the only slave states remaining on Saturday were Missouri and Arkansas. Douglas then received the nomination from the remaining delegates. The convention chose Benjamin Fitzpatrick of Alabama for vice president, but he later turned it down. The Democrats replaced him with Herschel V. Johnson of Georgia. And so the official national Democratic Party had become a sectional party representing the North, with Stephen A. Douglas at its head.

Southerners were not going to enter the election of 1860 without a candidate. Thus the bolters from both Charleston and Baltimore traveled to Richmond, and on Tuesday, June 26, they nominated John C. Breckinridge for president and Joseph Lane of Oregon for vice president. This group, claiming to be the official Democratic Party but actually lacking a name, now represented the South. The Democratic Party had split into sectional halves.

All of the nominations for the election of 1860 were fundamentally bizarre. The candidates had backgrounds that clashed with the cultural attributes of the majority of adherents to their party. The Republicans, supposedly reflecting New England morality, selected a nominee reared in a border slave environment and whose lack of church attendance was notorious. The Democratic nominee hailed from New England. The proslavery states' rights faction nominated Breckinridge, but he, it was reported, "*is rich, lives in the South, and owns not a cent's worth of slave property!*" John Bell, the candidate willing to place the Union above slavery, "is no richer than John C. Breckinridge but every cent he has accumulated after a long life, has been invested in the peculiar institution of the South."[15] Except for Douglas, personalities did not necessarily play a dominant role in the election of 1860. The platforms did. Unlike many or even most elections in the United States, the 1860 contest had an ideological polarization that can be understood only by comparing the platforms, not by comparing the candidates.

The Campaign of 1860

Parties that divide into autonomous fragments during an election invite the Grim Reaper to their election watch party. When the Democrats split into northern and southern halves, everyone knew that the fate of the Democratic Party was sealed and that the likelihood was Republican victory. Douglas may have partially acknowledged his desperate situation, but it was not in his personality to brood, ponder, and moan. Douglas was a fighter. A victory was always possible with enough work and persuasion. He took to the national stage the way he took to the Illinois stage: a Herculean speech-making effort that would bring the population to his side by dint of his oratorical powers.

Douglas and his organization never exactly laid out their plan to capture the election, but certain parts of it can be deduced. He expected to reinvigorate the northern party and again win the northern states that had once hoisted the Jacksonian banner—Maine, New Hampshire, Rhode Island, Connecticut, and the Great Lakes states. He knew Pennsylvania, New York, and New Jersey were more problematic, but not lost. He expected to take much of the South—Missouri, Arkansas, Louisiana, Texas, Alabama, and Georgia. Perhaps his hopes were so high because of the illustrious people enlisting in his cause, like Alexander H. Stephens, and because his correspondence from these states was so promising. Early in the campaign, he misjudged the appeal of the Breckinridge Democratic Party, believing that the party could only win South Carolina and Mississippi. The rest of the South, he felt, belonged to the Constitutional Union Party. Behind these estimates was a reasoning based on the election of 1856. Then Buchanan had won because the Republicans had not captured the Fillmore vote (Know-Nothings), and many conservatives had voted for the Democrats. He would hammer a campaign message that he stood for conservatism and abhorred sectionalism, thereby swaying the Fillmore voters to his standard.

Republicans honed their strategy to a single point: winning the northern states they had lost in 1856—Illinois, Indiana, Pennsylvania, New Jersey, and California. They expected a bitter fight with Douglas in many of them, but they recognized that the two important states of Pennsylvania and New Jersey were susceptible to a tariff appeal. As one informed Lincoln, the tariff "*was the all absorbing question here in Pennsylvania*," and correspondents especially related how the political winds in that state were blowing.[16] Republicans did not fret much about the Constitutional Union Party, Lyman Trumbull calling it "a perfectly dead affair."[17]

Exactly how the Breckinridge Democrats expected to win is something of a mystery. The strong men of the Breckinridge party perhaps hoped that Douglas would agree to forgo his campaign and join in a general fusion movement behind another candidate to thwart Lincoln's election. As soon as the Baltimore convention ended, talk of fusion filled in the air, especially in the states on the East Coast. Early in the summer, Jefferson Davis had proposed that Breckinridge, Bell, and Douglas all withdraw in favor of some other candidate. Douglas refused; by this time, his supporters were so angry at the actions of the seceders that they would have defected to the Republicans if Douglas had withdrawn. Northern Democratic Party operatives seethed in anger at their southern brethren.

Douglas would fight fusion for the rest of the campaign, and except in New Jersey no adequate union of the anti-Republican forces occurred. Douglas might have resisted fusion at first because he initially thought he had a chance at winning, but later in September, he fought for the future of the Democratic

Party. The idea of a federal slave code for the territories was certain death for the northern Democratic Party; the only standard that could bridge the sectional divide for the national Democratic Party was nonintervention in the territories. At least in part, Douglas continued his campaign in 1860 to preserve the Democratic Party's ideological integrity.

In previous presidential elections, candidates stayed at home, made no speeches, and let others do the campaigning for them. Americans had developed a tradition that the office called "disinterested" men to government service, and it was unseemly for a presidential candidate to seek personally the votes of the people. Douglas at first intended to obey this custom but then reconsidered. In early July, he decided to conduct an extensive speaking tour of the nation, and in it he would lay before his countrymen the necessity of defeating extremism.

Douglas began by traveling to New England on July 14, ostensibly to visit his family and New England birthplace, but he commenced giving speeches, and everyone understood his real purpose. In his initial appearances, he established *most* but not *all* of the themes of his campaign. Crowds appeared when he arrived in cities, and he responded by talking to them from balconies at hotels. He delivered one of his long addresses at Boston on August 17. He naturally stressed popular sovereignty and self-government. He attacked sectionalists North and South for violating the principle of nonintervention. The nation had to move beyond the slavery issue, or the "irrepressible conflict" would become reality. He then belittled the slavery question for distracting Congress from other measures—the tariff, the homestead act, the Pacific Railroad bill, and internal improvements: "Thus you find that all the great measures which affect the commercial, the manufacturing and the industrial interests of the whole country are lost for the want of time!"[18] Wherever he went, he paid homage to the Whigs, who had once favored compromise to preserve the Union; at Boston, Douglas made a dutiful allusion to the "god-like Webster."[19] He hoped his praise for the old Whig giants would sway former Whig supporters to him.

From Boston Douglas traveled to Springfield, Massachusetts; to Saratoga and Troy, New York; to Concord, Nashua, and Manchester, New Hampshire; and then to Providence and Newport, Rhode Island. Toward the end of August, his New England tour ended. To his Boston speech, he added two other themes. At Concord, he put forward the race issue in the same fashion as he had in his debates with Lincoln: "In my opinion, this government is the white man's government. ('That's so.') It was made by white men for the benefit of white men, and it ought to be administered by white men."[20] When he was in Rhode Island, he attended a clambake, and he used the occasion to show people how the states had a variety of climates and conditions that necessitated local government—that is, popular sovereignty—to allow people to write laws pertinent to their own environment. This was the reason the federal government should be noninterventionist, because one set of laws could not possibly work over such a vast nation as the United States, where climate and geography differed so dramatically.

He set the tone for the Douglas Democrats and of course invited criticism from officials of the other parties. It did not go unnoticed that the subject of slavery in the territories seemed exceptionally hollow as a live political issue because no one knew of any territory where the question might produce a controversy. Breckinridge Democrats in the South refused to yield on the subject. Fitzpatrick, who had turned down the vice presidential nomination, explained that Douglas had "good qualities," and except for the territorial question, "no one among Northern Democrats has more boldly and manfully sustained the constitutional rights of the South." But, Fitzpatrick added, Douglas made slavery in the territories "*the* issue," and "I tell you, my friends, that the South, if she would preserve her equality and the equality of her citizens, can not and never should surrender it." So far as the Breckinridge supporters were concerned, Douglas made the question of the territories the major issue, and if "the Union is in danger from anybody, it is Douglas."[21]

In the South, Douglas forces were weak. Herschel Johnson, Douglas's running mate, simply wrote, "I do not think [Douglas] can carry a single Southern State."[22] The major battle was between the Bell and Breckinridge parties. They fought over which party could better protect slavery. Bell forces also painted the Breckinridge leaders as traitors seeking to destroy the Union.

Republicans found the Douglas campaign disconcerting, but it did not detract from their basic method of attack. Republicans stressed free labor principles, the damage slavery did to northern society, the power of slaveholders over national affairs, and the economic issues that the Panic of 1857 had resurrected. As for Douglas, Republicans ate away at his pronouncement that economic issues had failed in Congress because of the slavery issue. John Sherman in Ohio cried that Douglas was "the greatest dodger that ever was in Congress," because he dodged the issues of the tariff and homestead.[23] Republicans also belittled the principle of popular sovereignty, with Massachusetts Republican Charles F. Adams stating that the doctrine was "sadly lacking in morals."[24] A Wisconsin Republican denounced Douglas's use of Rhode Island clambakes to glorify the principle of popular sovereignty; how could any rational person compare decisions about a clambake with decisions about human slavery?[25]

A few Republicans were willing to concede much to the doctrine of popular sovereignty and express admiration for Douglas's willingness to take his message directly to the people. An editorialist for the *New York Times* wrote that popular sovereignty was in fact the ideal of nine-tenths of the population, and that popular sovereignty was making the territories into the land of free labor, not Republican demands for congressional prohibition of the peculiar institution. And Douglas had traits that endeared him to the public: "He represents more thoroughly than any other public man that quickness of intellect, vigor of will and pushing restlessness of temper which characterize American life." But, concluded the editor, victory for popular sovereignty in debating arenas and admiration for his great oratorical skills would not elevate him to the presidency. The people would vote for the Republicans because they represented "democratic conservatism."[26] It was, as Douglas well knew, an uphill battle for him regardless of his past debating triumphs.

When Douglas was in Newport, Rhode Island, he laid plans to take his message to the South, to enter Virginia and give a set of speeches to dispel the disunionism that filled southern oratory. He arrived at Norfolk on August 25 and was giving his usual speech when he was handed two questions from a reporter from the *Southern Argus*, the reporter being a Breckinridge supporter. The first was whether Douglas believed the South would be justified in leaving the Union if Lincoln were elected. "I emphatically answer No," he declared. As long as the election was conducted in a constitutional manner, no one was justified in taking such radical action. The second question was, if Lincoln were elected, and before he committed an overt act against the South and the South seceded, would Douglas advise or vindicate resistance by force to the act of secession: "I answer emphatically," Douglas thundered, "that it is the duty of the President of the United States and all others in authority under him, to enforce the laws of the United States, as passed by congress and as the Courts expound them. [Cheers.]" Douglas insisted that the Constitution was "a remedy for every grievance that may arise within the limits of the Union." While the right of revolution existed for all people, governments should not be altered for ephemeral reasons. If a president disobeyed the Constitution, as southerners feared, then Congress could drive him out of office by impeachment. Then he added a very key understanding of his rejection of secession. Under the Constitution, all obtained equal and just rights. Remedies for infractions existed and had to be used before any violence was employed. But the price for a Constitution and equal rights was "obedience to the constitution and the constituted authorities of the country."[27] The Norfolk speech was a thunderbolt to many southerners. It was one thing for Republicans to talk about the illegality of secession, but quite another for the nation's most prominent northern Democrat to do so.[28]

Douglas continued to warn southerners about precipitate action. At Raleigh, North Carolina, he gave a two-hour speech that stressed nationalism. The Union was built on emotional attachment: "You cannot sever this Union unless you cut the heart-strings that bind father to son, daughter to mother, and brother to sister in all our new States and territories." Moreover, the Union must be preserved because "we are the greatest nation on earth in many respects," and the future had more marvels in store; the United States "are the admiration of all who love free institutions, while we are the terror of all tyrants." So long as the Constitution was obeyed, no justification for secession existed.

While at Raleigh he delved into the issue that had divided the Democratic Party into sectional halves. He defended his idea of popular sovereignty in his usual way and then went into a subject that he never raised when in the North: southern property rights in slaves. Here he reiterated his belief that no state could write the laws of property for a territory, because all the states had different laws about property, and this cacophony of laws could not be made harmonious. Therefore it was better to leave such questions to the settlers themselves:

> I will accept no privileges for Illinois that I will not guarantee to North-Carolina; and I will not claim the right in the territories for my citizens or for my property that I will not guarantee for every other state in the Union. I believe in the absolute and unconditional equality of all the States of the Confederacy. (Applause.) But I claim that I have the right to go into the territories and to carry my property with me and hold it there, and to have it protected on the same terms that you have in the slaveholding states. ("Good.") But upon what terms, I ask, can I carry my property into the territories? I carry it there subject to the local law.[29]

And so Douglas justified the Freeport Doctrine before a southern audience.

At Raleigh and later at Baltimore, he provided an interesting insight as to how he viewed the peculiar institution. He said it was all determined by climate and geography. He reduced the question entirely to self-interest: "Slavery was a question of political economy. People bought where they could buy cheapest, and sold where they could get the best price. So in regard to the employment of negro labor: where it was cheapest it would be employed: where white labor was cheapest slave labor would be excluded."[30] His understanding of the economics of slavery was epitomized in a standard joke he delivered to southern audiences: Illinois abandoned slavery because it "was not profitable[;] they could not make any money out of it, hence they turned philanthropists and abolished it. [Laughter and applause.]"[31] In these sentiments, he was radically different from both Republicans and proslavery intellectuals. By this reasoning, he had no fears, as did Lincoln, that slavery could ever plant itself economically in the North. Black slaves were simply an economic choice, no different really than choosing whether to plant corn or oats.

His speaking tour took a heavy toll on his health. Not long after he entered the southern states, reporters noticed his voice becoming difficult to hear. When he went back into the northern states, audiences found his voice raspy and cracking, his appearance disheveled, and his face weary. He faced criticism for his open campaigning, but most often people understood his purpose: to argue for the Union and against secession. The crowds that greeted him were huge.

When he reached Harrisburg, Pennsylvania, in September, he altered his address to include the important tariff issue. The reason Congress, he shouted, never passed a "proper tariff" was that the "cry was 'the negro!' 'The negro!' and the tariff bill was lost."[32] Douglas's record on the tariff was well known, and according to one Republican at the event, his discussion of the defeat of the tariff "brought down a loud spontaneous *guffaw* from the crowd."[33] Douglas understood the needs of the Pennsylvanians—his mention of the tariff issue was unique in his oratorical efforts—but he evidently had turned his back on usual special interest appeals because of his struggle with southern radicals and the Buchanan administration. For Douglas, the crisis over slavery and the territories had to be resolved first if the Democrats were ever to rise again to national glory.

From Harrisburg, he traveled to numerous northern cities, finally arriving at Chicago on October 2. During his northern portion of the trip, he emphasized that he was the legitimate candidate of the Democratic Party, but most of his speeches were highly repetitive, only changing in some small way. Northern Democrats responded well to Douglas's efforts, but they did not mimic all his arguments. They did not forgo their heritage of hostility to banks, corporations, and large government. A few indicated their willingness to allow slavery to expand if climatic conditions permitted. Such arguments, however, were dwarfed by one attack the northern Democratic Party made: they charged that the Republicans believed in "Negro equality" and would make blacks equal to whites. As the election rolled into October, the Democrats grabbed the race issue and pressed it upon the public with all their might.

Douglas hoped that the New England Democratic Party would revive and provide encouragement to other Democrats when Maine and Vermont held state elections in September. Those elections gave the Republicans a thumping victory, and Democratic hopes evaporated. Efforts at fusing the tickets of the anti-Republican parties grew ever stronger, especially in the key states of New York, Pennsylvania, and New Jersey. Herschel V. Johnson came north to campaign for Douglas and came away impressed with the crowds that Douglas drew. "I have never seen such enthusiasm"; no living man "has so deep a place in the hearts of the N.W. Dem[ocracy] as Douglas." Johnson had always been pessimistic about the party's chances for victory, "but I must say I have hope of N.Y. Pa. Indiana and Ohio. The Ground Swell in the N West is tremendous."[34]

October was a cruel month for the Democrats. The large states of Ohio, Pennsylvania, and Indiana voted on state races on October 9, and two of these states had been won by Buchanan in 1856. Such was not to be the case in 1860: Pennsylvania yielded a 30,000 vote majority for the Republican gubernatorial candidate, in Indiana the Republicans won the governorship by a 10,000 vote majority, and in Ohio the Republican candidate won a state supreme court judgeship by 13,000 votes. Everyone knew the race was over. Lanphier editorialized, "The result of the recent elections has knocked the Democracy of Illinois into spasms."[35] In the South, talk of secession became serious and widespread.

Douglas rested a few days in Chicago during the first week of October, but he knew his travels were not over. He planned to visit several places in the Great Lakes states; when he learned of the Pennsylvania election, he knew that his chances for the presidency had died. He also knew that southerners did not jest when they talked of secession. Therefore, he would have to tour the South again, arguing for the Union and against secession. In October, he made speeches in Detroit; Springfield, Illinois; and St. Louis. He then turned south and went to Memphis, Huntsville, Nashville, and Atlanta, among other southern cities, and finished his sojourn at Mobile. By this time, secession sentiment and anger at the North were growing, especially in the Gulf states, and threats were made against Douglas taking his unionist message into the realm of King Cotton. On one occasion, a few eggs were thrown at him.

His speeches covered much the same ground he had covered previously. He presented his case for nonintervention in the territories and told the audience that the destruction of the Democratic Party at Charleston was the work of evil plotters. When in the South, he repeated his answers to the Norfolk inquiries to let southerners know that peaceable secession was a lunatic's dream. Moreover, he insisted that constitutional safeguards were still in place to stop any Republican from menacing slavery in the states. In his speech at Atlanta, lasting two hours and twenty minutes, he reiterated his belief that only local law determined what objects were to be considered property and given protection.

Increasingly, though, a special American Gordian knot about democratic equality was coming to the forefront. Douglas always had assumed that local government and democracy were nearly synonymous, that states' rights meant democratic government. Throughout the South, the cry was raised that the equality of the states was being destroyed, that states' rights were being violated. Yancey made the dilemma between states' rights and democracy clear. Yancey announced that the only issue in the presidential election was "*the existence of the union and the safety of the institution of slavery.*" He attacked Douglas for being a covert Republican because he believed "that majorities should rule by force of numbers. They [Republicans and Douglas] said that as the principle that the majority should rule was the fundamental principle of government, they would vote down the minority." After complaining about federal policy, "Mr. Yancey then proceeded to show that the doctrine of the supremacy of mere numbers would destroy the equality of the States."[36]

Yancey was not fair to Douglas, because Douglas's view of popular sovereignty always included minority rights and states' rights as spelled out in the Constitution, but he hit a basic Gordian knot concerning democracy. Douglas did believe in majority rule, probably the central theme of his life. He came face to face with those who would not accept majority rule, even when conducted wholly within the confines of the Constitution. This problem had been building since the Lecompton Constitution controversy, and now it could not be avoided. States' rights were possibly a democratic doctrine, but possibly not. And in the aftermath of 1860, the possibilities turned negative.

Douglas was in Mobile the day of the election, and two days later he left for New Orleans. The telegraph had given him enough information to know that Lincoln had been elected by sweeping the North and obtaining 180 electoral votes, quite a few more than the 152 needed for a majority in the electoral college. Douglas only won the state of Missouri and a portion of New Jersey's electoral vote due to a fusion formula, for a meager total of 12 electoral votes. But the total votes cast probably caught Douglas's eye as well: Lincoln 1,864,735; Douglas 979,425; Breckinridge 669,472; Bell 576,414; and fusion 595,846—the fusion vote coming primarily from New York, New Jersey, and Pennsylvania.[37] Most of the fusion votes were Democratic Party votes. Assuming that the fusion vote was largely a Douglas vote, the Little Giant garnered about 1.5 million suffrages, more than double the total earned by the Charleston bolters' candidate.[38]

Beyond these summary figures were some interesting results for the Democratic Party. The election saw a Republican sweep of the New England states, taking all the congressional races while earning 61 percent of the vote. Democrats fared poorly in congressional contests in the Great Lakes and Mid-Atlantic regions, where Republicans elected eighty congressmen to thirty-three for the Democrats, but did better than they had in 1858. But the popular voting figures showed a somewhat less dismal story. Lincoln won the North by taking 1,838,347 votes, or 53.9 percent of the northern popular vote. Douglas earned, when the fusion vote is added, about 41 percent of northern votes. The northern Breckinridge voters (3 percent) were still Democrats, and it was uncertain where the northern Bell supporters belonged. All totaled, then, the Democrats were still a powerful party, taking in some 45 percent of the northern electorate. This large portion of the North could not be ignored on any issue touching secession. If the Democrats had sided with peaceful secession, the Republicans would have been in a precarious position trying to prevent it.

Douglas had little time to muse over the numbers, however, because he faced the last and greatest Gordian knot of democratic equality of all: the right of a disaffected group to break the rules of democracy and leave the polity entirely.

Notes

1. Barksdale to Davis, February 20, 1860, in Dunbar, *Letters of Davis*, 4:196.
2. J. M. Cutts to SAD, February 27, 1860, Douglas Papers, Uchi, series 2, box 2, folder 12.
3. Murray McConnel to SAD, April 22, 1860, Douglas Papers, Uchi.
4. Charleton C. P. Culver to SAD, April 24, 25, 1860, Douglas Papers, Uchi.
5. David M. Potter, *Impending Crisis, 1848–1861*, ed. Don E. Fehrenbacher (New York, 1976), 409–10.
6. *New York Tribune*, May 1, 1860.
7. *Harper's Weekly*, 4 (May 12, 1860): 294.
8. Samuel Smith to SAD, April 30, 1860, Douglas Papers, Uchi.
9. Magnus Gross to SAD, May 1, 1860, Douglas Papers, Uchi.
10. Robert Toombs to A. H. Stephens, June 9, 1860, in Ulrich Bonnell Phillips, ed., *The Correspondence of Robert Toombs, Alexander H. Stephens, and Howell Cobb* (Washington, D.C., 1911), 481.
11. C. F. W. Bay to SAD, May 7, 1860, Douglas Papers, Uchi.
12. CG, 36-1, appendix, 316.
13. CG, 36-1, 2153, 2144–45.
14. John W. Cook to SAD, June 12, 1860, Douglas Papers, Uchi.
15. *Weekly Vicksburg Whig*, September 19, 1860.
16. William M. Reynolds to Lincoln, August 1, 1860, Lincoln Papers, LC.
17. Lyman Trumbull to Lincoln, June 8, 1860, Lincoln Papers, LC.
18. *Boston Herald*, July 18, 1860.
19. *Harper's Weekly*, 4 (July 28, 1860): 470.
20. *Boston Herald*, August 1, 3, 1860.
21. *Milledgeville Federal Union*, September 11, 1860.
22. H. V. Johnson to Judge Cochran, July 6, 1860, H. V. Johnson Papers, Duke University.
23. (Columbus) *Ohio State Journal*, September 3, 1860.
24. *North American and United States Gazette* (Philadelphia), August 29, 1860, clipping in Adams Family Papers, Massachusetts Historical Society, Boston.

25. John Potter, "A Few of Douglas' Sage Remarks in His Speech Delivered at Augusta, August 16, 1860," in John F. Potter Papers, SHSWisc.

26. *New York Times*, June 26, 1860.

27. *New York Times*, August 29, 1860.

28. *Lynchburg Daily Virginian*, August 29, 1860.

29. *(Raleigh) North Carolina Standard*, September 5, 1860.

30. *New York Times*, September 7, 1860.

31. Atlanta *Daily Southern Confederacy*, November 1, 1860, Douglas Papers, Uchi, box 44, folder 3, clipping.

32. *Philadelphia Evening Bulletin*, September 8, 1860.

33. Joseph Casey to David Davis, September 16, 1860, contained in Lincoln Papers, LC.

34. H. V. Johnson to Alexander H. Stephens, October 1, 1860, Herschel V. Johnson Papers, Duke University.

35. *Ill St Reg*, October 12, 1860.

36. *New York Times*, September 27, 1860.

37. Vote totals taken from Potter, *Impending Crisis*, 443.

38. The contemporary figures can be found in the *Tribune Almanac* for 1861, p. 64, which differ slightly.

~

CHAPTER SEVEN

Secession and the Limits of Democracy, 1860–1861

The last Gordian knot of democratic equality that Douglas faced was the subject of secession. In nineteenth-century political philosophy, republics or democratic forms of government possessed a special, unique quality: the basis for all political action was consent of the governed. Aristocratic, monarchical, or any other type of government operated by coercion—the few controlled the police power and forced the masses to obey their dictates. Republics operated on consent, not coercion. What happened, then, when one group became so disaffected with the will of the majority that they tried to withdraw from the body politic? Here was for democracies the most convoluted of all Gordian knots: the dilemma of consent versus coercion, of obtaining the consent of the citizenry to abide by majority rule without having to resort to coercive measures to obtain that obedience. Stephen A. Douglas had many fundamental differences with the Republicans, but not on the nature of the Union. It was his and his party's ideal of democracy that permitted a united North to war on the South. Without the northern Democratic Party's assent to use force against a seceded state, no war between the sections could have occurred.

The South Secedes

As Douglas was journeying back North after the election of 1860, he received a request from New Orleans leaders for guidance on the current national situation. He complied by writing a letter on November 13 that sounded the themes that many unionists would use over the next six months. First, Lincoln had been elected wholly within the rules of the Constitution, and therefore no rights had been abridged, and no one could claim the election as a just cause for dissolution. Moreover, Republicans did not have control of Congress; they had fared less well in the northern states in 1860 than they had in 1858, and so Democrats, aided by the southern opposition party, could thwart any impolitic laws that Republicans tried to pass. Moreover, Lincoln could not wield patronage powers without the consent of a Democratic Senate. If Lincoln did not execute the laws fairly, he could be impeached and removed. Therefore, southerners had no reason to secede. Some might indeed wish for a southern confederacy, but all who "regard the Union under the Constitution . . . the most precious legacy ever bequeathed to a free people by a patriotic ancestry" would disavow any recourse to a dissolution of the nation.[1]

A weary Douglas left New Orleans and went to Chicago for a few weeks before returning to Washington, D.C., on December 1 in preparation for the second session of the Thirty-sixth Congress. His mind was fixed on finding some compromise solution to the rift dividing the South and North. He would not countenance peaceable secession, and he abhorred the idea of federal coercion of a state; that left only the path of compromise. There were those who despaired of a solution. Douglas could be that way too, but not for long. He was a battler, pure and simple, and the necessity for compromise was simply another battle into which he had to pour all his talents and energies.

Attempts to compromise depended on an understanding of what was creating the division. Douglas was mired in the controversy of slavery in the territories and failed to see the powerful commitments and fears motivating that controversy. Douglas basically ascribed the problems of his time to hysterical emotionalism either for or against slavery; the demon he faced was fanaticism. He understood northern dislike of slavery, but he never understood northern fear of it. Both the "Slave Power" and the "free labor" viewpoints were alien to him. Likewise, southern trepidation over northerners tampering with their property failed to impress him. Douglas seemingly never extended southern fears about slavery beyond the territorial question—he never saw that the South's demand for an ironclad guarantee that their interpretation of property rights in slavery would reign supreme arose from their acute anxiety about the stability and longevity of the peculiar institution.

On the nature of the Union, Douglas had more opinions in common with the Republicans than with southerners. The Constitution was a government of mutual consent. Peaceable secession by the action of only one member of the consenting group was inadmissible; consent from all the members had to be obtained. Separation was indeed possible in the American framework, but not separation by individual states acting on their own.

Searching for Compromise, Winter of 1860–1861

When Congress convened on December 3, it did so under the dark cloud of an impending South Carolina secession. Immediately after Lincoln's election, the state legislature had called for an election of delegates to a state convention to determine its continuance in the Union. On December 20, South Carolina voted to end their membership in the United States of America.

President Buchanan offered no help in the impending crisis. His message to Congress stated that state secession was a false doctrine but that the federal government nevertheless had no power to coerce a state. Congress eventually created a House committee and a Senate committee to devise a compromise solution that would dissipate the fears of the states desirous of separation. The Senate committee was composed of thirteen members, Douglas being one of them; the group contained three northern Democrats, five Republicans, and five slave state senators.

In this Committee of Thirteen, John J. Crittenden of Kentucky took the lead in proposing a series of amendments to the Constitution that would end the slavery controversy. Among his suggestions were an extension of the Missouri Compromise line to the California border, a prohibition against any constitutional amendment seeking to abolish slavery, preservation of slavery in the District of Columbia, prohibition of federal regulation of the interstate slave trade, and new legislation on runaway slaves. The southerners on the committee would only agree to these amendments if northern Republicans agreed; it had been determined that a true compromise required more than a mere majority of the vote of the committee; both northerners and southerners had to accept the proposals. The Deep South senators, Jefferson Davis and Robert Toombs, said they would accept the proposals, but they wanted the Republicans to do so first. The Republicans on the committee, led by Benjamin F. Wade, did not accede to the compromise. The great sticking point for the Republicans was the resurrection of the Missouri Compromise line, because the party position was no further extension of slavery. The Republicans interpreted their victory in 1860 as a sign that their constituents wanted an absolute prohibition on the expansion of the peculiar institution.

Douglas attempted to bridge the gap with his compromise solution. He offered two complex amendments to the Constitution, much of which was similar to Crittenden's plan. However, parts of it reflected a concession to the race fears of southerners. He would not allow states and territories to legislate citizenship and voting rights to blacks, and free blacks would be set upon a path of colonization abroad by use of federal funds. The committee did not tarry long on Douglas's work and quickly scuttled it. By December 28, the committee reported to the Senate that it had been unable to formulate a working compromise.

Meanwhile, the health of the Union worsened. Other southern states soon followed South Carolina: Mississippi on January 9, Florida on January 10, Alabama on January 11, Georgia on January 19, Louisiana on January 26, and Texas on February 1. Douglas took Crittenden's proposals directly to the Senate in January in an effort to get some action. But the Republicans sat silent and unmoved by the plight of the nation. And slowly Republican power in both the House and the Senate increased because as southern states left the Union, their senators and representatives left the Congress of the United States, intending never again to return as elected officials of that government. Efforts to have the Senate pass the Crittenden resolutions failed in the face of Republican intransigence.

Southern explanations about why they were leaving the Union left no doubt that they were obsessed with the preservation of slavery. Southerners simply could not project a safe, profitable future for themselves with a Republican administration hostile to slavery and its expansion. They offered numerous rationales for their action, but at the bottom of their complaints was the conviction that their whole society—economically, socially, and politically—rested on the foundation that slaves were property, and they feared that northerners were willing to violate those rights of property. Wrote a Virginian to Douglas, all southerners were agreed "that negroes are property and should be treated as such."[2] In his memoirs, the New York Democrat John A. Dix admitted that the "cause of the secession movement was, beyond dispute, a belief on the part of the slave-holding States that their slave property was imperilled by their association with the Northern States."[3] And this is why southerners raved so much about northern fanaticism: fanatics cared nothing for property rights.

At the same time, the Republicans continued to fear the Slave Power and how slavery affected free labor societies. In their view, exemplified by the new president Abraham Lincoln, slavery's strength came from expansion. Allowing slavery to expand was equivalent to resuscitating the Slave Power and letting it endanger northern society. As Lincoln said, denying slavery further expansion put the institution on the path of "ultimate extinction." For this reason, as well as the enormous political one of keeping their northern constituency satisfied, Republicans could accept a constitutional amendment agreeing that slavery could never be ended by constitutional amendment. Republicans did not expect the demise of slavery via that path; they expected it to die as a result of nonextension.

Given the two sides, it becomes obvious why the Crittenden Compromise solution was unpalatable in one way or another to both Deep South southerners and Republicans. Resurrecting the 36°30' line gave slavery new life via potential expansion if the nation ever went into a Manifest Destiny phase again; Republicans therefore could not countenance it. For southerners, the amendments merely nibbled around their rights without guaranteeing them. They wanted an outright declaration from the North that slaves were property and would be treated as property by the federal government in all matters. That route led to the possible nationalization of slavery, which northerners absolutely abhorred. No compromise was possible, because the issue had escaped the bounds of the territorial question and now centered on the future of slavery itself.

Douglas's inability to grapple with the deeper roots of the problem was shown when the Republicans proposed the creation of three new territories, Colorado, Nevada, and Dakota. Republican leaders wrote statutes of territorial organization for the three areas without reference to slavery. Douglas chortled that here was proof that the Republicans accepted popular sovereignty. Republican senators turned red in embarrassment at Douglas's truthful assessment of the final disposition of the territorial issue. One Republican senator, Oregon's Edward D. Baker, admitted as much.

But what Douglas missed was why Republican submission to popular sovereignty was insufficient to end the sectional crisis. Douglas had always predicted that the outcome of popular sovereignty would be free states. The Republicans finally accepted Douglas's analysis and felt no need to prohibit explicitly the establishment of slavery in their legislation. The reason, though, was because Republicans knew they would win. And southerners knew by this time, that under popular sovereignty they would always lose. The losing side was not going to surrender by simply admitting that the electoral process made someone else a winner. Too much—the future—was at stake. If the Republicans had thought a territory might vote in slavery, then they would have rushed a Wilmot Proviso into the legislation. Southerners wanted guarantees about the sanctity of their property rights in slaves, and popular sovereignty gave them no such guarantees. For these reasons, Douglas's hopes for reconciliation based on popular sovereignty and federal nonintervention never had much chance of success.

As the days passed, and as a Confederate States of America took shape in Montgomery, Alabama, Douglas frantically tried to move Congress into passing some measure that would assuage the feelings of the South and bring the seceded states back into the Union. He supported Virginia's initiative in calling for a peace conference to be held in Washington, D.C., starting on February 4 and to be attended by delegates from all the states. The conference met but drew few delegates and produced only a reiteration of the Crittenden proposals. Douglas's greatest efforts to obtain a compromise was to goad the Senate into approving a constitutional amendment stipulating that slavery could never be abolished by a constitutional amendment. The measure had passed the House but was bottled up in the Senate. February turned into March, and on the last day of the session, Douglas pleaded for a vote on the amendment. He obtained it on March 4 (at 5 a.m., just before the inaugural), and the amendment passed by the needed two-thirds majority. Immediately thereafter, the other Crittenden Compromise measures were brought up and roundly defeated by the Senate Republicans.

Douglas found the Republicans almost incomprehensible in their stand against compromise. In some ways, he was right. By his willingness to accept the Missouri Compromise line as a new basis of settlement for the territorial issue, Douglas was sacrificing his doctrine of popular sovereignty. Why could Republicans not sacrifice some of their doctrines to save the Union? What he did not comprehend was the Republican fear of the effects of slavery. Douglas saw no warping of northern life because of the existence or expansion of slavery, so he could afford to jettison some of his doctrines to preserve the nation. For the Republicans, however, expansion of slavery was exactly the reason the North was in danger of losing its freedom and economic might; they therefore believed they could not abandon their stand of prohibiting the spread of slavery.

Douglas attempted desperately to thwart the separation of the states, fighting as he had both antislavery and proslavery radicals the whole of his congressional life. His war against extremism has to be positioned in the general framework of slavery's impact on the nation and what the future might bring. Douglas had his own version, but it was only one interpretation among several. To this day, evaluation of Douglas's efforts entirely depends on how one comprehends the framework of the sectional controversy and how one understands the power and longevity of slavery.

Douglas believed slavery was an impotent and transitory institution, or at least one can deduce that from his statements. He never subscribed to the Slave Power argument of the Republicans, and during the winter of secession, he and his correspondents blamed Buchanan and his political lieutenants more than southern fire-eaters. Free labor ideals did not pour from his lips. He assumed no natural antagonism between slavery and free labor societies, believing entirely in a climatic and racial theory of slavery. Certain politicians—individuals, not groups—sought dissolution for their own bizarre reasons and aroused irrational passions and fears among the people. These were the enemies: passion and unreason. If only the United States could get past the immediate issue of Kansas, time would prove those passions wrong. No necessary conflict existed between the sections; they were economic complements of each other, not economic competitors. In this interpretation, if Lincoln had not been elected in 1860, no civil war would have occurred. And the projection was essentially true: *if* Douglas had been elected in 1860, *then* the South would never have left the Union, not even South Carolina. Southerners might have fumed and fussed about popular sovereignty, but Douglas was a known friend, certainly no enemy, to the peculiar institution.

But this interpretation merely covers the immediate problem of 1860. What of 1864, or 1868, or 1872? Was the antagonism between slavery and the North more deeply rooted, such that the condition of hostility never relented? Other interpretations hold that a permanent conflict existed and that no single presidential election was ever going to remove it. Scholars have offered explanations of the sectional division based on a conflict of moral values, the necessity of white southerners to control race relations, the agricultural needs of the plantation South that demanded continuous landed expansion, the inherent conflicts between free and slave labor in a national market setting, and the need of southerners to control federal legislation so as to ensure no depreciation of their slave assets. All of these interpretations assume an unceasing conflict between a northern free labor society and a southern slave labor society.

Whose view of North-South differences was correct? Was there an inherent conflict between slavery and free labor, between slave societies and free societies, that no compromise could overcome? Or was the problem of slavery—especially slavery in the territories—a transitory issue that once gotten over would produce no further friction? A reader's assessment of Douglas's wisdom, actions, and solutions concerning the territorial issue all depend on the reader's assessment of the power and strength of the institution of slavery in the fabric of the nation.

Politicians, the Parties, and Secession

Congress did not compromise, and everyone knew that that avenue of escape from the actions of the Cotton States increasingly looked like a dead end. The options became acceptance of southern secession, resistance to it by armed force, a change in the popular mind of the South favorable to the Union, hope for a reunion in a few years, or some other as-yet-undreamed-of alternative. The question of the legitimacy of secession, begun during the election of 1860, now governed public discourse.

Radical southern views admitted no possibility of error in their analysis. Southerners had a theory about the Constitution, and their theory was the obvious transcendental truth of the matter. There was no Union; it was instead a confederation of sovereign states that could exercise their right to leave whenever they wanted. Secession was a "reserved right" of the states under the Tenth Amendment to the Constitution. So long as some states were grievously disaffected, the binding force of sentiment was gone anyway, and the Union was basically dissolved. Wrote J. C. Cabell to William Rives in Virginia, "I yet cannot avoid the conviction that there can be no union between Sovereign States without a cordial consent of both parties. That is no Union in the sense of the constitution which has to be maintained at the point of the bayonet."[4] When the desire to remain in the Union faded, in other words, the Union had already suffered a death, and peaceable secession was the preferable way to end the association with distraught members.

Southern moderates and others had their reservations. Most southerners believed that if a state truly wanted separation, it should be allowed to depart. Others recognized problems with secession. As Archibald Dixon, an old Whig, wrote to Kentucky governor Beriah Magoffin, "A government that cannot prevent its own dismemberment, or execute its own laws, ceases to have any binding force, or be of any value to those for whose benefit it was created."[5] One secession would beget another secession. One North Carolinian wrote Douglas that "a peaceable division of the Union is not admissable for if these States are suffered to Secede and set up a government for themselves, other States may do so without any fear of Consequences[. In] that event Our Government would be only a Government of form but destitute of the power."[6] Secession by the action of one state alone created anarchy; no government could survive under such a condition. On the other hand, if the federal government forced a state to remain in the Union, coercion replaced voluntarism, and the great ideal of a republic—voluntary consent—was lost.

Republicans disliked the principle of secession, though they were divided over the means to deal with their present situation. Republicans saw no just cause for secession—no rights violated, no property endangered. They believed the question of slavery in the territories was not a constitutional question but a subject left to officials elected to office, officials who represented the popular will as revealed in voting. Thus they were hostile to compromise, for the South "want us to concede everything—slavery protection in the territories, right of transit, and all."[7] Part of this angry reaction was a response to the recent past; when southerners controlled Congress and passed laws to their liking, they expected northerners to obey the law. Northerners were furious that now that the shoe was on a different foot, southerners announced their unwillingness to play the role of obedient citizen. This attitude was caught in a news article from England, a clipping that found its way into Douglas's hands. "Public opinion here is strongly opposed to the action of the south upon the election of Mr. Lincoln," wrote the author, "and it is argued that the north having always quietly submitted to the election of a President of adverse politics to their own, the south in turn should follow the example of submission and order."[8] Even still, the question of coercing a state troubled Republicans, and some decided that if distrust between the sections had grown to such a fever pitch, then perhaps separation was best.

On a more general level, Republicans believed secession slapped majority rule right in the face. "[T]he question now is whether the majority or the minority shall rule," wrote one constituent to Simon Cameron; "I go for the majority."[9] Beyond the repudiation of majority rule, Republicans found secession to be anarchy because it dissolved the bond that enabled government to enforce rules. A former congressman wrote to Benjamin Wade of Ohio that he "deplore[d] . . . the opinion so frequently uttered that if a State desires to go, she may be permitted to go. . . . Who has the power to *permit* dissolution, except the people in their sovereign capacity?"[10] If every state determined whether or not its citizens would obey congressional rules, then no central government would ever be possible, self-government would collapse, and the American experiment would be a failure.

Republicans recognized that much of their problem stemmed from the Constitution. The frame of government did not provide a specific mechanism for enabling disaffected citizens of a state to depart. An editor of the *New York Times* said that the only existing means of separation was by a constitutional amendment. Here was the key to the northern side of the situation. South Carolina *could* secede if the other states *consented*.[11] For the Republicans, that was the essential quality lacking in the secession of Deep South states in the winter of 1860-1861: there was no consent among parties, just an obstreperous individualism proclaiming that a state could do whatever it wanted regardless of its obligations to others.

The northern Democratic Party had grievous divisions over the actions of the Deep South states. Northern Democrats expected compromise, and they cursed Republicans for refusing to budge from their platform. More generally, they castigated Republicans for being the authors of all these constitutional problems because the Republicans had insulted and taunted the South for years. Many Democrats, nonetheless, were opposed to secession; disunion, "from any cause, is unpopular with the mass of people here, and with the Democratic party."[12] For most Democrats, the grievous difficulty was the one actually exposed by James Buchanan and for which he was commonly denounced: secession was illegitimate, but coercion of a state by the federal government was unthinkable. Franklin Pierce wrote in the midst of the crisis, "To my mind one thing is clear—no wise man can under existing circumstances dream of coercion."[13]

Douglas, Secession, and Coercion

This was the commentary that surrounded Stephen A. Douglas in the critical months after February 1861. He had hoped to consummate a great compromise like the ones that had saved the Union in the past, such as the Compromise of 1850, but was unable to do so. Like his fellow Democrats, he heaped blame upon the fanaticism of the Republicans, their religious zeal, and their unrealistic fears on the "Negro question." Once compromise failed, however, he had to confront the possibility of coercion. His decisions on these matters were crucial, for he was the titular head of the party. He had earned 41 percent of the suffrages of northern citizenry in the election of 1860, and it was impossible to think that the Republicans could force obedience to the law in a southern state if such action were not backed overwhelmingly by the northern Democrats.

Douglas's comments on secession prior to March 1861 resembled those of the Republicans. While much has been made of the nationalism of Republicans, more attention should be paid to the nationalism of Douglas and the northern Democrats. On questions of Manifest Destiny and the future of the republic, no one had waved the flag with more vigor than Stephen A. Douglas had, and some of the letters sent to him during the secession crisis reflected this nationalism. Moreover, during his tour of the South and in his letter to Democrats in New Orleans, he was already on record opposing secession, stating that southerners had no cause to secede as none of their rights had been violated, that separate state secession was revolution, that the Constitution did not sanction separate state secession, that secession could only be justified by the consent of all parties to the Constitution, that secession was a denial of majority rule, and that the executive had to execute the laws. He also added to this a topic economically vital to the northwest Democratic Party: the Mississippi River was too important an artery of commerce to fall into the hands of another government. Indeed, the fame of his Norfolk answers against secession had initially put Douglas in the "coercion" camp.

But there were vital differences between Douglas and the Republicans as well. For one thing, Douglas and his fellow Democrats never subscribed to the Slave Power interpretation, even during the winter of secession. For Douglas, a few zealots turned the South against the Union, but it was no widespread planter conspiracy, and slavery had not produced a special interest that defied democracy and constitutional government. Perhaps Douglas thought this way because he had such a heavy correspondence with southerners of a unionist persuasion, but even the letters from northerners did not betray a belief in a Slave Power. Northern Democrats found their attitude toward secession and coercion complicated because they agreed with white southerners about the inferiority of African Americans. "As a democrat," wrote one Douglas correspondent, "I do not feel free to engage in a Black Republican, Abolition, Negro fight."[14]

For Douglas and his Democratic following, there were two points about secession that rankled. First, secession obliterated the idea of consent. In a constitutional sense, consent meant agreement among parties; for secession to be legitimate, all parties had to agree to it. Democrats rejected, as did Republicans, the individualism that screamed that a state could do whatever it wanted regardless of the wishes of others. While castigating the Republican leadership to New York financier August Belmont, Douglas nonetheless wrote, "I must say however that I can never recognize or acquiesce in the Doctrine that any State can secede & separate from us without our consent."[15] Someone had evidently sent Douglas a letter written by James Madison about the doctrine of secession after the nation had passed through the Nullification Crisis in 1832–1833. Madison made consent of all parties the cornerstone of a working republic: "Nothing certainly ever passed between us [he and Jefferson], which left an impression that he considered a State, as having a Constitutional or any right to secede from its compact with the other parties, without their consent, or without a breach, or abuse of the compact as absolved the seceding party from the obligations imposed by it."[16] Much of the rising anger of all northerners, Democratic as well as Republican, was the southern dismissal of having to treat with northerners at all in the fate of the Union.

The second subject connected to secession that must have wounded Douglas most deeply was the violation of the principle of majority rule. As he said to the people of New Orleans, he disliked the Republican agenda, he disliked their policies for the West, and he was repelled by their fanaticism; but the Republicans had won the presidency by a legitimate process, and the majority must be obeyed. One individual from Geneva, Illinois, wrote him that "there are around me who feel as I do and as you do that if majorities are to rule and administer their government we will acquies [sic], and support the maintenance of such a government."[17] Douglas obeyed the principle of majority rule when he lost political battles; when he and his fellow Illinois Democrats failed to keep the state from enacting a free banking system, he counseled his party, "We as good democrats are forced to submit to the will of the people when expressed according to the forms of the constitution."[18] When outvoted, the duty of the minority was to obey the will of the majority until the law could be amended or repealed. It was this submission that made democracy and representative government work. If Douglas could do so on a subject close to the heart of all active Democrats—banking issues—why could not the South?

And here was a gaping divide between Douglas and the southern radicals that could not be bridged. The issue of slavery in the territories involved the future existence of slavery in the nation, its profitability, and the racial customs of the South. True, the great issues concerning slavery were about its future rather than its present, but southerners had found slavery so infused into their daily lives that they massively reacted to any threat, no matter how minute, about its future. For them, slavery was fundamental, beyond the machinery of a constitution. Douglas, it seems, never quite grasped the depth of the white South's commitment to slavery, and how for white southerners, that commitment overrode constitutional obligations and the right of majorities to rule.

One subject, however, gave secessionists a chance to succeed in their bid for separation: the fear of coercing a state. Among Democrats, the idea was pervasive that the Union was a collection of states living together by consent, not by force. As one of his Illinois constituents reminded him, the people of the state were "against *coercion*"; "when the North resort to that, farewell to freedom and to all the endearments connected with it."[19] Coercion of a state was the hard place, the right of majorities to rule and constitutional consent was the rock, and Stephen A. Douglas was between them.

Although Douglas seemed to favor state coercion, the passage of several months without incident seemed to wear down his resolve. By March, he was thinking of other options, believing that war would be so awful that it should be avoided. Basically, the more time passed that the seceded states were out of the Union and functioning on their own, the more northern Democrats—if Douglas is any example—came to believe that if the disaffection was too deep and widespread, then perhaps secession was best. Some of his advisers told him to seek reconstruction later when passions had cooled, while others stressed the necessity of keeping the Border South within the Union. Douglas himself had become interested in the German system of the Zollverein, which he had witnessed on his trip abroad in 1853. In the Zollverein, a free trade association was created among independent states; no central government was erected, but the economic benefits of free trade were derived. The United States obtained those benefits via the constitutional prohibition against states hindering interstate trade, and Douglas's Manifest Destiny was economically a way of expanding the American commercial free trade empire by conquest or acquisition. He began rearranging his Manifest Destiny ideas under the impact of Deep South secession. If a commercial empire could not be created by a Union, it might be made by a Zollverein arrangement.

It is important to stress again what was happening. As long as time passed without an incident between armed forces, the Democrats were slowly adapting to the fact of secession, to a dissolved Union. Fear of state coercion was winning over the principles of constitutional behavior by mutual consent and majority rule. The more days that passed without incident, the more likely southern secession would become official and recognized. If the northern Democrats had become accommodated to the Confederate States of America, no civil war would have occurred. Lincoln could not have taken a massively divided North into such a war without inducing internal northern revolt.

President Lincoln, Senator Douglas, and War

Lincoln did not intend to let the South leave the Union, at least not without some kind of consensual agreement ratifying it, and he probably did not see one in the offing. When he arrived in Washington, Douglas quickly asked for an audience and tried to divine Lincoln's policy toward the seceded states. He was not overly successful, as the new president was enigmatic, but many thought that the two Illinoisans were working in harness. On inauguration day, March 4, Lincoln swore the presidential oath of office and prepared to deliver his address. Finding Lincoln stumbling around trying to place his hat somewhere, Douglas, who was on the speaker's platform, stepped up to hold it during the address. Lincoln produced views on secession that were widely held: consent had to be mutual, majority rule was at stake, secession was never a constitutional doctrine, secession threatened anarchy, zealots in the South had deluded southerners into precipitate action, slavery in the territories along with other slavery-related issues were objects of congressional legislation because the Constitution never spelled out specifics, the nation could not be divided geographically, and the president had been charged to execute the laws. At the end of his speech, Lincoln put the decision of civil war squarely on the shoulders of the South. Lincoln would take no precipitate action, but he would hold on to and protect federal property from assault.

Douglas was heard to mutter agreement at various points of the speech, and afterwards he indicated satisfaction at Lincoln's policy. Upon some later consideration, he found himself confused as to what the administration was doing. And the reason for the confusion was simple: Lincoln did not in his inaugural reject the doctrine of coercion of a state. Among Democrats, there was widespread talk and fear of coercing a state; Lincoln's inaugural did not make his position clear except by implication. What Lincoln had said was that he was going to enforce the laws of the land, and he hoped Deep South southerners would reconsider their actions; he did not say that he would not send in troops to protect federal property.

At issue were the fates of forts in the Deep South, especially Fort Pickens in Florida and Fort Sumter in Charleston, South Carolina. Within the administration, there was an animated debate on what to do. Fort Pickens was not an immediate problem, as Florida Confederates and federal officials found a way to coexist momentarily without friction, but Charleston was the center of southern radicalism and immediatism. South Carolinians wanted the federal government out of their harbor. When Lincoln entered the White House, supplies at Fort Sumter were running out, and without resupply, the commander told Washington that he would have to surrender the fort. One supply ship, the *Star of the West*, had tried to take supplies to the Fort, but had been fired upon and had retreated.

Douglas favored evacuating the fort and avoiding a collision with the new Confederacy. He authored resolutions in the Senate to force Lincoln's policy out in the open, but the attempt came to naught. Douglas saw the nation drifting toward final dissolution and evidently was becoming acclimated to the idea, as he began working more on his proposal for a free trade association. Lincoln, though, stiffened on the matter of protecting federal property and Fort Sumter. For him, evacuation meant symbolically the end of federal authority in South Carolina, an action tantamount to acceptance of secession. On March 28, Lincoln determined to resupply the Fort. He sent messages to Charleston and to the Confederate government at Montgomery that the resupply contained no munitions and carried only provisions to prevent starvation of the troops.

And here came one of the great "ifs" of American history. Jefferson Davis, the new president of the Confederacy, met with his cabinet to determine the Confederacy's course of action in light of the Union's attempt to resupply Fort Sumter. Davis's opinion was that if federal authority remained on Confederate soil, it was equivalent to admitting that the Union still ruled the Deep South states, that the Confederacy did not possess sovereignty, and that secession had failed. Therefore, federal troops had to be forced out of Fort Sumter by military action to demonstrate the independence of the Confederate States of America. Robert Toombs, the Confederate secretary of state, warned against military action: it would arouse the North and end the sympathy that northerners had for southern grievances and secession. Toombs lost. On April 9, the Confederate cabinet agreed to end Union occupation of Fort Sumter by military action. The orders came to General P. T. G. Beauregard, and on April 12, his forces bombarded the fortress. It took only thirty-four hours for Major Anderson to surrender, and on April 14, the Confederate flag flew over Fort Sumter.

On the next day, April 15, Lincoln called for enlistments from the states totaling seventy-five thousand men to suppress the rebellion in Charleston. Davis had already been building an army, and Lincoln's proclamation asking for troops to suppress the South Carolina rebellion was greeted by a surge in enlistments. Within a few days, Lincoln's decision to coerce a state led to a second wave of secession, as the upper-South states of Tennessee, Virginia, North Carolina, and Arkansas voted in favor of secession ordinances and joined the Confederacy—but Delaware, Missouri, Kentucky, and Maryland did not. The American Civil War had begun.

Looking at events from a distance, Robert Toombs may have been right. As historian Kenneth M. Stampp has written, the North was gripped with "mass hysteria," superpatriotism, and a passion to avenge its honor by defeating the South.[20] But if the South had not fired on Fort Sumter and physically assaulted northern authority, the Confederacy might have made good on its bid to secede. The northern Democrats were slowly accepting a new status quo of a Union and a Confederacy. The more time played out and the more the hostility between the sections preyed on the idea of a government by consent, the more northerners could find ways to legalize secession of the Gulf states and adapt to new circumstances. If the South had taken no action, Lincoln, being as attentive as he was to political coalitions, might not have on his own forced the issue via military power; he needed the South to act first. A few more months' time, and the northern Democrats might have well let fear of state coercion trump their other principles. When that would have happened, Lincoln might not have been able to mobilize the North against the South, and secession would have become a reality.

The Last Act

After one and one-half decades of turmoil, debate, and sectional acrimony, more than a few northerners were willing to take their anger out on southern pretensions to independence and the flouting of northern constitutional ideas. Douglas was among them. He had not yet made the decision to abandon his beliefs in majority rule and constitutions by mutual consent in favor of the policy of noncoercion of state governments. Illinois had divided sentiments concerning a possible civil war, as many from the southern portion of the state hailed from slaveholding states. A special session of the legislature was called to meet on April 23 to take measures in line with Lincoln's proclamation. Douglas journeyed back to Illinois to address the legislature on April 25, giving short speeches along the way at Bellair, Columbus, and Indianapolis. In an emotional, heart-wrenching speech, he supported Lincoln's decision to use force to preserve the Union. Again, he said that the South had no worthy cause for their actions, that if injustices had been attempted, then constitutional remedies existed. And then the great proponent of popular sovereignty, a major creator of the Illinois Democratic Party, laid down the reason the Union was going to coerce a state: the fundamental principle of the political system of the United States was "that the decision of the people at the ballot-box, without a fraud, according to the forms of the Constitution, was to command the explicit obedience of every good citizen. (Loud applause.)"[21] When he returned to Chicago in early May, he addressed a crowd at the "Wigwam," repeated his insistence that democracy required losers in elections to submit to the will of the majority when constitutional forms were followed, and also said that secession was the work of an "enormous conspiracy" that had to be suppressed. Lurking in the shadows was more than a defeat of a government; the leaders of secession "have destroyed social order, upturned the foundations of society[;] you have inaugurated anarchy in its worst form."[22] Douglas's fear of secession was remarkable for being so similar to the apprehensions of Lincoln.

So ended Douglas's struggle with his last Gordian knot of democratic equality. Democracy was a system of establishing rules by following the principle that the majority of citizens determine policy, so long as those policies do not violate initial, fundamental conditions. What happens when a group becomes so disaffected that it does not obey majority rule? The answer is that democratic government fails. The losers in political contests must accept their loss of control of policy; they may rationalize their loss by trying to win future contests, by continuing to persuade the public, by convincing themselves that the policies they pursued were not so vital to everyday life, but on some level they simply must accept the right of the majority to rule. When a minority refuses obedience to majority rule, democracy ends. Douglas never solved this Gordian knot, but then neither has anyone else. The problem remains: democracy, as a political system, cannot solve fundamental differences in social relations, values, or property arrangements.

Douglas's political journey was over. It was probably best that he did not live to see the agony of his nation and the war's vast physical and human destruction. During the last half of the 1850s, his health had been deteriorating. The ardors of the elections of 1858 and 1860 probably weakened his system further. Soon after his address at the Wigwam, he fell ill, and though he had moments of recovery, his condition worsened throughout the month. Doctors said he had a case of acute, feverish rheumatism and lacked the strength to fight it. He had periods of delirium. In early June, his wife asked a Roman Catholic priest to see him; Douglas was asked if he wished to be baptized; he said, "Never." He had a second chance at seeking baptism and again refused. He then sank further and further into illness. On the morning of June 4, he told his two sons to "obey the laws and support the Constitution of the United States," and then slipped away.[23] He died at nine o'clock in the morning, having only attained the age of forty-eight.

The dilemmas of democracy are eternal, but the mortals who fight the battles are not. Douglas left the discord and reached peace, giving to succeeding generations the task of unraveling the Gordian knots of democratic equality.

Notes

1. "To Ninety-six New Orleans Citizens," November 13, 1860, in Douglas, *Letters*, 502.

2. R. R. Collier to SAD, December 25, 1860, Douglas Papers, Uchi.

3. John A. Dix, "Notes by John A. Dix," 1875, in John A. Dix, *Memoirs of John Adams Dix*, comp. Morgan Dix, 2 vols. (New York, 1883), 1:344.

4. J. C. Cabell to William Rives, November 13, 1860, William C. Rives Papers, LC.

5. Clipping, Arch'd Dixon to his Excellency, Gov. Magoffin, in John J. Crittenden Papers, LC, reel 12.

6. Teho. Williams to SAD, April 1, 1861, Douglas Papers, Uchi.

7. E. W. H. Ellis to Oliver P. Morton, February 7, 1861, in William D. Fouke Papers, IndStLib.

8. "Daily News-England," Douglas Papers, Uchi, box 39, folder 11, clipping.

9. W. Ewing to Simon Cameron, December 27, 1860, Simon Cameron Papers, LC.

10. C. Delano to Wade, December 21, 1860, Wade Papers, LC.

11. *New York Times*, November 13, 1860.

12. George M. Wharton to James Buchanan, November 16, 1860, Buchanan Papers, HSP.

13. Franklin Pierce to Jacob Thompson, November 26, 1860, Franklin Pierce Papers, LC.

14. R. M. Foster to SAD, May 10, 1861, Douglas Papers, Uchi.

15. SAD to August Belmont, December 25, 1860, in Douglas, *Letters*, 505.

16. James Madison to Thomas Jefferson Randolph, December 6, 1833, Douglas Papers, Uchi, box 7, folder 21, addenda.

17. G. Conway to SAD, April 16, 1861, Douglas Papers, Uchi.

18. SAD to Lanphier, December 30, 1851, in Douglas, *Letters*, 235.

19. R. J. Smith to SAD, February 12, 1861, Douglas Papers, Uchi.

20. Kenneth M. Stampp, *And the War Came: The North and the Secession Crisis, 1860–1861* (Baton Rouge, 1950), 288.

21. *New York Tribune*, May 1, 1860.

22. Chicago Address, May 1861, in Flint, *Life of Douglas*, 218, 219.

23. Johannsen, *Douglas*, 871–72.

~

Essay on Sources

Reading both secondary and primary literature over the past thirty years has informed much of the writing of this book. It would be pointless to list all those works here. Instead, I shall give attention only to those works that I found most informative about Douglas and his era.

Douglas Biographies and Primary Material

Rather than start with primary source material, it is perhaps best to begin with the biographies of the Little Giant. There are several good ones, including Gerald M. Capers, *Stephen A. Douglas: Defender of the Union* (Boston, 1959); George Fort Milton, *The Eve of Conflict: Stephen A. Douglas and the Needless War* (Boston, 1934); and Damon Wells, *Stephen A. Douglas: The Last Years, 1857–1861* (Austin, TX, 1971). A surprisingly solid early piece on Douglas was Allen Johnson, *Stephen A. Douglas: A Study in American Politics* (New York, 1908). Douglas's legal and judicial years were revealingly explored by Harry E. Pratt, "Stephen A. Douglas, Lawyer, Legislator, Register and Judge: 1833-1843," parts 1 and 2, *Lincoln Herald* 51 (December 1949): 11-16, and 52 (February 1950): 37-43. However, they have all been superseded by Robert W. Johannsen, *Stephen A. Douglas* (New York, 1973). The Johannsen biography is overwhelming in its mastery of detail, the setting of the context of the age in which Douglas lived, and its exploration into contemporaries' understanding of the Illinoisan. Johannsen also raises important questions probing into the sincerity of Republican appeals and the logic of their argument. For some insightful views of Douglas and the building of Chicago, see Robin Einhorn,

Property Rules: Political Economy in Chicago, 1833–1872 (Chicago, 1991 and 2001). On the fate of Douglas and his control over the inherited Mississippi plantations, see the provocative article, Anita Clinton, "Stephen Arnold Douglas—His Mississippi Experience," *Journal of Mississippi History* 50 (Summer 1988): 56-88. Contained within the biographies of Abraham Lincoln are some interesting observations on Douglas. The most important of recent publications is Stewart Winger, *Lincoln, Religion, and Romantic Cultural Politics* (DeKalb, IL, 2003). Winger gives much information about Young America and stresses correctly Douglas's market orientation, but then pushes it too far.

The primary materials used to write about Douglas include manuscripts, newspapers, and congressional publications. The most important body of papers of Douglas's are now housed at the University of Chicago, and they are massive; a smaller but still valuable set of Douglas Papers resides at the Illinois State Historical Library. The Douglas Papers at the University of Chicago deserve special mention, because while they are so massive and extensive, they yet are in some ways disturbingly silent on many subjects. The national character of Douglas can simply be gleaned from the extent of his papers; they rival the holdings of presidential collections. Yet for a U.S. senator, the letters are surprisingly quiet on political movements during election times, the moment at which most other manuscripts of political leaders gain their bulk. This may be the result of Douglas's extensive speaking engagements, but nonetheless it is striking how few letters detailing political strategy there are in the collection. What is also striking is the enormous demand for Douglas speeches; there are hundreds if not thousands of letters asking for printings of his senatorial performances. Yet few letters discussed issues concretely with him. This difference becomes obvious when the collection in 1858 is compared to the Abraham Lincoln papers (Library of Congress, Washington, D.C.). Correspondents peppered Lincoln with advice about the prominent issues in 1858 and how to handle the Little Giant; by my reading, I don't think the name of Lincoln was mentioned once between August and October 1858 in the Douglas Papers. My impression is that the collection has some large holes in it. The indispensable companion to the letters received by Douglas are the ones he wrote; these are now conveniently collected in Robert W. Johannsen, ed., *The Letters of Stephen A. Douglas* (Urbana, IL, 1961).

Papers of other politicians are important in understanding the context of Douglas's activities and the views that others had of his motivations. Presidential papers were most helpful, as well as those of his fellow Illinoisans. I found especially beneficial the following: from the Illinois State Historical Library at Springfield, Illinois: Nathaniel P. Banks Papers, William H. Bissell Papers, Sidney Breese Papers, Charles H. Lanphier Papers, John A. McClernand Papers, Richard Yates Papers; from the Historical Society of Pennsylvania, Philadelphia, Pennsylvania: James Buchanan Papers; from the Clements Library, University of Michigan, Ann Arbor, Michigan: Lewis Cass Papers; from the Ohio Historical Society, Columbus, Ohio: Joshua R. Giddings Papers and Benjamin Tappan Papers; from the Indiana Historical Society, Indianapolis, Indiana: John Givan Davis Papers and William H. English Papers; from the State Historical Society of Wisconsin, Madison, Wisconsin: James R. Doolittle Papers and John F. Potter Papers; from the Library of Congress, Manuscripts Division, Washington, D.C.: William Allen Papers, Edmund Burke Papers, James H. Hammond Papers, Franklin Pierce Papers, James K. Polk Papers, Alexander H. Stephens Papers, Lyman Trumbull Papers, Martin Van Buren Papers, and Benjamin Franklin Wade Papers.

Given that after 1843 Douglas dealt almost entirely with national issues, congressional sources are absolutely essential to understanding his career. His speeches are contained in the *Congressional Globe*, and his writings on the territories in the Serial Set (publications of the reports and findings of the various committees, as well as communications from the executive branch). Most of this information can now be easily obtained online by going to the Library of Congress website and to the American Memory section (www.loc.gov).

For the numerical details about early Illinois population, occupations, and politics, I relied largely on the census information in published form. Voting statistics came from the *Tribune Almanac* (title varies) and John L. Moore, ed., *Congressional Quarterly's Guide to U.S. Elections*, 2nd ed. (Washington, D.C., 1985). This was at times supplemented by Howard W. Allen and Vincent A. Lacey, *Illinois Elections, 1818–1990: Candidates and County Returns for President, Governor, Senate, and House of Representatives* (Carbondale, IL, 1992); and Theodore Calvin Pease, ed., "Illinois Election Returns, 1818-1848," *Collections of the Illinois State Historical Library*, vol. 18 (Springfield, IL, 1923).

Newspapers served many vital services in plotting out Douglas's career. Not only was the opinion of party leaders found in their columns, but often they were the only places where speeches were recorded. The great New York papers were indispensable: the *New York Times*, the *New York Tribune*, and the *New York Herald*. A biography of Douglas is impossible without the Illinois newspapers, especially the Springfield *Illinois Daily State Register* (earlier the Vandalia *Illinois Daily Register*), the Springfield *Illinois Daily State Journal* (earlier the *Sangmo Journal*), the *Quincy Whig*, the *Chicago Democrat*, and the *Chicago Daily Times* (title varies). Complimenting the Illinois newspapers were Democratic newspapers in the North. They include the following: the *Boston Post*, the *Cincinnati Daily Inquirer*, the *Cleveland Daily Plain Dealer*, the *Detroit Democratic Free Press* (*Detroit Free Press*), the *Hartford Connecticut Times*, the

Pittsburgh Post, the Philadelphia Public Ledger, and the Washington Daily Union. Among the southern papers most informative for this study were the Augusta Daily Constitutionalist (Georgia Weekly Constitutionalist), the Charleston Mercury, the Huntsville Southern Advocate (Alabama), the Jackson Mississippian, the Louisville Daily Courier, the Milledgeville Southern Recorder (Georgia), the Mobile Daily Register (Mobile Register and Journal), the Nashville Union, the Natchez Mississippi Free Trader, the New Orleans Picayune, the Richmond Enquirer, and the North Carolina Gazette. Virginia papers recorded Douglas's speeches during the campaign of 1860 when he went into that state: the Lexington Valley Star, the Staunton Spectator, and the Lynchburg Daily Virginian, as well as the Richmond Enquirer. Monthly and weekly magazines also housed much interesting material; those most useful for a study of Douglas include the American [Whig] Review, Atlantic Monthly, De Bow's Review, Harper's Weekly, Harper's Monthly, Southern Literary Messenger, and the United States Magazine and Democratic Review (United States Review).

Several contemporary books are pertinent to a study of the Little Giant, often because they include several of his more notable speeches. These include James W. Sheahan, The Life of Stephen A. Douglas (New York, 1860); and H. M. Flint, Life of Stephen A. Douglas, to Which Are Added His Speeches and Reports (Philadelphia, 1865). A condensation of Douglas's mature political views can be gleaned from James Madison Cutts, A Brief Treatise upon Constitutional and Party Questions . . . from the Late Senator Stephen A. Douglas, of Illinois (New York, 1866). Other sources yielding information on Douglas include Daniel Roberts, "A Reminiscence of Stephen A. Douglas," Harper's New Monthly Magazine 87 (November 1893): 957–59; Jeremiah Bonham, Fifty Years' Recollections with Observations and Reflections on Historical Events (Peoria, IL, 1883).

Published Collections

Fortunately for historians, the letters and writings of a number of important politicians in the antebellum years have been published. Those most applicable to a study of Douglas would include James Buchanan, The Works of James Buchanan: Comprising His Speeches, State Papers, and Private Correspondence, ed. John Bassett Moore, 12 vols. (1908–1911; reprint, New York, 1950); John C. Calhoun, Works of John C. Calhoun, ed. Richard K. Crallé, 6 vols. (New York, 1856); John C. Calhoun, The Papers of John C. Calhoun, ed. Robert L. Meriwether et al., 25 vols. to date (Columbia, SC, 1959–); Jefferson Davis, Jefferson Davis: Constitutionalist; His Letters, Papers, and Speeches, ed. Dunbar Rowland, 10 vols. (Jackson, MS, 1923); Jefferson Davis, The Papers of Jefferson Davis, ed. Haskell M. Monroe Jr. and James T. McIntosh, 6 vols. at present

(Baton Rouge, 1971–); and Abraham Lincoln, *The Collected Works of Abraham Lincoln*, ed. Roy P. Basler, Marion Dolores Pratt, and Lloyd A. Dunlap, 9 vols. (New Brunswick, NJ, 1953–1955); James K. Polk, *Correspondence of James K. Polk*, ed. Herbert Weaver et al., 7 vols. to date (Nashville, 1969–); Daniel Webster, *The Papers of Daniel Webster*, ed. Charles M. Wiltse and Harold D. Moser, 4 vols. to date (Hanover, NH, 1974). Collections of documents are also important to understanding the era Douglas lived in; ones that I found beneficial were Dwight L. Dumond, ed., *Southern Editorials on Secession* (New York, 1931); Robert W. Johannsen, ed., *The Lincoln-Douglas Debates of 1858* (New York, 1965); and William W. Freehling and Craig M. Simpson, eds., *Secession Debated: Georgia's Showdown in 1860* (New York, 1992).

Biographies

Douglas's great adversary in Illinois was, of course, Abraham Lincoln, and there is no lack of Lincoln scholarship. Among the biographies that are most informative are Don E. Fehrenbacher, *Prelude to Greatness: Lincoln in the 1850s* (Stanford, CA, 1962); Benjamin P. Thomas, *Abraham Lincoln: A Biography* (New York, 1952); Stephen B. Oates, *With Malice toward None: The Life of Abraham Lincoln* (New York, 1977); Brian R. Dirck, *Lincoln and Davis: Imagining America, 1809–1865* (Lawrence, KS, 2001); and Kenneth J. Winkle, *The Young Eagle: The Rise of Abraham Lincoln* (Dallas, TX, 2001). Other biographies of merit include William J. Cooper Jr., *Jefferson Davis, American* (New York, 2000); Lara Gara, *The Presidency of Franklin Pierce* (Lawrence, KS, 1991); Philip Shriver Klein, *President James Buchanan: A Biography* (University Park, PA, 1962); Elbert B. Smith, *The Presidency of James Buchanan* (Lawrence, KS, 1975); Roy Franklin Nichols, *Franklin Pierce: Young Hickory of the Granite Hills* (Philadelphia, 1931); Willard Carl Klunder, *Lewis Cass and the Politics of Moderation* (Kent, OH, 1996); Joel H. Silbey, *Martin Van Buren and the Emergence of American Popular Politics* (Lanham, MD, 2002); Donald B. Cole, *Martin Van Buren and the American Political System* (Princeton, NJ, 1984); Robert V. Remini, *Martin Van Buren and the Making of the Democratic Party* (New York, 1959); Paul H. Bergeron, *The Presidency of James K. Polk* (Lawrence, KS, 1987); William Dusinberre, *Slavemaster President: The Double Career of James K. Polk* (New York, 2003).

Histories of the Period

Of the general histories of the period, the enduring classics are Allan Nevins, *Ordeal of the Union*, 2 vols. (New York, 1947) and *The Emergence of Lincoln*, 2 vols. (New York, 1950); and Roy Franklin Nichols, *The Disruption of American*

Democracy (New York, 1948). The last half century has seen its contributions to antebellum period history as well, probably the most formidable being David M. Potter, *The Impending Crisis, 1848–1861*, ed. Don E. Fehrenbacher (New York, 1976). Also of merit is James M. McPherson, *Ordeal by Fire*, 2nd ed. (New York, 1992). Two recent studies stressing the control of slaveholders over the federal government are Leonard L. Richards, *The Slave Power: The Free North and Southern Domination, 1780–1860* (Baton Rouge, 2000); and Don E. Fehrenbacher, *The Slaveholding Republic: An Account of the United States Government's Relation to Slavery*, completed and edited by Ward M. McAfee (New York, 2001). To round out the critique of slavery, also see Eric Foner, *Free Soil, Free Labor, Free Men: The Ideology of the Republican Party Before the Civil War*, 2nd ed. (New York, 1995).

Works on Illinois

Antebellum Illinois politics has been covered in a number of ways, but the recent literature has been excellent. See James E. Davis, *Frontier Illinois* (Bloomington, IN, 1998); Gerald Leonard, *The Invention of Party Politics: Federalism, Popular Sovereignty, and Constitutional Development in Illinois* (Chapel Hill, NC, 2002); John Mack Faragher, *Sugar Creek: Life on the Illinois Prairie* (New Haven, CT, 1986); Arthur Charles Cole, *The Era of the Civil War, 1848–1870* (1919; reprint, Freeport, NY, 1971); Stephen L. Hansen, *The Making of the Third Party System: Voters and Parties in Illinois, 1850–1876* (Ann Arbor, MI, 1978); Einhorn, *Property Rules*; and James Simeone, *Democracy and Slavery in Frontier Illinois: The Bottomland Republic* (DeKalb, IL, 2000). A book that is standard in the bibliography of Illinois but that is almost incomprehensible to me is Theodore Calvin Pease, *The Frontier State, 1818–1848* (Springfield, IL, 1918).

Jacksonian Politics

The birth of the Jacksonian political system is covered in any number of good works. For the party system as a system, the following historians are vital: Joel H. Silbey, *The American Political Nation, 1838–1893* (Stanford, CA, 1991); Silbey, *The Partisan Imperative: The Dynamics of American Politics before the Civil War* (New York, 1985); Paul Kleppner, *The Third Electoral System, 1853–1892: Parties, Voters, and Political Cultures* (Chapel Hill, NC, 1979); and Richard P. McCormick, *The Second American Party System: Party Formation in the Jacksonian Era* (New York, 1966). All histories of Jacksonian politics start with Arthur M. Schlesinger Jr., who still holds a grasp on the imaginations and the writings of historians; with him began the class analysis of Jacksonian politics and the emphasis on its agrarian, redistributive nature: *The Age of Jackson* (Boston, 1949). Those who have developed Schlesinger's themes or have combated them include the following: John Ashworth, *'Agrarians' and 'Aristocrats': Party Political Ideology in the United States, 1837–1846* (Cambridge, UK, 1983); Ashworth, *Slavery, Capitalism, and Politics in the Antebellum Republic*, vol. 1, *Commerce and Compromise, 1820–1850* (Cambridge, UK, 1995); Harry L. Watson, *Liberty and Power: The Politics of Jacksonian America* (New York, 1990); Charles Sellers, *The Market Revolution: Jacksonian America, 1815–1846* (New York, 1991); Lawrence Frederick Kohl, *The Politics of Individualism: Parties and the American Character in the Jacksonian Era* (New York, 1989). Different depictions of the Jacksonian age can be gleaned from Daniel Feller, *The Jacksonian Promise: America, 1815–1840* (Baltimore, 1995); Robert V. Remini, *The Legacy of Andrew Jackson: Essays on Democracy, Indian Removal, and Slavery* (Baton Rouge, 1988) and Remini, *The Revolutionary Age of Andrew Jackson* (New York, 1976). For the Whigs, one can now turn to Michael F. Holt's encyclopedic *The Rise and Fall of the American Whig Party: Jacksonian Politics and the Onset of the Civil War* (New York, 1999). For the political culture of the Democrats, the best study remains Jean Baker, *Affairs of Party: The Political Culture of Northern Democrats in the Mid-Nineteenth Century* (Ithaca, NY, 1983). The vexed subject of states' rights is given some clarity in Forrest McDonald, *States' Rights and the Union: Imperium in Imperio, 1776–1876* (Lawrence, KS, 2000). Two books are especially informative on the issues of banking and internal improvements: William Gerald Shade, *Banks or No Banks: The Money Issue in Western Politics, 1832–65* (Detroit, 1972); and John Lauritz Larson, *Internal Improvement: National Public Works and the Promise of Popular Government in the Early United States* (Chapel Hill, NC, 2001). The struggle for democracy itself has been somewhat lost, interestingly, among current histories of the first half of the nineteenth century. For a corrective, see Robert H. Wiebe, *Self-Rule: A Cultural History of American Democracy* (Chicago, 1995); a more critical assessment has been made by Stephen John Hartnett, *Democratic Dissent and the Cultural Fictions of Antebellum America* (Urbana, IL, 2002).

In the nineteenth century, religion played a vital role in the life of the nation; its role in the life of Stephen A. Douglas is a more questionable subject deserving more scrutiny. For the general background of religious activity, see Richard H. Carwardine, *Evangelicals and Politics in Antebellum America* (New Haven CT, 1993); Nathan O. Hatch, *The Democratization of American Christianity* (New Haven, CT, 1989); and Daniel Walker Howe, "The Evangelical Movement and Political Culture in the North during the Second Party

System," *Journal of American History* 77 (March 1991): 1216–39. On Douglas
and religion, besides the biographies, see James L. Huston, "Democracy by
Scripture vs. Democracy by Process: A Reflection on Stephen A. Douglas and
Popular Sovereignty," *Civil War History* 43 (September 1997): 189–200.

Manifest Destiny

Manifest Destiny remains a subject undergoing continuous evaluation, much
of it unfavorable to the stand of Douglas and the 1840s Democrats. For favorable views, see Robert W. Johannsen, "The Meaning of Manifest Destiny,"
in *Manifest Destiny and Empire: American Antebellum Expansionism*, ed. Sam
W. Haynes and Christopher Morris (College Station, TX, 1997), 7–20; and
Johannsen, "Stephen A. Douglas and the American Mission," in *The Frontier
Challenge: Responses to the Trans-Mississippi West*, ed. John G. Clark (Lawrence,
KS, 1971), 111–40. Some of the earlier work on Manifest Destiny remains the
best: Albert K. Weinberg, *Manifest Destiny: A Study of Nationalist Expansionism in American History* (Baltimore, 1935); Frederick Merk, *Manifest Destiny
and Mission in American History: A Reinterpretation* (New York, 1963); and
Norman A. Graebner, ed., *Manifest Destiny* (Indianapolis, 1968). Perhaps the
turning point in the historiography came with the analysis of Thomas Hietala,
who stressed that anxiety over eastern conditions rather than optimism about
the West drove the movement; *Manifest Design: Anxious Aggrandizement in
Late Jacksonian America* (Ithaca, NY, 1985). Other informative studies include
Anders Stephanson, *Manifest Destiny: American Expansionism and the Empire
of Right* (New York, 1995); and Linda S. Hudson, *Mistress of Manifest Destiny:
A Biography of Jane McManus Storm Cazeneau, 1807–1878* (Austin, TX, 2001);
Frank Lawrence Owsley Jr. and Gene A. Smith, *Filibusters and Expansionists:
Jeffersonian Manifest Destiny, 1800–1821* (Tuscaloosa, AL, 1997). How Mani-
fest Destiny fit into the general culture of the nineteenth century is presented
by Steven W. Usselman, *Regulating Railroad Innovation: Business, Technology,
and Politics in America, 1840–1920* (New York, 2002). For late-period Manifest
Destiny, see Robert W. Johannsen, *To the Halls of the Montezumas: The Mexi-
can War in the American Imagination* (New York, 1985); and Robert E. May,
The Southern Dream of a Caribbean Empire, 1854–1861 (Baton Rouge, 1973).
An excellent examination of James K. Polk's role in expansionism is Sam W.
Haynes, *James K. Polk and the Expansionist Impulse* (New York, 2002); but also
see Thomas M. Leonard, *James K. Polk: A Clear and Unquestionable Destiny*
(Wilmington, DE, 2001); Dusinberre, *Slavemaster President*; Bergeron, *James
K. Polk*. Questions about Manifest Destiny and the Mexican War are included
in general histories of the westward movement, histories that at times take a

longer view of the forces at work rather than focusing on reactions to contemporary events. The earlier histories tended to be laudatory of the pioneer, the later ones more willing to see the westward movement as a war of conquest and subjugation: Ray Allen Billington, *Westward Expansion: A History of the American Frontier* (New York, 1967); Thomas D. Clark, *Frontier America: The Story of the Westward Movement*, 2nd ed. (New York, 1969); Patricia Nelson Limerick, *The Legacy of Conquest: The Unbroken Past of the American West* (New York, 1987); Richard White, *"It's Your Misfortune and None of My Own": A History of the American West* (Norman, OK, 1991). In this vein, for extra information about Young America, see Stewart Winger, *Lincoln, Religion, and Romantic Cultural Politics* (DeKalb, IL, 2003).

Closely connected with Manifest Destiny was the presence of racist views toward blacks, especially within the Democratic Party. On this subject, see Alexander Saxton, *The Rise and Fall of the White Republic: Class Politics and Mass Culture in Nineteenth-Century America* (London, 1990); Noel Ignatiev, *How the Irish Became White* (New York, 1995); Jean Baker, *Affairs of Party*; Justin Walsh, "Radically and Thoroughly Democratic; Wilbur F. Storey and the Detroit *Free Press*, 1853 to 1861," *Michigan History* 47 (September 1963): 193–225.

Civil War Causation

Douglas's life became most renowned for his attempt to dampen the sectionalism threatening to divide the nation, and thus he figures prominently in works dealing generally with the coming of the Civil War. Many of the interpretations of the causes of the war can be gleaned from the readings in Kenneth M. Stampp, ed., *The Causes of the Civil War*, 2nd ed. (Englewood Cliffs, NJ, 1974). Recent scholarship takes many directions: the breakdown of the political system due to ethnocultural forces among others is given in Michael F. Holt, *The Political Crisis of the 1850s* (New York, 1978); the role of personalities, in John Aldrich, *Why Parties? The Origin and Transformation of Political Parties in America* (Chicago, 1995); the southern need for western land, in Eugene D. Genovese, *The Political Economy of Slavery: Studies in the Economy and Society of the Slave South* (New York, 1965) and Roger L. Ransom, *Conflict and Compromise: The Political Economy of Slavery, Emancipation, and the American Civil War* (Cambridge, UK, 1989); the fear of southerners losing their capital gains from Republican tinkering, in Gavin Wright, *The Political Economy of the Cotton South: Households, Markets, and Wealth in the Nineteenth Century* (New York, 1978); the southern demand for sanctity of property rights in slaves, in James L. Huston, *Calculating the Value of the Union: Slavery, Property Rights, and the Origin of the Civil War* (Chapel Hill, NC, 2003); irrational religious revivalism, in Robert W. Fogel, *Without Consent or Contract: The Rise and Fall of American Slavery* (New York, 1989); the southern code of honor, in Bertram Wyatt-Brown, *Yankee Saints and Southern Sinners* (Baton Rouge, 1985); southern belief in rural, republican values, in Michael A. Morrison, *Slavery and the American West: The Eclipse of Manifest Destiny and the Coming of the Civil War* (Chapel Hill, NC, 1997) and Lacy K. Ford, *The Origins of Southern Radicalism: The South Carolina Upcountry, 1800–1860* (New York, 1988); the fear of southern domination of the nation, in Richards, *The Slave Power*, and Fehrenbacher, *Slaveholding Republic*; the moral issue of slavery, in Potter, *Impending Crisis*; the struggle between wage labor and slave labor in ideological terms, in Eric Foner, *Free Soil, Free Labor, Free Men*, and John Ashworth, *Slavery, Capitalism, and Politics in the Antebellum Republic*, vol. 1, *Commerce and Compromise, 1820–1850* (Cambridge, UK, 1995); and southern demands for sanctity of the domicile, in Stephanie McCurry, *Masters of Small Worlds: Yeoman Households, Gender Relations, and the Political Culture of the Antebellum South Carolina Low Country* (New York, 1995). Historians stressing the institutional weakness of the United States under conditions of acquisition of more land include Brian Holden Reid, *The Origins of the American Civil War* (London, 1996), and Peter J. Parish, *The American Civil War* (New York, 1975). A special issue currently receiving more attention is the developing nationalism in both sections; however, this literature curiously ignores the Democrats at times and especially the 1840s in favor of looking at southern nationalism and northern nationalism: Paul C. Nagel, *One Nation Indivisible: The Union in American Thought, 1776–1861* (New York, 1964); Major L. Wilson, *Space, Time, and Freedom: The Quest for Nationality and the Irrepressible Conflict, 1815–1861* (Westport, CT, 1974); Avery O. Craven, *The Growth of Southern Nationalism, 1848–1861* (Baton Rouge, 1953); John McCardell, *The Idea of a Southern Nation: Southern Nationalists and Southern Nationalism, 1830–1860* (New York, 1979); Susan-Mary Grant, *North over South: Northern Nationalism and American Identity in the Antebellum Era* (Lawrence, KS, 2000).

Most of the general works on the coming of the Civil War cover the train of events in the 1850s, but there are specialized studies to consult. On the Wilmot Proviso, see Chaplain W. Morrison, *Democratic Politics and Sectionalism: The Wilmot Proviso Controversy* (Chapel Hill, NC, 1967); and Eric Foner, "The Wilmot Proviso Revisited," *Journal of American History* 56 (September 1969): 262–79; Frederick J. Blue, *The Free Soilers: Third Party Politics, 1848–54* (Urbana, IL, 1973); and Peter B. Knupfer, *The Union as It Is: Constitutional Unionism and Sectional Compromise, 1787–1861* (Chapel Hill, NC, 1991). On the Compromise of 1850, the standard account is Holman Hamilton, *Prologue to Conflict: The Crisis and Compromise of 1850* (New York, 1964), but now should be supplemented with Mark J. Stegmaier, *Texas, New Mexico, and the Compromise of 1850: Boundary Dispute and Sectional Crisis* (Kent, OH, 1996); see also William R. Brock, *Parties and Political Conscience: American Dilemmas 1840–1850* (Millwood, NY, 1979). On the rise of the Republican Party and the confusions with Know-Nothingism, see William E. Gienapp, *The Origins of the Republican Party, 1852–1856* (New York, 1987), and for reassessments of the Know-Nothings and their influence, consult Tyler Anbinder, *Nativism & Slavery: The Northern Know Nothings & the Politics of the 1850s* (New York, 1992); and Mark Voss-Hubbard, *Beyond Party: Culture of Antipartisanship in Northern Politics before the Civil War* (Baltimore, 2002). A good article on Douglas and the Know-Nothings is Stephen Hansen and Paul Nygard, "Stephen A. Douglas, the Know-Nothings, and the Democratic Party in Illinois, 1854–1858," *Illinois Historical Journal* 87 (Summer 1994): 109–30. On Kansas affairs, see Nicole Etcheson, *Bleeding Kansas: Contested Liberty in the Civil War Era* (Lawrence, KS, 2004); and Paul W. Gates, *Fifty Million Acres: Conflicts over Kansas Land Policy, 1854–1890* (1954; reprint, Norman, OK, 1997).

For the influence of the Panic of 1857, read James L. Huston, *The Panic of 1857 and the Coming of the Civil War* (Baton Rouge, 1987). Somewhat interestingly, the Democrats do not have much of a historiography for the antebellum decade except for a very old one; two recent additions are Jerome Mushkat, *Fernando Wood: A Political Biography* (Kent, OH, 1990); and Jonathan H. Earle, *Jacksonian Antislavery and the Politics of Free Soil, 1824–1854* (Chapel Hill, NC, 2004). The primary study of the *Dred Scott* decision is now Don E. Fehrenbacher, *The Dred Scott Case: Its Significance in American Law and Politics* (New York, 1978). On the elections of 1858 and the Lincoln-Douglas debates, see Richard Allen Heckman, *Lincoln vs. Douglas: The Great Debates Campaign* (Washington, D.C., 1967); Harry V. Jaffa, *Crisis of the House Divided: An Interpretation of the Issues in the Lincoln-Douglas Debates* (New York, 1959), and Jaffa, *A New Birth of Freedom: Abraham Lincoln and the Coming of the Civil War* (Lanham, MD, 2000); Robert W. Johannsen, *Lincoln, the South and Slavery: The Political Dimension* (Baton Rouge, 1991). The effects of the John Brown invasion of Harpers Ferry are fully covered in Steven A. Channing, *Crisis of Fear: Secession in South Carolina* (New York, 1974), and see the contributions in Paul Finkelman, ed., *His Soul Goes Marching On: Responses to John Brown and the Harpers Ferry Raid* (Charlottesville, VA, 1994). For the election of 1860, see Ollinger Crenshaw, *The Slave States in the Presidential Election of 1860* (Baltimore, 1945); Daniel Crofts, *Reluctant Confederates: Upper South Unionists in the Secession Crisis* (Chapel Hill, NC, 1989); and Reinhard Henry Luthin, *The First Lincoln Campaign* (Cambridge, MA, 1944). Of course, biographies of Lincoln, Douglas, and Davis all cover the election of 1860 as well. The secession winter has been investigated by insightful historians: David M. Potter, *Lincoln and His Party in the Secession Crisis*, 2nd ed. (New Haven, CT, 1962); Maury Klein, *Days of Defiance: Sumter, Secession, and the Coming of the Civil War* (New York, 1997); Jeffrey Rogers Hummel, *Emancipating Slaves, Enslaving Free Men: A History of the American Civil War* (Chicago, 1996); Kenneth M. Stampp, *And the War Came: The North and the Secession Crisis, 1860–61* (Baton Rouge, 1950).

Index

~

About the Author

James L. Huston was born in Canton, Illinois and raised in Moline, Illinois where he attended public schools. He obtained his B.A. from Denison University (Granville, Ohio) and earned his A.M. and Ph.D. from the University of Illinois. He has been at Oklahoma State University–Stillwater since 1980, recently being promoted to Regents Distinguished Professor. He has authored nearly thirty articles in journals of history and three previous books: *Calculating the Value of the Union: Slavery, Property Rights, and the Economic Origins of the Civil War* (2003), *Securing the Fruits of Labor: The American Concept of Wealth Distribution, 1765-1900* (1998), and *The Panic of 1857 and the Coming of the Civil War* (1987). His area of concentration is economic and political history in the middle decades of the nineteenth century.